President Kennedy Should Have Survived Dallas

The Secret Service and the JFK Assassination

VINCE PALAMARA

Author of *Survivor's Guilt*

PRESIDENT KENNEDY SHOULD HAVE SURVIVED DALLAS: THE SECRET SERVICE AND THE JFK ASSASSINATION © VINCE PALAMARA 2025. ALL RIGHTS RESERVED

Published by:
Trine Day LLC
PO Box 577
Walterville, OR 97489
1-800-556-2012
www.TrineDay.com
trineday@icloud.com

Library of Congress Control Number: 2025934837

Palamara, Vince.
PRESIDENT KENNEDY SHOULD HAVE SURVIVED DALLAS:—1st ed.
p. cm.

Epub (ISBN-13) 978-1-63424-512-8
TradePaper (ISBN-13) 978-1-63424-511-1
1. Kennedy, John F. 1917-1963 Assassination. 2 United States. Secret Service History 20th century. 3. PRESIDENTS PROTECTION UNITED STATES. 4. United States. Secret Service Officials and employees. I. Palamara, Vince. II. Title

FIRST EDITION
10 9 8 7 6 5 4 3 2 1

Distribution to the Trade by:
Independent Publishers Group (IPG)
814 North Franklin Street
Chicago, Illinois 60610
312.337.0747
www.ipgbook.com

This book is dedicated to my dear wife Amanda,
my late mother Patricia
and to the memory of President John F. Kennedy.

Author's Note

With the many JFK assassination file releases from 2017-2025, interest in the Kennedy murder has reached a crescendo with both the media and the public. In fact, there hasn't been a buzz about this case this high since the 50th anniversary in 2013. It is heartening to see the level of interest and inquiry from both John Q. Citizen and the news media. Regular stories on the files have been seen on CNN, MSNBC, Fox, NewsNation and a host of other outlets, not to mention countless online forums and social media networks.

While most of these files have been both from and about the CIA and the FBI, no doubt thanks to the many Secret Service files that were deliberately and unlawfully destroyed by the agency in 1995, there have been a couple Secret Service-related stories of interest. In addition to former Secret Service agent Abraham Bolden being pardoned by President Biden in 2022, the following is of interest.

TABLE OF CONTENTS

INTRODUCTION

With word that former Kennedy agent's Clint Hill and Paul Landis have major documentaries forthcoming (*Clint Hill: Agent Number 9* and *The Final Witness*, respectively), I thought it imperative to address their past, present and future propaganda before the truth was lost to history. Former Secret Service agents Gerald Blaine, Clint Hill[1] and Paul Landis are the three still-living men who have done most of the whitewashing of the Secret Service's poor performance in Dallas. Through a detailed analysis of their books, their testimony and the record, I believe the true story of the Kennedy assassination will become quite clear. Simply put: Oswald or no Oswald, conspiracy or no conspiracy, if the Secret Service would have done their normal protective function, President Kennedy would have and should have survived Dallas.

Powerful statement? Read on.

In addition to a thorough look at the Secret Service through the eyes of the investigations conducted by the Warren Commission, the House Select Committee on Assassinations, and the Assassination Records Review Board, the previously mentioned books (most co-authored by Hill's wife Lisa McCubbin-Hill), testimony and records, all of my many interviews and correspondence with the vast majority of the Kennedy agents (years before the Blaine, Hill and Landis books saw the light of day) will tell the real story of what did and did not happen in Dallas on that fateful day on 11/22/63.

Furthermore, the many recently released and remastered films and photos of Kennedy motorcades (many of which I discovered and are featured on my YouTube channel, my blogs and other social media platforms), often just discovered in the last 5-15 years, gives the lie to the notion that Kennedy did not receive good protection before Dallas. It also debunks the notion that Kennedy was to blame for the lack of security. The buck stops with the Secret Service.

Vince Palamara

12/4/2024

---

1   Hill passed away 2/21/25 as this book was going to press. However, the documentary on his life will still come out.

CHAPTER ONE

FORMER JFK SECRET SERVICE AGENT GERALD BLAINE'S BOOK *THE KENNEDY DETAIL*

JERRY BLAINE

On June 1, 2005, I sent a 22-page registered letter, signed receipt required, to former Secret Service agent Clint Hill[2] (infamous for his leap onto the back of the limousine during the assassination of President Kennedy on November 22, 1963). My letter was, in essence, a "Cliff Notes" version of my own book *Survivor's Guilt: The Secret Service & The Failure To Protect President Kennedy*,[3] focusing mainly

2   See my first book *Survivor's Guilt: The Secret Service & The Failure to Protect President Kennedy* (2013).

3   Then available in self-published format.

on the issue of the agents' presence – or lack thereof – on the rear of the presidential limousine on 11/22/63, as well as the actions and inactions of three specific agents I have many misgivings about: Floyd Boring (the number two agent on the Kennedy Detail and the Secret Service planner of the Texas trip), Shift Leader Emory Roberts (the commander of the agents in the follow-up car in Dallas), and William Greer (the driver of JFK's limousine). When I phoned the gentleman on June 13, 2005, I received a very cantankerous "non-reply," so to speak: "[Referring to my letter:] About what? Yeah, I'm here. I'm just not interested in talking to you." I did not really expect much, but it was worth a try (having received an unexpected recommendation to talk to Mr. Hill from former agent Lynn Meredith, who was gracious enough to provide Mr. Hill's unlisted address and phone number).

On June 10, 2005, I phoned fellow former agent Gerald Blaine (having previously spoken to the gentleman on 2/7/04). Blaine confirmed his deep friendship with Hill and, much to my surprise, seemingly out of nowhere, said: "Don't be too hard on Emory Roberts. He was a double, even a triple-checker. He probably took Jack Ready's life into consideration." It was at that moment that I realized that Clint Hill shared the contents of my letter with Blaine, probably with a good dose of anger and indignation, as well. When I received word, that Blaine was coming out with a book called *The Kennedy Detail* and that Clint Hill was writing the Foreword, I knew that I was responsible, as a catalyst, for their endeavors! Blaine and Hill are now on a book tour together, as well as appearing jointly on several news and media outlets, including an upcoming Discovery Channel documentary, based on the book.

In fact, Blaine even admitted to *Grand Junction Sentinel* reporter Bob Silbernagel that it was during this exact time that he "began contacting all he could of the 38 agents who were in the Kennedy Detail on Nov. 22, 1963," adding further that once "he began seeing all the misinformation and outright deceit about the assassination on the Internet, as well as in books and films, he decided, "Essentially, it was a book that had to be written."[4]

There was no question in my mind that I ruffled feathers with Blaine and Hill. If all this weren't enough, Blaine's attorney even sent me a certified letter in November 2009, a year before his book was to appear, asking me to take down a blog that Blaine noticed on my main Secret Service blog[5] that merely announced their forthcoming book. Blaine thought I

---

4   *The Daily Sentinel,* Summer 2005. See also page 364 of The Kennedy Detail.
5   Vince Palamara's main SECRET SERVICE blog: JFK, ZERO FAIL, The Kennedy Detail, and more (https://www.youtube.com/watch?v=btGfV71NJbc&t=10s)

was trying to say that I was the co-author, which was the furthest thing from the truth – I was innocently telling my readers of a book they might find of interest. In any event, after writing back to Blaine and his lawyer, I decided to take that specific blog down... but this incident let me know, in no uncertain terms: Blaine and Hill were men on a mission.

This is further evidenced by what Blaine himself wrote on his blog[6]: "At the annual conference of the 2,500 member former Secret Service Agents Association [AFAUSSS] last week (8/26-8/28/10) in New York City, Lisa McCubbin and I [Gerald Blaine] presented an overview of the book at the business meeting to ensure the agents that the publication was "Worthy of Trust and Confidence."; "At the conference opening reception Clint Hill, Lisa McCubbin and I [Gerald Blaine] met with Secret Service Director [Mark] Sullivan and discussed the book from the perspective of today's operations. Clint Hill, who lives in the Washington DC area, had previously briefed the Director on the accuracy and purpose of writing the book."; "I [Gerald Blaine] am the sole surviving charter member and a past president of the organization. The association was conceived by Floyd Boring and Jerry Behn with the assistance of fifteen charter members. Jerry Behn was the Special Agent in Charge of the Kennedy Detail and Floyd Boring was an Assistant Agent in Charge. The organization's mission is to maintain social and professional relationships, to liaison with the Secret Service and other law enforcement agencies."[7]

To quote from a popular commercial, "Can you hear me now?"

I knew their "mission" was to circle the wagons, so to speak, and attempt to counter my prolific research on the failings of the Secret Service on November 22, 1963, specifically, the statements by many of their colleagues – including BLAINE himself – that President Kennedy was a very nice man, never interfered with the actions of the Secret Service and, to the point, did NOT order the agents off his limousine... ever! These men, as well as several important non-agency personnel (such as Dave Powers, Congressman Sam Gibbons, and Cecil Stoughton, among others), provided information, on the phone and/ or in writing, to a total stranger – me – with no trepidation whatsoever. "Official" history – the *Warren Report*, the *HSCA Report*, William Manchester's *The Death of a President*, and Jim Bishop's *The Day Kennedy Was Shot* – espouses a decidedly different verdict: President Kennedy was reckless with his security and did order the agents off his limousine-not in Dallas, but during the

---

6   About The Authors | The Kennedy Detail, (http://kennedydetail.com/about-the-authors/)
7   https://kennedydetail.blogspot.com/2010/09/association-of-former-agents-of-united.html

major trip before, in Tampa, FL, on 11/18/63, which allegedly had grave consequences for JFK's protection on the day he was assassinated.

First, a detailed look at the contents of *The Kennedy Detail* is in order.

The book gets off on the wrong foot with me and others right away with the bold pronouncement: "JFK's Secret Service Agents Break Their Silence" (which is also the subtitle of the book). This is hogwash: not only did several agents, including Clint Hill, testify to the Warren Commission, many of the agents spoke to the aforementioned William Manchester (including Blaine and Hill), Jim Bishop, and the HSCA, as well as to, among others, Prof. Philip Melanson (for his book *The Secret Service: The Hidden History of an Enigmatic Agency*), several prominent Secret Service television documentaries between 1995 and 2004 (Hill was involved in all of these productions that made their way to VHS and/ or DVD, as well[8]), and, last but certainly not least, to myself, Vince Palamara, between 1992 and 2006 (again, including Blaine and Hill)! Things only get worse once one gets to the inside flap jacket: Blaine writes that JFK "banned agents from his car," which is patently false – as Winston Lawson, the lead advance agent for the fateful Dallas trip, wrote to me in a letter dated 1/12/04: "I do not know of any standing orders for the agents to stay off the back of the car. After all, footholds and handholds were built into that particular vehicle... it never came to my attention as such. I am certain agents were on the back on certain occasions." For his part, ATSAIC (Shift Leader) Art Godfrey told this reviewer on May 30, 1996, regarding the notion that JFK ordered the agents not to do certain things which included removing themselves from the rear of the limousine: "That's a bunch of baloney; that's not true. He never ordered us to do anything. He was a very nice man ... cooperative." Godfrey reiterated this on June 7, 1996. In a letter dated November 24, 1997, Godfrey stated the following: "All I can speak for is myself. When I was working with President Kennedy, he never asked me to have my shift leave the limo when we were working it," thus confirming what he had also told the author telephonically on two prior occasions. As we shall see, Blaine makes much ado about this issue ... for obvious reasons (*Thou Protest Too Much*).

Although very well written and containing some nice photographs, *The Kennedy Detail* provides the reader a generous dose of fact, "faction"

---

8   For the record, Clint Hill was interviewed by: Warren Commission (March 9, 1964), for Manchester, *The Death of a President* (November 18, 1964; May 20, 1965), and 60 Minutes (December 7, 1975; November 1993); December 1963 newsreel regarding Treasury award (with C. Douglas Dillon as presenter); *Who Killed JFK: The Final Chapter?* (CBS, November 19, 1993); *The Secret Service* and *Inside the Secret Service* videos (1995); *Inside the U.S. Secret Service* documentary (2004); Larry King Live (March 22, 2006); and now, numerous TV shows since.

(playing hard and loose with alleged 'facts' and encompassing reconstructed dialogue and supposed meetings that allegedly occurred without documentation) and fiction. In fact, there are no footnotes, endnotes, sources, or a bibliography to be found (although, to his credit, Blaine did include an impressive index). It is important to note that many important former agents and officials, such as "the brass" – Treasury Secretary Douglas Dillon, Asst Sec. G. d'Andelot Belin, Chief James Rowley, Aide to the Chief Walter Blaschak, Deputy Chief Paul Paterni, Assistant Chief Russell Daniels, Assistant Chief Ed Wildy, Chief U.E. Baughman, Special Agent In Charge (SAIC) Gerald Behn, ASAIC Floyd Boring (the planner of the Texas trip), ASAIC Roy Kellerman (rode in JFK's limo), ASAIC John Campion, ATSAIC (Shift Leader) Emory Roberts (rode in follow up car), ATSAIC Stu Stout (on Texas trip), ATSAIC Art Godfrey (on Texas trip), SAIC of Personnel Howard Anderson, SAIC of PRS Robert Bouck, ASAIC of LBJ Detail (and former JFK agent) Rufus Youngblood, Head Inspector of PRS Elliot Thacker, Chief Inspector Jackson Krill, Inspector Thomas Kelley, Inspector Gerard McCann, & Inspector Burrill Peterson – and many "privates," such as Bill Bacherman, Glen Bennett (of PRS; rode in motorcade), Andy Berger (on the Texas trip), Bert deFreese (on the Texas trip), Jerry Dolan, Paul Doster, PRS Dick Flohr, Morgan Gies, William Greer (the driver of JFK's limo), Dennis Halterman (on the Texas trip), Ned Hall II (on the Texas trip), Harvey Henderson, George Hickey (rode in the follow-up car), Andy Hutch, Jim Jeffries, Sam Kinney (drove the follow-up car), PRS Elmer Lawrence, James Mastrovito, John "Muggsy" O'Leary (on the Texas trip), Bill Payne (on the Texas trip), PRS Walter Pine, Wade Rodham,[9] Henry Rybka (on the Texas trip), Thomas Shipman (deceased 10/14/63!), PRS Frank Stoner, & PRS Walter Young – not to mention countless agents from field offices (such as the SAIC of the Dallas Office Forrest Sorrels and his assistant Robert Steuart *and* Charlie Kunkel), died years before this book was even a thought. In addition, since there are no specific references, it is hard to know exactly *who* among the living *was* interviewed, as Blaine recently admitted that "three agents still cannot discuss the emotional aspects of that day in Dallas" and he was unable "to contact three other agents who served." In addition, several other agents (such as Lynn Meredith, Bob Foster, Paul Burns, Jerry Kivett and Stu Knight) passed away during the time Blaine was writing his book, so we are unable to know if they were contacted, as well.

---

9   Rodham was Hillary Rodham Clinton's first cousin who she thought of as an uncle due to his age! I received confirmation of this via former agent Don Cox.

That said, it is most telling that Blaine admitted that three agents – Larry Newman, Tony Sherman, and Tim McIntyre (rode in the follow-up car) – were not contacted because they had "responded to Seymour Hirsch's [sic] book, *The Dark Side of Camelot*, which violated the code of silence." Yet, the fourth agent, Joe Paolella, apparently *was* interviewed for Blaine's volume. Why wasn't he banished from his work, as well? Using this "code of silence" criteria, several (perhaps many) of the agents who spoke to myself, and others should have been ignored, as well (example: former agent Walt Coughlin told me that LBJ was "a first-class prick"). It was obvious why Blaine ignored former agent Abraham Bolden: the controversial nature of Bolden's beliefs and so forth.[10] So, it appears a little selectivity, necessary and otherwise, was used regarding former agent interviews for *The Kennedy Detail*.[11]

As for the aforementioned Newman, Sherman, McIntyre, and Paolella, they waxed on to Seymour Hersh (and others, including the December 1997 ABC/Peter Jennings special *Dangerous World: The Kennedy Years*) about their anger and disgust over JFK's private lives. Incredibly, even Emory Roberts' concerns over these issues were voiced by McIntyre. This is very disturbing because it shows a motive for inaction on 11/22/63. For his part, McIntyre told ABC News, regarding JFK's private life: "Prostitution – that's illegal. A procurement is illegal. And if you have a procurer with prostitutes paraded in front of you, then, as a sworn law enforcement officer, you're asking yourself, 'Well, what do they think of us?'" McIntyre felt this way after having only spent a very brief time with JFK before the assassination: he joined the White House Detail in the fall of 1963.[12] McIntyre also told Hersh: "His shift supervisor, the highly respected Emory Roberts, took him aside and warned … that 'you're going to see a lot of shit around here. Stuff with the President. Just forget about it. Keep it to yourself. Don't even talk to your wife.' … Roberts was nervous about it. Emory would say, McIntyre recalled with a laugh, 'How in the hell do you know what's going on? He could be hurt in there. What if one bites him' in

---

10   Bolden is also the author of *The Echo from Dealey Plaza* (2008).

11   The agents we **DO** know were involved in *The Kennedy Detail*, based on the text of the book and Blaine's online blogs and so forth (and the upcoming Discovery tv documentary), are the following: Gerald Blaine, Clint Hill, Joe Paolella, Chuck Zboril, Robert Faison, Hamilton Brown, Walt Coughlin, Richard Johnsen, Ken Wiesman, Radford Jones, Winston Lawson, Toby Chandler, Ron Pontius, David Grant (Clint Hill's brother-in-law!), Paul Rundle, Eve Dempsher, Tom Wells and Paul Landis. That leaves, from the Texas trip, Sam Sulliman, John Ready, Warren "Woody" Taylor, Lem Johns, Jerry Bechtle, Donald Bendickson, Jim Goodenough, Bill Duncan, PRS Dale Wunderlich, Mike Howard (Dallas office), John Joe Howlett (Dallas office), Roger Warner, Bob Burke, Frank Yeager, Don Lawton, Ken Giannoules, and Ernest Olsson as still living and eligible to have been interviewed... *maybe*.

12   Author's interview with Gerald Blaine 6/10/05.

a sensitive area? Roberts 'talked about it a lot', McIntyre said. 'Bites' ... In McIntyre's view, a public scandal about Kennedy's incessant womanizing was inevitable. 'It would have had to come out in the next year or so. In the campaign, maybe.' McIntyre said he and some of his colleagues ... felt abused by their service on behalf of President Kennedy ... McIntyre said he eventually realized that he had compromised his law enforcement beliefs to the point where he wondered whether it was 'time to get out of there. I was disappointed by what I saw.' "[13] Blaine chose to ignore these men and this issue entirely in his book: is this good history? I think not. It might not be pleasant, but these men said what they said – to ignore this matter speaks of a cover up of guilty knowledge. I did not ignore it.

From the first photo section and page 19 of his book (and, later, on pages 240 and 288), we learn something I had already reported years before: that SAIC Gerald Behn "always traveled with the president. In the three years since Kennedy had been elected, Jerry Behn had not taken one day of vacation.... He took his first vacation in four years the week JFK was assassinated." Quirk of fate or convenient absence? You decide. I have.

Also on page 19, Blaine begins to (using a lawyer's term) "lay the foundation," as it were, for blaming the victim (JFK) and, in the process, makes a real whopper: Blaine writes, "the Secret Service was not authorized to override a presidential decision." Wrong! Ample proof to the contrary abounds. Chief James J. Rowley testified under oath to the Warren Commission: "No President will tell the Secret Service what they can or cannot do."[14] In fact, Rowley's predecessor, former Chief U. E. Baughman, who had served under JFK from Election Night 1960 until September 1961, had written in his 1962 book Secret Service Chief: "Now the Chief of the Secret Service is legally empowered to countermand a decision made by anybody in this country if it might endanger the life or limb of the Chief Executive. This means I could veto a decision of the President himself if I decided it would be dangerous not to. The President of course knew this fact."[15] Indeed, an Associated Press story from November 15, 1963, stated: "The (Secret) Service can overrule even the President where his personal security is involved." Even President Truman agreed, stating, "The Secret Service was the only boss that the President of the United States really had."[16] Finally, In an 11/23/63 UPI story written by Robert

13   *The Dark Side of Camelot* by Seymour Hersh (1997), pages 240-241.
14   Warren Commission Volume 5, page 570: 5H 570.
15   U. E. Baughman, *Secret Service Chief* (New York: Harper & Row, Popular Library edition, January 1963), p. 70.
16   Rowley oral history, LBJ Library, January 22, 1969, p. 2. See also David Seidman, *Extreme Careers – Secret Service Agents: Life Protecting the President* (New York: The Rosen Publishing Group,

J. Serling from Washington entitled "Secret Service Men Wary of Motorcade," based in part on "private conversations" with unnamed agents: "An agent is the only man in the world who can order a President of the United States around if the latter's safety is believed at stake ... in certain situations an agent outranks even a President."

One major myth down, one major one left to demolish.

Peppered throughout the book, but starting on page 74, Blaine begins to bring up the issue of the agents' presence (or lack thereof) on the back of JFK's limousine (in Tampa on 11/18/63, in Dallas on 11/22/63, and elsewhere – further "laying the foundation" for his false premise of blaming the victim), accurately stating for the record, after revealing his knowledge of the Joseph Milteer threat received via the Miami Police Department before JFK's trip to Florida: "...the only way to have a chance at protecting the president against a shooter from a tall building would be to have agents posted on the back of the car." Indeed, on pages 81-84, as various films and photos confirm, Blaine tells of his having ridden on the rear of President Kennedy's limousine in Rome and Naples, Italy (7/2/63). In addition, his first photo section depicts Blaine and his colleagues on or near the rear of JFK's car in Costa Rica (March 1963), Berlin, Germany (June, 1963) and Ireland (also in June 1963), while his second photo section depicts yet another photo of the agents on the car in Ireland, as well as in Tampa, Florida (11/18/63) and even agent Clint Hill on the rear of the car in Dallas, Texas on 11/22/63, albeit before the motorcade reached Dealey Plaza.

It is on pages 100-101, in his zeal to set up his premise, that Blaine makes a costly error. Blaine writes: "Fortunately, they'd have SS100X [JFK's special 1961 Lincoln Continental] in Dallas, which had the rear steps and handholds so two agents could be perched directly behind the president and could react quickly. He'd [Win Lawson would] be sure to tell Roy Kellerman, the Special Agent in Charge for the Texas trip, that when the motorcade was driving through downtown, agents would need to be on the back of the car." However, as we have seen, and it bears repeating, Win Lawson wrote to this reviewer on 1/12/04, before this book was even a thought, and said: "I do not know of any standing orders for the agents to stay off the back of the car. After all, foot holds and handholds were built into that particular vehicle... it never came to my attention as such." This is in direct contradiction to these statements, attributed to Lawson by Blaine, in *The Kennedy Detail*.

Inc., 2003), p. 11. Rowley himself said: «Most Presidents have responded to our requests ....»

Blaine makes much of the 11/18/63 trip JFK took to Tampa as 'evidence' that President Kennedy ordered the agents off the car (as did the Secret Service, exactly five months after the assassination, via five reports submitted to the Warren Commission by Chief Rowley[17]). As with SAIC Behn's first-time absence, we now supposedly have another instance of a brand-new notion, as Blaine writes on page 148: "In the three years he'd been with JFK, he'd never heard the president call the agents off the back of the car in the middle of a motorcade." Indeed, on page 162, Blaine reports that agent Ron Pontius stated: "I've never heard the president say anything about agents on the back of the car," registering his astonishment based on allegedly hearing this, for the first time, on 11/21/63 from long-deceased agent Bert deFreese (in a 47-year-old reconstructed conversation – faction? fiction? – that Blaine makes in the book). Blaine is alleging that JFK ordered the agents (specifically, agents Don Lawton and Chuck Zboril) off the back of the car in Tampa, allegedly using the phrase made infamous by William Manchester[18]: "Floyd [Boring], have the Ivy League charlatans drop back to the follow-up car." Blaine later adds on page 184: "None of the agents understood why he [JFK] was willing to be so reckless." If that weren't enough, Blaine also stated (on the upcoming Discovery Channel documentary airing on 11/22/10): "President Kennedy made a decision, and he politely told everybody, 'You know, we're starting the campaign now, and the people are my asset,'" said agent Jerry Blaine. "And so, we all of a sudden understood. It left a firm command to stay off the back of the car."[19] Huh? "Everybody"? *That* alleged statement "left a firm command"? In any event, once again, we have a major conflict with reality – not only do many films and photos depict the agents (still) riding on (or walking/ jogging very near) the rear of the limousine in Tampa,[20] Congressman Sam Gibbons, who actually rode a mere foot away *in* the car with JFK, wrote to me in a letter dated 1/15/04: "'I rode with Kennedy every time he rode. I heard no such order. As I remember it the agents rode on the rear bumper all the way. Kennedy was very happy during his visit to Tampa. Sam Gibbons." Also, photographer Tony Zappone, then a 16-year-old witness to the motorcade in Tampa (one of whose photos for this motorcade was ironically used in *The Kennedy Detail*!), told me that

---

17   CE1025: 18 H 803-809. I have dealt with these reports exhaustively in my own book (*Survivor's Guilt*: see Chapter one in entirety).

18   *The Death of a President* by William Manchester, pp. 37-38 (all references to Manchester's book are from the 1988 Perennial Library edition.)

19   *The Kennedy Detail* DVD.

20   Excellent security for President Kennedy 11/18/63 Tampa and Miami, Florida, (https://www.youtube.com/watch?v=VShezymzQVc&t=60s)

the agents were "definitely on the back of the car for most of the day until they started back for MacDill AFB at the end of the day."[21]

As for the "Ivy League Charlatans" remark JFK allegedly uttered to ASAIC Floyd Boring and, again, first made famous by Manchester, Boring told this author, "I never told him [Manchester] that." As for the merit of the quote itself, as previously mentioned, Boring said, "No, no, no – that's not true," thus contradicting his own report in the process, stating further: "He actually – No, I told them.... He didn't tell them anything ... He just – I looked at the back and I seen these fellahs were hanging on the limousine – I told them to return to the car ... [JFK] was a very easy-going guy ... he didn't interfere with our actions at all."[22] In a later interview, Boring expounded further: "Well that's not true. That's not true. He was a very nice man; he never interfered with us at all."[23] If that weren't enough, Boring also wrote the author: "He [JFK] was very cooperative with the Secret Service."[24] Incredibly, Boring was not even interviewed for Manchester's book! We may never know Mr. Manchester's source for this curious statement: he told the author on August 23, 1993, that "... all that material is under seal and won't be released in my lifetime" and denied the author access to his notes (Manchester has since passed away). Interestingly, Manchester did interview the late Emory Roberts – an agent this

---

21   E-mail to Vince Palamara from Tony Zappone dated 10/20/10. This was also confirmed by lead motorcycle officer Russell Groover.

22   Author's interview with Floyd Boring 9/22/93.

23   Author's interview with Floyd Boring dated 3/4/94.

24   Floyd Boring letter to Vince Palamara dated 11/22/97.

reviewer is most suspicious of[25] – and GERALD BLAINE, Manchester's probable "source(s)."[26]

As for Blaine, this is what he told this reviewer: On February 7, 2004, Blaine said that President Kennedy was "very cooperative. He didn't interfere with our actions. President Kennedy was very likeable – he never had a harsh word for anyone. He never interfered with our actions." When I asked Blaine how often the agents rode on the back of JFK's limousine,

---

25   Manchester, p. 667. Of the 21 agents/officials interviewed by Manchester, only Roberts, Greer, Kinney, and Blaine were on the Florida trip. Blaine was the advance agent for Tampa (riding in the lead car), Greer drove JFK's car, Kinney drove the follow-up car, and Roberts was the commander of the follow-up car. That said, in the author's opinion, Roberts is still the main suspect of the four as being Manchester's dubious source for this quote: after all, he was asked to write a report about JFK's so-called desires, citing Boring as the source for the order via radio transmission. The others – Greer, Kinney, and Blaine – were not asked to write a similar report. In addition, Manchester had access to this report while writing his book (see next footnote). Also, unlike the other three, Roberts was interviewed twice and, while Greer never went on record with his feelings about the matter, one way or the other, Kinney adamantly denied the veracity of Manchester's information, while Blaine denied the *substance* of the information, although he *did* mention the «Ivy league charlatan» remark coming from a secondary source. Finally, of the 21 agents interviewed by Manchester, Blaine is the only agent – save two headquarters Inspectors (see next footnote) – whose interview comments are not to be found in the text or index. Since, in addition to Blaine, three other agents – Lawton, Meredith and Newman – also mentioned the remark to this reviewer strictly as *hearsay*, in some fashion or another, it is more than likely that Manchester seized upon the remark and greatly exaggerated its significance ... and attributed it to Boring, while his actual source was likely Roberts and/or Blaine. Again, since Boring wasn't interviewed, the comment had to come second-hand from another agent, who, in turn, received the remark second-hand from Boring. Ultimately, the question is: did Boring really give out this order on instructions from JFK?
26   Interestingly, Manchester, having interviewed 21 different agents/officials for his book (pp. 660–9), chose to include interviews with *Secret Service Inspectors Burrill Peterson and Jack Warner*. What's the problem? Well, these men, not even associated with the Texas trip in any way, were interviewed more than any of the other agents: four times each (Peterson: October 9, 1964, November 17, 1964, November 18, 1964, February 5, 1965; Warner: June 2, 1964, November 18, 1964, February 5, 1965, May 12, 1965)! Only Emory Roberts, Clint Hill, Roy Kellerman, and Forrest Sorrels had two interviews apiece, while all the other agents/officials garnered just one inter-view each. And, more importantly, unlike all the other 19 agents, save one, Gerald Blaine (a Texas trip WHD agent), these two Inspectors are not even mentioned in the actual text or the index; their comments are "invisible" to the reader. It appears, then, that Manchester's book was truly a sanitized, "official" book, more so than we thought before (as most everyone knows, the book was written with Jackie Kennedy's approval – it was her idea, in fact [p.ix]. Manchester even had early, exclusive access to the Warren Commission itself: "At the outset of my inquiry the late Chief Justice Earl Warren appointed me an ex officio member of his commission ... and provided me with an office in Washington's VFW building, where the commission met and where copies of reports and depositions were made available to me." [p. xix]) Inspector Peterson figured prominently in the post-assassination press dealings (or lack thereof) – as Agent Sorrels testified: ".. I don't think at any time you will see that there is any statement made by the newspapers or television that we said anything because Mr. Kelley, the Inspector, told me, 'Any information that is given out will have to come from Inspector Peterson in Washington.'" [7 H 359] Peterson became an Assistant Director for Investigations in 1968 [*20 Years in the Secret Service* by Rufus Youngblood (New York: Simon & Schuster, 1973), p. 220], while Inspector Warner would go on to become Director of Public Affairs (a position he held until the 1990s), acting as a buffer to critical press questions during the assassination attempts on President Ford and other related matters [*The Secret Service: The Hidden History of an Enigmatic Agency* (New York: Carroll & Graf, 2003) by Philip Melanson with Peter Stevens, pp. 101, 201, 224, 237]. Warner would also later become a consultant to the 1993 Clint Eastwood movie *In the Line of Fire*.

the former agent said it was a "fairly common" occurrence that depended on the crowd and the speed of the cars. In fact, just as one example, Blaine rode on the rear of JFK's limousine in Germany in June 1963, along with fellow Texas trip veterans Paul A. Burns and Samuel E. Sulliman. Blaine added, in specific reference to the agents on the follow-up car in Dallas: "You have to remember, they were fairly young agents," seeming to imply that their youth was a disadvantage, or perhaps this was seen as an excuse for their poor performance on November 22, 1963. Surprisingly, Blaine, the WHD advance agent for the Tampa trip of November 18, 1963, said that JFK did make the comment "I don't need Ivy League charlatans back there," but emphasized this was a "low-key remark" said "kiddingly" and demonstrating Kennedy's "Irish sense of humor." However, according to the "official" story, President Kennedy allegedly made these remarks only to Boring while traveling in the presidential limousine in Tampa: Blaine was nowhere near the vehicle at the time, so Boring, despite what he conveyed to this reviewer, had to be his source for this story! In addition to Emory Roberts, one now wonders, as mentioned previously, if Blaine was a source (or perhaps the source) for Manchester's exaggerated "quote" attributed to Boring, as Agent Blaine was also interviewed by Manchester. Blaine would not respond to a follow-up letter on this subject. However, when the author phoned Blaine on June 10, 2005, the former agent said the remark "Ivy League charlatans" came "from the guys ... I can't remember who [said it] ... I can't remember." Thus, Blaine confirms that he did not hear the remark from JFK. That said, Blaine's memory got a whole lot "better" 5 years later: he writes on page 148: "The message came through loud and clear on Blaine's walkie-talkie." Incredible.

As for ASAIC Floyd Boring, this reviewer has no doubt that Boring DID INDEED CONVEY the fraudulent notion that JFK had asked that the agents remove themselves from the limo between 11/18-11/19/63, but that the former agent was telling the TRUTH of the matter when he spoke to me years later. You see, Clint Hill wrote in his report:

"I ... never personally was requested by President John F. Kennedy not to ride on the rear of the Presidential automobile. I did receive information passed verbally from the administrative offices of the White House Detail of the Secret Service to Agents assigned to that Detail that President Kennedy had made such requests. I do not know from whom I received this information.... No written instructions regarding this were ever distributed ... [I] received this information after the President's return to Washington, D.C. This would have been between November 19,

1963, and November 21, 1963 [note the time frame!]. I do not know specifically who advised me of this request by the President."

Mr. Hill's undated report was presumably written in April 1964, as the other four reports were written at that time. Why Mr. Hill could not "remember" the specific name of the agent who gave him JFK's alleged desires is very troubling – he revealed it on March 9, 1964, presumably before his report was written, in his (obviously pre-rehearsed) testimony under oath to the future Senator Arlen Specter, then a lawyer with the Warren Commission[27]:

Specter: "Did you have any other occasion en route from Love Field to downtown Dallas to leave the follow-up car and mount that portion of the President's car [rear portion of limousine]?" Hill: "I did the same thing approximately four times." Specter: "What are the standard regulations and practices, if any, governing such an action on your part?" Hill: "It is left to the agent's discretion more or less to move to that particular position when he feels that there is a danger to the President: to place himself as close to the President or the First Lady as my case was, as possible, which I did." Specter: "Are those practices specified in any written documents of the Secret Service?" Hill: "No, they are not." Specter: "Now, had there been any instruction or comment about your performance of that type of a duty with respect to anything President Kennedy himself had said in the period immediately preceding the trip to Texas?" Hill: "Yes, sir; there was. The preceding Monday, the President was on a trip to Tampa, Florida, and he requested that the agents not ride on either of those two steps." Specter: "And to whom did the President make that request?" Hill: "Assistant Special Agent in Charge Boring." Specter: "Was Assistant Special Agent in Charge Boring the individual in charge of that trip to Florida?" Hill: "He was riding in the Presidential automobile on that trip in Florida, and I presume that he was. I was not along." Specter: "Well, on that occasion would he have been in a position comparable to that occupied by Special Agent Kellerman on this trip to Texas?" Hill: "Yes sir; the same position." Specter: "And Special Agent Boring informed you of that instruction by President Kennedy?" Hill: "Yes sir, he did." Specter: "Did he make it a point to inform other special agents of that same instruction?" Hill: "I believe that he did, sir." Specter: "And, as a result of what President Kennedy said to him, did he instruct you to observe that Presidential admonition?" Hill: "Yes, sir." Specter: "How, if at all, did that instruction of President Kennedy affect your action and – your action in

---

27   2 H 136–7.

safeguarding him on this trip to Dallas?" Hill: "We did not ride on the rear portions of the automobile. I did on those four occasions because the motorcycles had to drop back and there was no protection on the left-hand side of the car."

However, keeping in mind what Boring told this reviewer, the ARRB's Doug Horne – at the request of this reviewer – interviewed Mr. Boring regarding this matter on 9/18/96. Horne wrote: "Mr. Boring was asked to read pages 136–137 of Clint Hill's Warren Commission testimony, in which Clint Hill recounted that Floyd Boring had told him just days prior to the assassination that during the President's Tampa trip on Monday, November 18, 1963, JFK had requested that agents not ride on the rear steps of the limousine, and that Boring had also so informed other agents of the White House detail, and that as a result, agents in Dallas (except Clint Hill, on brief occasions) did not ride on the rear steps of the limousine. Mr. Boring affirmed that he did make these statements to Clint Hill, but stated that he was not relaying a policy change, but rather simply telling an anecdote about the President's kindness and consideration in Tampa in not wanting agents to have to ride on the rear of the Lincoln limousine when it was not necessary to do so because of a lack of crowds along the street."

This reviewer finds this admission startling, especially because the one agent who decided to ride on the rear of the limousine in Dallas anyway – and on at least four different occasions – was none other than Clint Hill himself.

This also does not address what the agents were to do when the crowds were heavier, or even what exactly constituted a "crowd," as agents did ride on the rear steps of the limousine in Tampa on November 18, 1963 anyway! (Agents Donald J. Lawton, Andrew E. Berger, and Charles T. Zboril, to be exact. Perhaps this is why Blaine felt the need to caption a photo of Boring with the following: "[Boring] was highly respected by all the agents, as well as by JFK.")

"Presidential admonition" (as Specter said to Hill)? Simply an "anecdote" of "the President's kindness" (what Boring said to Horne)? "Not true" (what Boring said to this reviewer)? You decide. I have... and so has Blaine: twice, in fact – what he told this reviewer and what he now claims in *The Kennedy Detail* (see the flap jacket, pages 148-150, 162, 183-184, 206, 208, 209, 232)."

On page 162, Blaine alleges that SAIC Gerald Behn, from his office in the White House, told agent Ron Pontius on 11/21/63: "[JFK] wanted the agents off the back of the car [in Tampa and Dallas] in order for the people to get an unobstructed view." However, in a contradiction Blaine doesn't even notice (although he previously mentioned it on page 19 and in the first photo section), Behn was on vacation during this time! Perhaps most importantly, Behn told this reviewer on 9/27/92: "I don't remember Kennedy ever saying that he didn't want anybody on the back of his car. I think if you watch the newsreel pictures, you'll find agents on there from time to time." In fact, many former agents and White House aides told this reviewer the same thing Lawson, Boring, and Behn all said![28]

And yet, despite all of this defensive posturing, faction, and fabricating, Blaine states, with regard to the agents' not being on the rear of the car in Dealey Plaza (on page 209): "It was standard procedure – regardless of the president's request – for all agents to fall back to the follow-up car in this situation." (see also page 289) But Blaine wasn't done just yet.

In what this reviewer regards as a clever fabrication with "faction" (reconstructing alleged dialogue, 47 years later, from long-dead colleagues), Blaine claims (on pages 285-289 & 360) that there was a meeting at 8 A.M. on 11/25/63, the morning of JFK's funeral, in which the issue of JFK's alleged orders to remove the agents from the car in Tampa (and Dallas) was allegedly covered up so the public would not blame the president for his own death, something this book, and especially this "tale," dies with vigor! Blaine claims that this meeting was attended by himself, Chief James Rowley (deceased 11/1/92), Rowley's secretary Walter Blaschak (long deceased), ASAIC Floyd Boring (deceased 2/1/08 and in ill health long beforehand), SAIC Jerry Behn (as noted previously, deceased 4/21/93), ATSAIC Stu Stout (deceased December 1974)[29], and ATSAIC Emory Roberts (deceased 10/8/73). ASAIC Roy Kellerman (deceased 3/22/84) allegedly did *not* attend and, while Blaine mentions that "every supervising agent" was in attendance, he does not mention

---

28   See my first book *Survivor's Guilt: The Secret Service & The Failure to Protect President Kennedy* (2013).

29   Stout's son, Stu Stout III, wrote this reviewer on 11/1/10: "Vince. Thought I would mention that one of the influential people that attended the advance planning meetings for the Dallas trip was the Mayor of Dallas in 63 and I think it was Earle Cabell or Eric? Doesn't really matter. I distinctly ...remember during a conversation at the dinner table weeks following (that surreal day), my father telling my mother that "the mayor thought agents riding on the back of the car (which was common protocol) would send a message and did not want his city to appear dangerous to the world though the media. He asked for subtle security exposure if and where possible." On that day only two individuals would have been able to direct such an order and that would have been the President himself or Floyd Boring SAIC. In my opinion, and you know about opinions, if you find out who else was in that chain of command "during that moment" you will be able to rationally determine why the agents jumped down for a portion of that politically motivated route through the city. Take care Vince and please don't give up."

ATSAIC Art Godfrey (deceased 5/12/2002) by name, although it is 'inferred' that he was there, as well.

It must be said forcefully: There is no documentation whatsoever that this alleged meeting occurred and all the participants, save Blaine (imagine that), are long dead *and* many of them said and wrote things to this reviewer contradictory to the substance of this alleged meeting. On page 288, Blaine writes, speaking for SAIC Behn: "Jim, after Floyd told me about the incident [the alleged JFK orders to remove the agents 11/18/63 in Tampa], I told him to relay the information to the shift leaders – Emory Roberts, Art Godfrey, and Stu Stout – and I know that he did that. They in turn told the men on their shift, which included the agents out on advances." Incredible.

We already know what Behn, Boring, Blaine, Godfrey, and Lawson said to this reviewer; Stout and Kellerman never said anything officially, one way or the other on the matter. Roberts' report confirms nothing except that ASAIC Boring told him to remove the agents from the car on 11/18/63; nothing about JFK or anything else. What about the other "agents out on advances?" Frank Yeager, Blaine's advance partner in Tampa, in a letter to this reviewer dated December 29, 2003, Yeager wrote: "I did not think that President Kennedy was particularly 'difficult' to protect. In fact, I thought that his personality made it easier than some because he was easy to get along with...." Regarding the author's question "Did President Kennedy ever order the agents off the rear of his limousine?" Yeager responded: "I know of no 'order' directly from President Kennedy. I think that after we got back from Tampa, Florida where I did the advance for the President, a few days before Dallas, Kenny O'Donnell, Chief of Staff, requested that the Secret Service agents not ride the rear running board of the Presidential car during parades involving political events so that the president would not be screened by an agent. I don't know what form or detail that this request was made to the Secret Service who worked closely with O'Donnell. I also do not know who actually made the final decision, but we did not have agents on the rear of the President's car in Dallas."

Like Hill's report mentioned above, please note the timing. Further, regarding the notion of JFK's staff having a hand in this matter, in a letter to the author dated January 15, 2004, former agent Gerald O'Rourke, who was on Blaine's shift on the Texas trip, wrote: "Did President Kennedy order us (agents) off the steps of the limo? To my knowledge President Kennedy never ordered us to leave the limo. You must remember at times we had to deal with the Chief of Staff." The agent added: "President Kennedy was easy to protect as he completely trusted the agents of the Secret Service. We always had to be entirely honest with him and up front so we did not lose his trust." So, while both agents say JFK was easy to protect and that no order came from JFK, they imply, or seem to imply, that the Chief of Staff – O'Donnell – had something to do with this. More on this crucially important matter in a moment, as we shall look at the other advance agents and what they conveyed to this reviewer.

J. Walter Coughlin, who helped do the San Antonio advance with the late Dennis Halterman (deceased 1988), wrote this reviewer: "In almost all parade situations that I was involved with we rode or walked the limo." Coughlin later wrote: "We often rode on the back of the car." (For the record, Ned Hall II, who helped with the advance in Fort Worth, passed away in 1998; his son, Ned Hall III, had no comment to make on the matter. The other agent on the Fort Worth advance, Bill Duncan, never has said a thing regarding this issue, officially or otherwise, and it is not apparent if he was even contacted for Blaine's book or not). Ronald Pontius, who helped advance the Houston stop with the late Bert deFreese (died sometime in the 1980's), wrote this reviewer that JFK *did* convey these alleged orders "through his staff," and here is why this "staff" notion is so important: This is a notion that Blaine doesn't even touch in the book! For the record, Presidential Aide (Chief of Staff/Appointments Secretary) Kenneth P. O'Donnell does not mention anything with regard to telling the agents to remove themselves from the limousine (based on JFK's alleged "desires") during his lengthy Warren Commission testimony (nor to author William Manchester, nor even in his or his daughter's books, for that matter); the same is true for the other two Presidential aides: Larry O'Brien and Dave Powers. In fact, Powers refutes this whole idea – he wrote this reviewer in a letter dated 9/10/93 that "they never had to be told to 'get off' the limousine."

JFK's staff is not mentioned as a factor during any of the agents' Warren Commission testimony, nor in the five reports submitted in April 1964. Furthermore, Helen O'Donnell wrote this reviewer on 10/11/10: "Suffice to say that you are correct; JFK did not order anybody off the car, he never interfered with my dad's direction on the Secret Service, and this is much backed up by my Dad's [audio] tapes. I think and know from the tapes Dallas always haunted him because of the might-have-beens – but they involved the motorcade route [only]." In addition, former agents Art Godfrey and Kinney denounced the "staff/O'Donnell" notion to this reviewer, despite what a small minority of the agents I contacted – Yeager, O'Rourke, and Pontius – suggested (although, again, Yeager and O'Rourke agreed that JFK was easy to protect and that no order came from him).

Just *why* are these seemingly contradictory accounts of this minority of agents' Yeager, O'Rourke, and Pontius (seemingly contradictory, that is, to this reviewer *and* definitely contradictory to Blaine) so very important? Because Blaine's alleged 11/25/63 "meeting" mentions not a thing about staff interference or input, his book mentions not a thing about staff interference or input, and, in fact, on page 352, Blaine even writes: "If ever asked about whether JFK had ordered them [the former agents] off the back of his car, the answer was always, "Oh, no. President Kennedy was wonderful. He was very easy to protect. No, I don't remember him ever ordering agents off the back of his car." This is simply false. In addition to the three agents (Yeager, O'Rourke, and Pontius), several agents contacted by the author would not comment, several would claim not to remember, and three (one, contacted by myself, the other two, via the HSCA) gave hazy second-hand information (of dubious quality) seeming to blame JFK after all! If that weren't enough, Rufus Youngblood in his book[30] and Emory Roberts in his report[31], claimed it was the motorcycles that got in the way of the agents (Ready especially) getting onto the rear of the car … geez.

Finally, in addition to Blaine, former agents Lynn Meredith, Larry Newman, and Don Lawton mentioned the "Ivy League Charlatan" remark to myself, although none claimed to have heard it from JFK (Meredith told me: "I must admit that I was not along on the trip and was back at the White House with Caroline and John, Jr. .. I do not know first-hand if President Kennedy ordered agents off the back end of his limousine." The former agent said that "No Secret Service agents riding on the rear of the limousine" was the number one reason JFK was killed! Newman, not interviewed for Blaine's book, said "supposedly, I didn't hear this directly" and that Manchester's book was "part of myth, part of truth." Newman added: "There was not a directive, per se" from President Kennedy to remove the agents from their positions on the back of his limousine. For his part, Lawton told me: "I didn't hear the President say it, no. The word was relayed to us – I forget who told us now – you know, 'come back to the follow-up car.' " Lawton also added: "Everyone felt bad. It was our job to pro-

---

30   *20 Years in the Secret Service* (New York: Simon & Schuster, 1973), p. 111.
31   18 H 783.

tect the President. You still have regrets, remorse. Who knows, if they had left guys on the back of the car ... you can hindsight yourself to death."[32])

You see, almost none of these former agents were contacted by anyone other than this reviewer, as the agents had unlisted addresses and phone numbers; only the hospitality of a couple former agents led me to these men. Blaine's comments on page 352 (and, indeed, his whole book) were aimed squarely at myself and my 22-page letter mentioned at the beginning of this review. After calling me a "self-described "Secret Service expert" – without actually naming me – on page 359 (guilty as charged; that said, The History Channel, Vince Bugliosi, the Assassination Records Review Board, and many authors and researchers have given me this tag), Blaine saves his special ire for me on page 360: "This same "expert" who had been interviewed for many conspiracy theory books relentlessly blamed the Secret Service for JFK's death by using their own statements against them [no theories, just facts – it is what it is: they said what they said, they wrote what they wrote, and to a total stranger, to boot]. In many cases he called agents and recorded their conversations without their knowledge [not "in many cases": only in a very few instances many years ago and these agents are now deceased. That said, thank God I did: *Who* would choose to believe my word now, especially with Blaine's book out now for public consumption?]" And here is the kicker, in the context of the alleged "meeting" Blaine detailed on pages 285-289 (and on page 352), Blaine continues (still on page 360): "When asked whether President Kennedy had ever ordered the agents off the back of his car, the agents gave him the standard line that Chief Rowley requested they give. And as the agents upheld their code, Rowley's words from the day of President Kennedy's funeral resonating in their minds, the Secret Service "expert" turned around and used their words to stab them – and their brothers – in the back with baseless accusations." Incredible.

There was no morning-of-JFK's-funeral-meeting to cover for the dead president so he wouldn't be blamed for ordering the agents off his car – this was used as a clever device to diffuse and cast aside the damning evidence of just what all these men (including Blaine himself!) said and wrote to me, many of whom died years before this book – and this alleged meeting – was even a figment of Blaine's imagination. Again, there is no documentation for this 47-year-old meeting – we must take Blaine, the "sole survivor" of this alleged meeting, at his word. And, what – all these

32   See my first book *Survivor's Guilt: The Secret Service & The Failure to Protect President Kennedy* (2013).

men are liars now for what they said and wrote to me? In the context of my 22-page letter, I believe this "meeting" to be a total fabrication. But it IS clever for another reason: I am sure there *was* most likely a meeting regarding the security detail's coverage of all the dignitaries and their walk with Jackie to St. Matthew's Cathedral and so forth; a clever cover story, indeed.

That said, there are two major reasons why Blaine's 47-year-old cover story is patently false: first, several important non-Secret Service agents (Dave Powers, Congressman Sam Gibbons, Marty Underwood, Helen O'Donnell, and Pierre Salinger, among others, such as various newsmen on 11/22/63, etc.[33]) also told this reviewer that JFK did *not* interfere with the Secret Service or order the agents off his car – what "code" would *they* have been following, Mr. Blaine? Why would they be "lying" to me? (Yes, I am being facetious.) Perhaps this is why Blaine chose to ignore the other cover story of blaming the staff: He had no control over *their* refutations.

The second reason also reveals an embarrassing error on Blaine's part – he writes on page 360: "If these "experts" [me!] and "researchers" had only read some of the documents that were released in 1992 and available online, they would have found a letter from Chief James J. Rowley written in response to J. Lee Rankin, general counsel on the Warren Commission, in which Rowley admitted what he so desperately did not want to become public. He did not want it to look as if the Secret Service was in any way blaming President Kennedy for his own death." (see also page 289 of Blaine's book) Epic Fail – not only does this book achieve Rowley's "non-goal" of blaming JFK for the security inefficiencies in Dallas, but these "documents" were released in 1964 in the Warren Commission Volumes: 18 H 803–9, to be exact! In addition, Rowley's alleged "desperation" to 'hide' JFK's own alleged culpability in his own death was a monster failure of epic proportions: as we know, Clint Hill testified to the Warren Commission[34] and this testimony was mentioned in the Warren Report, a massive best-seller which was also quoted by many major newspapers and magazines the world over and, if that weren't enough, the five reports were mentioned by Jim Bishop in his own massive best-seller *The Day Kennedy Was Shot*. Many other books mention these reports (and/or Hill's testimony). And just WHY would Rowley even need these five after-the-fact reports? Why didn't he just tell Rankin, in "confidence," about the meeting they all supposedly had on the matter on 11/25/63?

---

33   See my first book *Survivor's Guilt: The Secret Service & The Failure to Protect President Kennedy* (2013).

34   2 H 136–7.

Why, indeed. For what it's worth, Blaine (on pages 360-363) proceeds to quote from the five reports but does NOT state what they each say in verbatim fashion. Interestingly, nothing is mentioned specifically about JFK's alleged desires regarding the Dallas motorcade of November 22, 1963, as was requested by the Commission. And, of the five Secret Service reports, four have as their primary source for JFK's alleged request Agent Boring, including one by Boring himself, while the remaining report, written by SAIC Behn, mentions the same November 18, 1963 trip with Mr. Boring as the others do (Boring's report was the first one written, then came one each from Roberts, Ready, Behn, and Hill, respectively). Again, both Behn and Boring totally contradicted the contents of their reports at different times, independent of each other, to the author, while Roberts report is nothing more than his having heard Boring telling him to have the agents removed from the car on 11/18/63; Ready and Hill freely admit they weren't even *on* the Tampa trip in the first place in these reports (and, as Blaine omits), Hill wrote "I do not know from whom I received this information … I do not know specifically who advised me of this request by the President." In addition, agents did ride on the rear of the limousine on July 2, 1963 and November 18, 1963 anyway, despite these alleged Presidential requests, as the film and photo record proves.[35] Needless to say, with Boring joining Behn in refuting the substance of their reports, the official Secret Service 'explanation' falls like a house of cards.

All these reports are supposedly evidence of JFK expressing his desire to keep Secret Service agents off the limousine, particularly in Tampa, Florida on November 18, 1963.

Importantly, no mention is made of any alleged orders via President Kennedy's staff.

And, again, there is nothing about what JFK said or "requested" on November 22, 1963, the critical day in question!

As a "postscript" to Blaine's cover stories about the agents removal from the car, on page 343 of his book, Blaine makes yet another embarrassing error: "When it came to the agents and whether they should or should not have been on the back of the car, the [Warren] report stated that "the configuration of the presidential car and the seating arrangements of the Secret Service agents in the car did not afford the Secret Service agents the opportunity they should have had to be of immediate assistance to

---

35   Exclusive: All President Kennedy Motorcades & Secret Service Protection 1961-1963 JFK assassination, (https://www.youtube.com/watch?v=RlxkEDbTbWg&t=4131s)

the president at the first sign of danger," but this was in reference to Agent Roy Kellerman's position in the front seat and the obstacles he may have faced, not the agents who should have been on or near the rear of the car using the unobstructed grab-handles!

Regarding the issue of the bubbletop, although Blaine (on page 188) states that agent Lawson conveyed to Sam Kinney, the driver of the follow-up car, that the bubbletop was to be removed in Dallas, Sam told this reviewer on 10/19/92 and, again, on 3/4/94 and 4/15/94: "It was my fault the top was off [the limousine in Dallas] – I am the sole responsibility of that."[36] In addition, Kinney's oft-ignored report dated November 30, 1963 confirms this fact[37], as does the former agent's recently-released February 26, 1978 HSCA interview: "...SA Kinney indicated that he felt that his was the responsibility for making the final decision about whether to use the bubble-top."[38] Blaine later states, on page 244, that the bubble-top "was meant to shield the passengers from the weather – he [agent Sam Kinney] could count on one hand how many times it had been used," but this is simply untrue on two counts: the bubbletop was often used in nice weather conditions and was used more frequently than Blaine, speaking for the long-deceased Kinney (died 7/21/97), admits.[39] On page 193, Blaine states that agent Henry J. Rybka "never worked [the] follow-up [car], other than driving," yet the record indicates otherwise.[40]

Predictably, on pages 306-307 & 312-313, Blaine covers up the infamous drinking incident involving nine agents of the Secret Service, including Clint Hill, Paul Landis, Glen Bennett, and Jack Ready! Interestingly, they were all from Shift Leader Emory Roberts' particular shift. Significantly, none of the agents from the V.P. LBJ detail were involved in the drinking incident.[41]

Blaine doesn't even touch the issue of the Secret Service and their involvement of removing motorcycle coverage for JFK on 11/22/63. During a November 19, 1963 security meeting in Dallas, with no Secret Service men present, it was agreed that eighteen motorcycles would be used, some positioned alongside the limousine, similar to the plan used

---

36   Author's three interviews with Sam Kinney 1992-1994.
37   18 H 730.
38   RIF#180–10078–10493.
39   The JFK bubble top: Sam Kinney's decision + all the times it was used (1/3 of all motorcades),(https://www.youtube.com/watch?v=QbBH_ZYBlKg&t=76s)
40   Advance man Jerry Bruno's notes from the JFK Library in Boston. Agent Henry Rybka was also on the follow-up car team in San Antonio on November 21, 1963(as had driver agent George Hickey in Tampa and in Dallas). Rybka was *not* the driver.
41   The Secret Service drinking incident of 11/22/63, (https://www.youtube.com/watch?v=btGfV71NJbc&t=10s)

in the prior Texas cities of San Antonio, Houston, and Fort Worth.[42] However, there was another meeting on November 21, 1963 in which those plans were changed.[43] Captain Perdue Lawrence of the Dallas Police testified to the Warren Commission: "I heard one of the Secret Service men say that President Kennedy did not desire any motorcycle officer directly on each side of him, between him and the crowd, but he would want the officers to the rear."

And yet:

Mr. Dulles: "... do you recall that any orders were given by or on behalf of the President with regard to the location of those motorcycles that were particularly attached to his car?"

Mr. Lawson: "Not specifically at this instance orders from him." [44]

The House Select Committee on Assassinations (HSCA) summed up the situation best:

> The Secret Service's alteration of the original Dallas Police Department motorcycle deployment plan prevented the use of maximum possible security precautions.... Surprisingly, the security measure used in the prior motorcades during the same Texas visit shows that the deployment of motorcycles in Dallas by the Secret Service may have been uniquely insecure.[45]

Blaine *also* does not deal with the issue of the press and photographer's displacement from the motorcade. *Dallas Morning News* reporter Tom Dillard testified to the Warren Commission:

> We lost our position at the airport. I understood we were to have been quite a bit closer. We were assigned as the prime photographic car which, as you probably know, normally a truck precedes the President on these things [motorcades] and certain representatives of the photographic press ride with the truck. In this case, as you know, we didn't have any and this car that I was in was to take photographs which was of spot-news nature.[46]

42   11 HSCA 527; 7 H 577–580; 21 H 567; RIF#180-10093-10320: May 31, 1977, Memorandum from HSCA's Belford Lawson to fellow HSCA members Gary Cornwell and Ken Klein (revised August 15, 1977).

43   7 H 580-1; 11 HSCA 527, 529; RIF#180-10093-10320: May 31, 1977, Memorandum from HSCA's Belford Lawson to fellow HSCA members Gary Cornwell and Ken Klein (revised August 15, 1977).

44   4 H 338.

45   See also RIF#180-10093-10320: May 31, 1977 Memorandum from HSCA's Belford Lawson to fellow HSCA members Gary Cornwell and Ken Klein (revised August 15, 1977) – the original language used for this passage: "But in comparison with what the SS's own documents suggest were the security precautions used in prior motorcades during the same Texas visit, the motorcade alteration in Dallas by the SS may have been a unique occurrence."

46   6 H 163. As the author presented at the COPA '96 and Lancer '97 conferences, the press

On pages 221-222, Blaine, referring to the president's physician, Admiral George Burkley, writes:

> Normally the admiral rode in a staff car in the motorcade, or in the rear seat of the follow-up car, but he and the president's secretary, Evelyn Lincoln, had misjudged the timing of the motorcade's departure from Love Field and wound up scurrying to the VIP bus. He was furious for not having been in his normal seat but had nobody to blame but himself. His sole purpose for being in the motorcade was to be close to the president in case anything happened, but who could have predicted this?"

Again, the record indicates otherwise: "Dr. George Burkley ... felt that he should be close to the President at all times ... Dr. Burkley was unhappy ... this time the admiral protested. He could be of no assistance to the President if a doctor was needed quickly."[47] Burkley also said: "It's not right ... the President's personal physician should be much closer to him," even to the extent of .".. sitting on an agent's lap."[48] Burkley stated a few years after the assassination:

> I accompanied President Kennedy on every trip that he took during his time as President ... I went on all trips ... we had a regular setup ... all the possible angles were covered by cooperation with the Secret Service, in that we knew the areas of most likely danger. We knew where additional medical aid would be available, and things of that nature.... When we were in Fort Worth, Mrs. [Evelyn] Lincoln and I were in the second car in the motorcade ... [in Dallas] I complained to the Secret Service that I should be either in the follow up car or the lead car ... this was brought to their [the Secret Service's] attention very strongly at the foot of the stairway from the airplane [Air Force One] ... Most of the time, however, I was within one or two cars of the President. This was one of the few times that this did not occur.[49]

---

photographers frequently rode in a flatbed truck in front of the motorcade pro-cession [films courtesy JFK Library; see also *John F. Kennedy: A Life in Pictures*, pp. 178–180, 183, 231]. Photographer Tony Zappone confirmed to the author on December 18, 2003, that a flatbed truck was used for the photographers in Tampa, Florida, on November 18, 1963.

47   Bishop, pp. 109–110, 134.

48   Manchester, pp. 131–2. See also *The Flying White House*, p. 209 (O'Donnell seems to get the blame for Burkley's lack of proximity).

49   Manchester, pp. 131–2. See also *The Flying White House*, p. 209 (O'Donnell seems to get the blame for Burkley's lack of proximity). Burkley's October 17, 1967, JFK Library oral history.

In fact, Burkley rode in the lead car in Miami on November 18, 1963.[50] "The only other time that it did not occur, to my direct recollection, is when we were in Rome [July 2, 1963],"[51] which was a model of very good security in every other respect.

Evelyn Lincoln, JFK's secretary, confirmed Burkley's feelings on the matter to the HSCA:

> Mrs. Lincoln also mentioned what she thought was a curious incident in Dallas prior to the assassination. She said she was with Dr. Burkley ... when they left Love Field for the beginning of the motorcade. She said they were somewhat surprised at being 'shoved' back in the motorcade into a bus. She said they usually rode in an automobile a few cars behind the car carrying the President.[52]

It appears even Jackie Kennedy and, by extension, Dave Powers, were wondering about this situation regarding Burkley: On the weekend after President Kennedy's funeral, Powers showed Mrs. Kennedy the color still frames from the Zapruder film as displayed in that week's Life magazine. The pictures, of course, depict Jackie leaving the rear seat to crawl onto the back of the car. "Dave, what do you think I was trying to do?" she asked. Dave could only suggest that maybe she was searching for the President's doctor, Rear Admiral George G. Burkley, who was in a bus at the rear of the motorcade."[53]

Incredibly, as documented in agent Andy Berger's report[54], Blaine writes on page 233, regarding Parkland Hospital: "A representative of the CIA appeared a while later." Also, as Blaine never even mentions, JFK's Military Aide, General Godfrey McHugh, a devout Kennedy loyalist was relegated to the distant VIP car in the Dallas motorcade,[55] stated that he was asked by the Secret Service "for the first time" to "ride in a car in the back [of the motorcade], instead, as normally I would do, between the driver and the Secret Service agent in charge of the trip."[56]

Indeed, McHugh had just occupied this very spot on JFK's previous trip to Florida, not to mention countless other times beforehand when ei-

---

50   RIF#154–10002–10422.
51   Burkley's October 17, 1967, JFK Library oral history.
52   July 5, 1978, HSCA interview of Evelyn Lincoln.
53   *Johnny, We Hardly Knew Ye*, p. 31.
54   18 H 795; See also see Bill Sloan, *Breaking the Silence*, pp. 181–5; *The Man Who Knew Too Much*, pp. 570–1; Michael Benson, Who's *Who in the JFK Assassination* (1993), pp. 40–41.
55   Along with General Ted Clifton, the other military aide who often rode in the front seat of the limousine between the driver and the agent in charge.
56   CFTR radio (Canada) interview 1976 Interview with McHugh conducted late 1975 via phone.

ther he or fellow military aide, General Ted Clifton, rode in this position. (Greer admitted that many times an aide rode in the front seat of the limo with the driver and the supervisor[57], as the film and photo record bears out.) McHugh admitted that this was "unusual": "That's exactly what I thought." The reason? "To give the President full exposure … they told me it would be helpful politically to the President."[58]

There's that qualifier again: "politically." The HSCA's Mark Flanagan, who interviewed McHugh, reported: "Ordinarily McHugh rode in the Presidential limousine in the front seat. This was the first time he was instructed not to ride in the car so that all attention would be focused on the President to accentuate full exposure."[59]

In yet another matter Blaine chose to ignore, Dallas Sheriff Bill Decker, who rode in the lead car with Lawson and Sorrels, told his men to in no way participate in the security of the motorcade.[60] As verified in several films and photos, Decker's men were standing idle at the corner of Main and Houston as mere spectators, nothing more. Indeed, Deputy Sheriff Luke Mooney told author Larry Sneed: "I was merely a spectator with a number of other plain clothes officers on Main Street just north of the Old Red Court House. We in the sheriff's department had nothing to do with security."[61]

Decker had given this unusual order to his men after telling Forrest Sorrels the previous day that he had agreed to incorporate additional personnel for security purposes, and even offered his full support to the agent: Decker had agreed to furnishing fifteen of his men for duty![62] Incredibly, the *Dallas Morning News* on October 26, 1963 reported the following, based on an interview with DPD Chief Jesse Curry: "LARGE POLICE GUARD PLANNED FOR KENNEDY – Signs Friday pointed to the greatest concentration of Dallas police ever for the protection of a high-ranking dignitary when President Kennedy visits Dallas next month…. The deployment of the special force, he [Curry] said, is yet to be worked out with the U.S. Secret Service."[63] Yet Homicide Detective Gus Rose said: "I didn't hear of any extraordinary security measures being set up thus we continued our normal rotation."[64]

---

57   2 H 129.
58   CFTR radio (Canada) interview 1976 Interview with McHugh conducted late 1975 via phone.
59   May 11, 1978, interview with the HSCA's Mark Flanagan (RIF#180–10078–10465 [see also 7 HSCA 14]).
60   Roger Craig, *Two Men in Dallas* video.
61   *No More Silence* by Larry Sneed (1998), p. 224.
62   21 H 547, 572: DPD Stevenson Exhibit.
63   22 H 626
64   *No More Silence*, p. 337.

Blaine also is seemingly unaware of the following, as noted by report-er Seth Kantor: "Will Fritz's men called off nite (sic) before by SS. Had planned to ride closed car w/ machine guns in car behind Pres." (Which could mean someplace behind JFK's car, as was the case in Chicago, IL, on 3/23/63 & New York on 11/15/63.)[65]

Furthermore, Milton Wright, a Texas Highway Patrolman who was the driver of Mayor Cabell's car, wrote this reviewer: "As I recall, prior to the President arriving at the airport we were already staged on the tarmac. I do not recall what position I was in at that time, but it was not #1[the number taped to his car's windshield]. At the last minute there was a lot of shuffling, and I ended up in the 5th vehicle. My vehicle was the last to leave downtown after the shooting because the police set up a roadblock behind my car."[66]

On page 224, Blaine writes: "It was very rare for both the president and vice president to be together at the same time in the same place." This is an understatement – being in the same MOTORCADE was unique![67] Agent Youngblood later wrote: "It is strictly taboo, from the security standpoint, for the President and the Vice President to ride together in the same car, boat, plane, wagon, or anything else."[68] As J.F. terHorst (from the White House Press Corps), a man who covered every major presidential trip – including November 22, 1963 – both at home and abroad, and Colonel Ralph Albertazzie (Nixon's Air Force One pilot) observed in their book: Beyond the Environs of Washington, the Vice President rarely accompa-nies the President. The reason is not only a matter of physical security but one of politics.... But Texas was a special case, the exception that proved the rule."[69] As HSCA attorney Belford Lawson succinctly put it: "Why for the first time in American history were the President and Vice-President together in the same motorcade?"[70]

Blaine also ignores the fact that the roofs along the route were not manned or checked. SAIC of the Nashville office Paul Doster told the *Nashville Banner* back on May 18, 1963, that "a complete check of the en-tire motorcade route" was done for JFK's trip to Nashville. In addition, Doster stated: "Other [police] officers were assigned atop the municipal

65   3/23/63 Secret Service Survey Report: RIF#154-10003-10012. 20 H 391; see also 4 H 171-172 (Curry); 11 HSCA 530.

66   9/3/98 e-mail to the author.

67   Author's interview with Bolden, September 16, 1993; Lawson: 4 H 336. SA Kinney told the HSCA on February 26, 1978, that it was "unusual for LBJ to be along."

68   *My Life Protecting Five Presidents* by Rufus Youngblood, p. 199.

69   *The Flying White House*, pp. 214–5.

70   RIF#180-10093-10320: May 31, 1977, Memorandum from HSCA's Belford Lawson to fellow HSCA members Gary Cornwell and Ken Klein (revised August 15, 1977).

terminal and other buildings along the route. These men took their posts at 8 A.M. and remained at their rooftop stations until the president and his party passed." The roofs of buildings were also guarded on November 18, 1963[71], four short days before Dallas, in addition to San Antonio on November 21, 1963,[72] just the day before, as well as in Fort Worth on the morning of the assassination.[73]

On page 201, regarding agent Bill Greer, the driver of JFK's car in Dallas, Blaine writes: "And, God forbid, if he [Greer] ever did have to make a sudden getaway, he knew the 7,500-pound car with its 300-horsepower engine just didn't gather speed as quickly as he would like." If that wasn't enough, Blaine adds on page 212: "[Greer, after the shooting commenced] quickly tapped on the brake to see how the car would respond." Finally, on page 356, Blaine delivers the coup de grace: "Yes, Bill Greer put his foot on the brake after the first shot. But for God's sake, it had nothing to do with a conspiracy, or negligence – he was merely responding as any professionally trained driver would respond."

Oh, really? Over 70 witnesses and the Zapruder film document Secret Service agent William R. Greer's deceleration of the presidential limousine, as well as his two separate looks back at JFK during the assassination[74] (Greer denied all of this to the Warren Commission[75]). By decelerating from an already slow 11.2 mph, Greer greatly endangered the President's life, and as even Gerald Posner admitted, Greer contributed greatly to the success of the assassination. When we consider that Greer disobeyed a direct order from his superior, Roy Kellerman, to get out of line before the fatal shot struck the President's head, it is hard to give Agent Greer the benefit of the doubt. As ASAIC Roy H. Kellerman said: "Greer then looked in the back of the car. Maybe he didn't believe me."[76] Kellerman also testified to the Warren Commission: "I have driven that car many times, and I never ceased to be amazed even to this day with the weight of the automobile plus

71   RIF#154–10002–10423: Secret Service Final Survey Report, Tampa, FL – underpasses controlled by police and military units; Sheriff's office secured the roofs of major buildings in the downtown and suburban areas; agents on limo; Salinger with Kilduff; close press and photographers (including Stoughton in follow-up car); McHugh in between Secret Service agents in front seat of limo).

72   RIF#154–10002–10424: Final Survey report, San Antonio – Forty members of the military police from Fort Sam Houston, Texas: traffic control, motorcade route security, and intersection control; police helicopter utilized along route; many flanking motorcycles.

73   See also Constance Kritzberg and Larry Hancock, *November Patriots* (Colorado, Undercover Press, 1998), p. 423.

74   *Honest Answers About the Murder of President John F. Kennedy* by Vince Palamara (2021), Chapter 10.

75   2 H 112–132 (Greer): see his entire testimony.

76   Manchester, p. 160.

the power that is under the hood; we just literally jumped out of the God-damn road."[77] Ken O'Donnell stated: "Greer had been remorseful all day, feeling that he could have saved President Kennedy's life by swerving the car or speeding suddenly after the first shots."[78] In addition, Greer told Jackie the following on November 22, 1963 at Parkland Hospital, shortly after the murder: "Oh, Mrs. Kennedy, oh my God, oh my God. I didn't mean to do it, I didn't hear, I should have swerved the car, I couldn't help it. Oh, Mrs. Kennedy, as soon as I saw it, I swerved. If only I'd seen it in time! Oh!"[79] Finally, Dave Powers confirmed Greer's guilt to CBS newsman Charles Kuralt on November 22, 1988, also adding that if Greer would have sped up before the fatal headshot, JFK might still be alive today.[80]

When this reviewer asked Richard Greer, the surviving son of Bill Greer, on 9/17/91: "What did your father think of JFK?" Richard did not respond the first time. When this author asked him a second time, Greer responded: "Well, we're Methodists ... and JFK was Catholic." Bill Greer was born and raised in County Tyrone, Ireland, coming to America in February 1930 and, if that weren't enough, "worked one summer on the estate of Henry Cabot Lodge,"[81] JFK's two-time political opponent (a staunch Republican defeated twice by Kennedy) and Ambassador to Saigon during the CIA and U.S. government–sponsored assassination of President Diem of Vietnam on November 2, 1963 (Lodge was principally involved[82]). Obviously, Greer, just from his association with Lodge, as well as his work in and around Boston, had to have known about Kennedy, as well as his rich family, Ambassador father Joe, and their controversial heritage of alleged bootlegging, Nazi sympathizing, and political history in Boston.[83]

The sequence is crucial:

First shot (or shots) rings out: the car slows.

Greer turns around once.

Kellerman orders Greer to "get out of line; we've been hit!"

---

77   2 H 74.

78   *Johnny, We Hardly Knew Ye* by Dave Powers & Ken O›Donnell w/ Joe McCarthy, p. 44.

79   Manchester, p. 290 (and 386). See also *The Day Kennedy Was Shot* (1992 edition) by Jim Bishop, p. 196.

80   See also Mikita Brottman, *Car Crash Culture* (New York: Palgrave, 2001), p. 173 (chapter authored by Pamela McElwain-Brown): USPP Motorcycle Officer Nick Prencipe spoke to Greer on the night of the murder and said that the agent was quite distressed that evening. JFK aide and friend Dave Powers on Secret Service agent Bill Greer 11/22/88, (https://www.youtube.com/watch?v=OupcoytOznA)

81   2 H 113.

82   See the book by O'Leary and Seymour, *Triangle of Death* (Nashville, TN: WND Books, 2003).

83   *Crossfire* by Jim Marrs (1988), p. 2.

Greer disobeys his superior's order and turns around to stare at JFK for the second time, until after the fatal headshot finds its mark! As stated before, Greer was responsible, at fault, and felt remorse. In short, Greer had survivor's guilt.

But, then, stories and feelings changed.

Agent Greer to the FBI, November 22, 1963: "Greer stated that he first heard what he thought was possibly a motorcycle backfire and glanced around and noticed that the President had evidently been hit [notice that, early on, Greer admits seeing JFK, which the Zapruder proves he did two times before the fatal head shot occurred]. He thereafter got on the radio and communicated with the other vehicles, stating that they desired to get the President to the hospital immediately [in reality, Greer did not talk on the radio, and Greer went on to deny ever saying this during his Warren Commission testimony] ... Greer stated that they (the Secret Service) have always been instructed to keep the motorcade moving at a considerable speed inasmuch as a moving car offers a much more difficult target than a vehicle traveling at a very slow speed. He pointed out that on numerous occasions he has attempted to keep the car moving at a rather fast rate, but in view of the President's popularity and desire to maintain close liaison with the people, he has, on occasion, been instructed by the President to 'slow down.'[84] Greer stated that he has been asking himself if there was anything he could have done to avoid this incident, but stated that things happened so fast that he could not account for full developments in this matter..."[85] [The "JFK-as-scapegoat" theme – and so much for Greer's remorse from earlier the same day.]

Finally, what did Jacqueline Kennedy think of Greer's performance on 11/22/63? Mary Gallagher reported in her book: "She mentioned one Secret Service man who had not acted during the crucial moment, and said bitterly to me, 'He might just as well have been Miss Shaw!' "[86] Jackie also told Gallagher: "You should get yourself a good driver so that nothing ever happens to you."[87] Secret Service agent Marty Venker confirmed that the agent Jackie was referring to was Agent Greer: "If the agent had

---

84   Ironically, in former Chief U. E. Baughman's book, *Secret Service Chief*, it is written (p. 69): "It is a cardinal principle of Presidential protection never to allow the president to stop his car in a crowd if it can possibly be avoided."

85   Sibert and O'Neil Report, November 22, 1963.

86   Mary Barelli Gallagher, *My Life with Jacqueline Kennedy* (New York: David McKay, 1969), p. 342: Secret Service Agent Marty Venker (Rush, p. 25) and Jackie biographer C. David Heymann [*A Woman Called Jackie* (New York: Lyle Stuart, 1989), p. 401] confirm that this unnamed agent was indeed Greer. See also Edward Klein, *Just Jackie: Her Private Years* (Ballantine Books, 1999), pp. 58, 374.

87   Gallagher, p. 351.

hit the gas before the third shot, she griped, Jack might still be alive."[88] Later, authors C. David Heymann and Edward Klein further corroborated that the agent Mrs. Kennedy was referring to was indeed Greer.[89] Manchester wrote: "[Mrs. Kennedy] had heard Kellerman on the radio and had wondered why it had taken the car so long to leave."[90] In addition, Jackie "played the events over and over in her mind…. She did not want to accept Jack's death as a freak accident, for that meant his life could have been spared – if only the driver in the front seat of the presidential limousine [Agent William R. Greer] had reacted more quickly and stepped on the gas … if only the Secret Service had stationed agents on the rear bumper…"[91]

Incredibly, ASAIC Roy Kellerman told the following to FBI agents' Sibert & O'Neil on the night of the murder: "The advanced security arrangements made for this specific trip were the most stringent and thorough ever employed by the Secret Service for the visit of a President to an American city."[92] Perhaps *this* is why JFK reassured a worried San Antonio Congressman Henry Gonzalez on 11/21/63 by saying: "The Secret Service told me that they had taken care of everything – there's nothing to worry about."[93] If that weren't enough, President Kennedy told an equally concerned advance man, Marty Underwood, on 11/21/63: in Houston, "Marty, you worry about me too much."[94]

On pages 230-231, Blaine seeks to pass the blame on to others once again, this time in the form of JFK's Chief of Staff, Ken O'Donnell: "Ken O'Donnell agreed … that Johnson should return to Washington as soon as possible and that yes, he should leave Dallas on Air Force One." However, O'Donnell denied this, telling author William Manchester: "The President and I had no conversation regarding Air Force One. If we had known he was going on Air Force One, we would have taken Air Force Two. One plane was like the other."[95] In fact, when Arlen Specter of the Warren Commission asked O'Donnell, "Was there any discussion about his [LBJ] taking the presidential plane, AF–1, as opposed to AF–2?"

---

88   Secret Service Agent Marty Venker (Rush, p. 25).

89   *A Woman Called Jackie* (New York: Lyle Stuart, 1989), p. 401; Edward Klein, *Just Jackie: Her Private Years* (Ballantine Books, 1999), pp. 58, 374.

90   Manchester, p. 163.

91   Edward Klein, *Just Jackie: Her Private Years* (Ballantine Books, 1999), pp. 58–59, 374, based on an interview Klein had with Kitty Carlisle Hart regarding Hart›s conversation with Jackie.

92   FBI RIF#124-10012-10239; Kellerman would go on to deny ever saying such a thing: 18 H 707-708.

93   *High Treason*, page 127; *Two Men in Dallas* video by Mark Lane, 1976.

94   *Evening Magazine* video 11/22/88; interview with Marty Underwood 10/9/92.

95   Jim Marrs, *Crossfire*, pp. 296–7. See also Bishop, p. 259, and Manchester, pp. 234–5.

O'Donnell responded: "There was not."[96] In this regard, O'Donnell later wrote in his book *Johnny, We Hardly Knew Ye* that a Warren Commission attorney – the aforementioned Arlen Specter – asked him to "change his testimony so that it would agree with the President's": an offer O'Donnell refused.[97] With this in mind, author Jim Bishop reported: "Emory Roberts suggested that Johnson leave at once for Air Force One ... Roberts asked Kenny O'Donnell and he said: 'Yes.' Johnson refused to move. Roberts returned to O'Donnell and asked again: 'Is it all right for Mr. Johnson to board Air Force One now?' 'Yes,' O'Donnell said, 'Yes.' "[98]

This author believes O'Donnell when he says he had no part in LBJ going to Air Force One over Air Force Two. This was a Secret Service (Emory Roberts) decision. Presidential aides Ken O'Donnell and Dave Powers best summed up the situation when they wrote: "Roberts, one of President Kennedy's agents ... had decided to switch to Johnson as soon as Kennedy was shot."[99] In addition, four other authors have noted Agent Roberts' "switch of allegiance," including Chief Curry.[100] Incredibly, Roberts was the President's receptionist during the Johnson administration while still a member of the Secret Service, receiving a Special Service Award from the Treasury Department for improving communications and services to the public in 1968![101] LBJ thought highly of Roberts, and the feeling was mutual – President Johnson told a gathering that "Emory Roberts, who I am sorry can't be here today – he greets me every morning and tells me good-bye every night."[102] (For the record, LBJ didn't think much of Roy Kellerman: "This fellow Kellerman ... he was about as loyal a man as you could find. But he was about as dumb as an ox."[103])

Also predictably, on pages 334-335 & 356-357, Blaine seeks to minimize former agent Abraham Bolden's claims of Secret Service negligence and conspiracy.[104]

---

96   7 H 451. See also *Johnny, We Hardly Knew Ye*, pp. 35, 38.
97   Marrs, p. 297. In fact, as noted by researcher David Starks in his 1994 video *The Investigations*, while Specter's name appears in the hardcover version of O'Donnell's book, it was deleted from the mass-market paperback (p. 41)!
98   Bishop, p. 244.
99   *Johnny, We Hardly Knew Ye*, p. 34.
100   Manchester, pp. 165, 175; Curry, pp. 36–37; Hepburn, *Farewell America*, p. 229; *The Flying White House*, p. 215. (https://www.presidency.ucsb.edu/documents/remarks-the-secret-service-and-presentation-award-james-j-rowley)
101   *The Washington Post*, October 11, 1973.
102   Remarks of LBJ 11/23/68 – see http://www.presidency.ucsb.edu/ws/index.php?pid=29254
103   Michael R. Beschloss, *Reaching for Glory: Lyndon Johnson's Secret White House Tapes, 1964–1965* (New York: Simon & Schuster, 2002), p. 703.
104   See Bolden's excellent 2008 book *The Echo from Dealey Plaza*.

Blaine (on pages 350 and 352) seeks to cast away *any* notion that the Secret Service agents believed there was a conspiracy, yet there is the record that says differently:

> From the February 22, 1978 House Select Committee on Assassinations (HSCA) interview of Miami SAIC John Marshall, former White House Detail agent who conducted all the advance work on President Kennedy's frequent trips to Palm Beach: "Twice during the interview, Mr. Marshall mentioned that, for all he knew, someone in the Secret Service could possibly have been involved in the assassination. This is not the first time an agent has mentioned the possibility that a conspiracy existed, but it is the first time that an agent has acknowledged the possibility that the Secret Service could have been involved."

In addition, former agents Jerry O'Rourke, Sam Kinney, Abraham Bolden, and Maurice Martineau believed there was a conspiracy, as well![105]

The Kennedy Detail, a book firmly rooted in the "Oswald-did-it-alone" camp, also contains contradictory evidence of conspiracy in its pages. On page 216, Blaine describes the shooting sequence in this manner: "...the first shot strikes the president, the second shot strikes Governor Connally, and the third shot strikes JFK in the head..." There is no acknowledgement of the Warren Commission's fictional single bullet theory or the known missed shot that struck bystander James Tague! This is a pattern Hill and Blaine repeat on national television.[106] On page 217, Blaine writes that agent Clint Hill saw "a bloody, gaping, fist-sized hole clearly visible in the back of his head," clear evidence that JFK was struck by a shot from the FRONT, as also confirmed by Hill's report[107] and Warren Commission testimony[108], not to mention the reports (plural) from fellow agent Paul Landis (whose contents were confirmed by Landis to the HSCA[109]), no matter what Landis or Blaine say now (see pages 225 & 352-353), as well as the statements made by agent Sam Kinney to myself (and, ironically, in Blaine's own book, pages 216 & 218, regarding blood hitting his windshield!) and agent Win Lawson, who also "saw a huge hole

105   *Survivor's Guilt*, numerous.
106   Fox News 11/12/10.
107   Hill's November 30, 1963, report: 18 H 740–5. (See also the 2004 National Geographic documentary, *Inside the U.S. Secret Service*.)
108   2 H 141, 143.
109   Landis's report dated November 27, 1963: 18 H 758–9; Landis's detailed report dated November 30, 1963: 18 H 751–7; HSCA Report, pp. 89, 606 (referencing Landis's interview, February 17, 1979, outside contact report, JFK Document 014571).

in the back of the president's head."[110] Blaine also uses this same language later in the book (page 258):

Now the men who just four and a half hours earlier had seen the back of President Kennedy's head blown off hauled the casket holding his dead body..." Finally, regarding Hill, Blaine describes his friends' recollections of the autopsy (page 266): "Six inches down from the neckline, just to the right of the spinal column, there was a small wound, a hole in the skin... All Clint could see was that the right rear portion of President Kennedy's head was completely gone.

On page 261, Blaine writes: "[7:55 P.M., 11/22/63] For about twenty minutes [Chief James J] Rowley gave [the agents] what could only be called a pep talk... There was no feeling that he blamed anyone or that the assassination could somehow have been prevented." On page 275, Blaine says of SAIC Behn (deceased 4/21/93): "From everything Jerry Behn had heard about the tragedy in Dallas, nobody was to blame." Blaine carries this incredibly dumb statement even further during television interviews for the book – he told MSNBC's Chris Matthews on 11/12/10: "No, there was nothing that could have been done to stop it."

On pages 264-265, Blaine related how he almost shot President Johnson on 11/23/63 with his Thompson submachine gun, a tale of dubious merit that garnered much press before the release of the book.

Blaine seems to be unaware of the following, as reported by the Assassination Records Review Board in 1998: "Congress passed the JFK Act of 1992. One month later, the Secret Service began its compliance efforts. However, in January 1995, the Secret Service destroyed presidential protection survey reports for some of President Kennedy's trips in the fall of 1963. The Review Board learned of the destruction approximately one week after the Secret Service destroyed them, when the Board was drafting its request for additional information. The Board believed that the Secret Service files on the President's travel in the weeks preceding his murder would be relevant."[111]

On page 359, Blaine identifies the agent recalled at Love Field as SA Don Lawton, the other agent (along with SA Henry Rybka) "ostensibly" left to secure Love Field for the President's departure and takes this reviewer to task for his misidentification. In the interest of time, please see this reviewer's online videos wherein he fully explains himself, his rationale, and his belief that, regardless of who the agent is (and he is willing

---

110   See article in *The Virginian-Pilot*, June 17, 2010, by Bill Bartel.
111   ARRB Final Report (1998), p. 149.

to concede that it was probably Lawton after all), the substance of what is being depicted in the video – the essence – remains the same. Suffice to say that many people were "fooled" by this footage – former JFK agent Larry Newman, the ARRB, The History Channel, Rybka's family, millions of YouTube viewers, countless authors and researchers, and even a December 2009 Discovery Channel Secret Service documentary *Secrets of the Secret Service*!

Although very well written, along with some nice photographs, as well, *The Kennedy Detail* is really a thinly veiled attempt to rewrite history (a la Gerald Posner and Vince Bugliosi, who believe 11/22/63 was the act of a single lone man) and absolve the agents of their collective survivor's guilt (and to counter the prolific writings of a certain reviewer). In the eyes of those from *The Kennedy Detail*, the assassination was the act of *two* "lone men": Oswald, who pulled the trigger, and JFK, who set himself up as the target. Simply put: President Kennedy *was* indeed a very nice man, did not interfere with the actions of the Secret Service, did not order the agents off his limousine (in Tampa, in Dallas, or elsewhere), and did not have his staff convey any anti-security sentiments, either. The sheer force and power of what these men all told me, a complete stranger, in correspondence and on the phone, is all the more strong because, not only did they have a vested interest to protect themselves, the vast majority believe that Oswald acted alone and that all official "stories" are correct.

In light of the work of this reviewer, future pensions, professional and personal reputations, and so forth, *The Kennedy Detail* makes perfect sense. After the reviewer's letter to Clint Hill, it truly *was* "a book that *had* to be written." A postscript: Gerald Blaine stated on 11/11/10 on MSNBC's *Morning Joe*: "We felt we were 100% failure."

Finally, you said something we can ALL agree on, Mr. Blaine.

CHAPTER TWO

FORMER KENNEDY SECRET SERVICE
AGENT CLINT HILL'S BOOK
MRS. KENNEDY & ME

CLINT HILL

I so wanted to dislike this book. As the leading civilian literary expert on the Secret Service, I had previously----and rightfully---lambasted Lisa McCubbin's prior effort entitled *The Kennedy Detail* for its rewriting of history, blaming JFK for his own death and putting words in the late president's mouth that he never once uttered, as verified by the prior accounts of numerous top agents and White House aides, many of whom were there in Dallas (unlike former agent Gerald Blaine). As previously stated, it was my 22-page letter to former agent Clint Hill that angered him and his best friend to whom I had also spoken to, the aforementioned Blaine, that directly led to the writing of *The Kennedy Detail* and, by extension, the need to write a follow-up tome, *Mrs. Kennedy & Me* (whenever a book is even a mild best-seller, which their first effort was, it is almost a guarantee that, if there is any gas left in the tank, so to speak, a further literary work will be forthcoming). In fact, both agents Blaine and Hill debated the merits of my research on television and, if that weren't enough, I was mentioned on pages 359-360 of *The Kennedy Detail* (without naming me, of course). One could argue several other pages refer to my work, directly or indirectly, but I digress from the matter at hand.

Simply put, *Mrs. Kennedy & Me* is excellent: a literary home run, second only to another brand-new work, the outstanding 2012 book *Within Arm's Length* by former agent Dan Emmett, as attaining the mantle of being the best book on the Secret Service by a former agent ever to date (1865-2012 and counting). I have to say in all honesty: Mr. Hill and Ms. McCubbin have a lot to be proud of in this book. It is consistently everything *The Kennedy Detail* is not: truthful, honest, no axe to grind, not dry or boring, well written, and coming from the perspective of a brave and dedicated public servant who *was* truly there. (To be fair, even *The Kennedy Detail,* and certainly the documentary it was based on, had its moments, although my judgment is rightfully clouded by what I and others feel are the purposeful untruths and propaganda contained throughout, as well as the exasperating third-person narrative interwoven throughout the book, making it hard to pin down exactly *who* was responsible for specific passages. President Kennedy did *not* order the agents off his limousine in Tampa, in Dallas, or anywhere else, for that matter- SAIC Behn, ASAIC Boring, ATSAIC Godfrey, many of their colleagues, and several prominent White House aides said so). Do I still have misgivings about some of the agents on the Kennedy detail? Sure; that will never change. Am I also an ardent admirer of the Secret Service? You bet: the agency has a whole lot to be proud of. Clint Hill at least *tried* to do something that fateful day in Dallas and carried much guilt and depression over the sad events of that time and place. That is a whole lot more than several of his colleagues can lay claim to. That aside, *Mrs. Kennedy & Me* is highly recommended to everyone for its honesty and rich body of true, first-hand accounts of guarding First Lady Jacqueline Kennedy. Too bad this book wasn't even longer, and *The Kennedy Detail* did not exist, but one cannot ask for everything.

The assassination-related part of this book aside, I obviously quite liked this book- there are no if's, and's, or but's about it. However, upon reflection, there are several items in the assassination-related section (and elsewhere) that should be noted. (Indeed, I later added a disclaimer to my online review noting this dissent). On pages 55-56, Hill talks about the benefits of Jackie Kennedy keeping a low profile during her trip to New York as beneficial to security: "The fewer people who know your intended destination or route, the better. A police escort would have just drawn attention to us, so we kept the motorcade to as few vehicles as possible." Indeed, on yet another trip to New York in early 1963, this one involving both Jackie and JFK, Hill records Jackie as stating: "We want to keep it private...No police escorts, no motorcades, no official functions. We just want to enjoy the city like we used to." However, this very same situation for President Kennedy in New York, the very same city, in mid-November 1963 was viewed not as a virtue but as a detriment to his safety and welfare by several writers after his assassination. Today, these kinds of trips are known by the Secret Service as "OTR" s, or "off the records," and they are quite effective, now as then, in their element of surprise from potential assassins. Indeed, Hill writes: "It was a real challenge for the Secret Service agents to keep these presidential movements private yet still maintain an adequate amount of protection, without police escorts or blocking the streets, but we managed." That was their job, and they did it well...until November 22, 1963. In addition, this book vividly demonstrates that Jackie DID indeed travel with JFK on many trips other than the fateful Texas venture in November 1963: New York, Florida, Boston, Mexico, Costa Rica, Canada, Germany, etc. Page 136 has an item of much interest to those contrasting the measures used in Dallas: "The lead vehicle in the motorcade was a press truck---an open flatbed truck with rails around the outside---filled with about a dozen photographers. This was typical when you expected large crowds along a motorcade route for a president, but I'd never seen it, prior to this trip [Pakistan], for a first lady." *Dallas Morning News* reporter Tom Dillard testified to the Warren Commission: "We lost our position at the airport. I understood we were to have been quite a bit closer. We were assigned as the prime photographic car which, as you probably know, normally a truck precedes the President on these things [motorcades] and certain representatives of the photographic press ride with the truck. In this case, as you know, we didn't have any and this car that I was in was to take photographs which was of spot-news nature."[112]

---

112   6 H 163. As the author presented at the COPA 1996 and Lancer 1997 conferences, the

On page 202, there is a photo of the agents surrounding the presidential limousine at the Orange Bowl in Miami in December 1962: agents Gerald Blaine (of *Kennedy Detail* infamy), Ken Giannoules, Clint Hill, Paul Landis, Frank Yeager (uncredited), Ron Pontius (uncredited), and Bob Lilley (also uncredited). Hill writes: "I and the other agents jogged alongside the car, constantly scanning the crowd for any sign of disturbance or disruption, as we headed toward the waiting helicopter outside the arena." On page 212, Hill says: "There would always be at least five or six Secret Service agents around the president and trailing close behind the president's limousine was the not so unobtrusive follow-up car."

Still, all things considered, smooth sailing so far- a good book about Jackie Kennedy and Clint Hill, great human-interest anecdotes and dialogue. However, the party ends briefly on pages 270-271, wherein Hill does his best Gerald Blaine "imitation" and seeks to rewrite a little history to suit his own ends. Hill states that it was November 20, 1963, when he saw ASAIC Floyd Boring (the planner of the Texas trip) and, conveniently,[113] fellow ASAIC Roy Kellerman (the agent nominally in charge of the Dallas trip) by the Secret Service office in the White House, as he correctly notes that SAIC Gerald Behn was on vacation at the time. It was here that Boring – with Kellerman strangely silent by his side---conveyed to Hill that JFK allegedly ordered the agents off the limousine in Tampa on 11/18/63, something this author is adamant, based on years of research and interviews with Boring, Behn, and many of their colleagues, never happened. When asked if Hill was aware of what allegedly went down in Tampa, Hill states: "I didn't recall anything out of the ordinary [on the radio]." Hill, "quoting" Boring (who passed away 2/1/08), writes: "(as Boring) We had a long motorcade in Tampa, and it was decided that we should keep two guys on the back of the car for the entire route---just for added precaution." Hill further writes (as himself): "I nodded. That wasn't all that unusual." Then, in a little jumbled thought/ sentence, Hill (once again as Boring), adds: "So, we had Chuck Zboril and Don Lawton on the back of the car the *entire* way," Floyd said. "But *partway* through the motorcade, in an area where the crowds had thinned, the president requested we remove the agents from the back of the car." On page 271, Hill writes: "Really? I asked. I had *never* heard the president ever question

press photographers frequently rode in a flatbed truck in front of the motorcade procession [films courtesy JFK Library; see also *John F. Kennedy: A Life in Pictures*, pp. 178–180, 183, 231]. Photographer Tony Zappone confirmed to the author on December 18, 2003, that a flatbed truck was used for the photographers in Tampa, Florida, on November 18, 1963.

113   Kellerman was conveniently absent from Blaine's alleged 11/25/63 meeting.

procedural recommendations by his Secret Service detail." Hill writes: "What was the reason?" Writing "as" Floyd Boring again (with, again, a strangely silent Roy Kellerman, assuming he was there and this really took place as written): "He said now that we're heading into the campaign, he doesn't want it to look like we're crowding him. And the word is [from whom?], from now on, you don't get on the back of the car unless the situation absolutely warrants it." "Okay," I said. "Understood." Nothing is in writing, Kellerman is silent, Behn is on vacation, and we are to just take Hill at his word that this 2012 reconstruction is the gospel. Congressman Sam Gibbons, who rode a mere foot away in the car with JFK, wrote to me in a letter dated 1/15/04: "I rode with Kennedy every time he rode. I heard no such order. As I remember it the agents rode on the rear bumper all the way. Kennedy was very happy during his visit to Tampa. Sam Gibbons." Also, photographer Tony Zappone, then a 16-year-old witness to the motorcade in Tampa (one of whose photos for this motorcade was ironically used in *The Kennedy Detail*!), told me that the agents were "definitely on the back of the car for most of the day until they started back for MacDill AFB at the end of the day." Win Lawson wrote to this reviewer on 1/12/04, before this book was even a thought, and said: "I do not know of any standing orders for the agents to stay off the back of the car. After all, foot holds and handholds were built into that particular vehicle... it never came to my attention as such." FLOYD BORING himself told me "[JFK] was a very easy-going guy … he didn't interfere with our actions at all." In a later interview, Boring expounded further: "Well that's not true. That's not true. He was a very nice man; he never interfered with us at all." If that weren't enough, Boring also wrote the author: "He [JFK] was very cooperative with the Secret Service." As for ASAIC Floyd Boring, this reviewer has no doubt that Boring did indeed convey the fraudulent notion that JFK had asked that the agents remove themselves from the limo between 11/18-11/19/63, but that the former agent was telling the truth of the matter when he spoke to me years later. You see, Clint Hill wrote in his report:

"I … never personally was requested by President John F. Kennedy not to ride on the rear of the Presidential automobile. I did receive information passed verbally from the administrative offices of the White House Detail of the Secret Service to Agents assigned to that Detail that President Kennedy had made such requests. I do not know from whom I received this information…. No written instructions regarding this were ever distributed … [I] received this information after the President's return to Washington, D.C. This would have been between November 19, 1963, and November 21, 1963 [note the time frame!]. I do not know specifically who advised me of this request by the President."

Mr. Hill's undated report was presumably written in April 1964, as the other four reports submitted to the Warren Commission were written at that time. Why Mr. Hill could not "remember" the specific name of the agent who gave him JFK's alleged desires is very troubling. He revealed it on March 9, 1964, presumably before his report was written, in his (obviously pre-rehearsed) testimony under oath to the future Senator Arlen Specter, then a lawyer with the Warren Commission[114]:

"Specter: Did you have any other occasion en route from Love Field to downtown Dallas to leave the follow-up car and mount that portion of the President's car [rear portion of limousine]? Hill: I did the same thing approximately four times. Specter: What are the standard regulations and practices, if any, governing such an action on your part? Hill: It is left to the agent's discretion more or less to move to that particular position when he feels that there is a danger to the President: to place himself as close to the President or the First Lady as my case was, as possible, which I did. Specter: Are those practices specified in any written documents of the Secret Service? Hill: No, they are not. Specter: Now, had there been any instruction or comment about your performance of that type of a duty with respect to anything President Kennedy himself had said in the period immediately preceding the trip to Texas? Hill: Yes, sir; there was. The preceding Monday, the President was on a trip to Tampa, Florida, and he requested that the agents not ride on either of those two steps. Specter: And to whom did the President make that request? Hill: Assistant Special Agent in Charge Boring. Specter: Was Assistant Special Agent in Charge Boring the individual in charge of that trip to Florida? Hill: He was riding in the Presidential automobile on that trip in Florida, and I presume that he was. I was not along. Specter: Well, on that occasion would he have been in a position comparable to that occupied by Special Agent Kellerman on this trip to Texas? Hill: Yes sir; the same position. Specter: And Special Agent Boring informed you of that instruction by President Kennedy? Hill: Yes sir, he did. Specter: Did he make it a point to inform other special agents of that same instruction? Hill: I believe that he did, sir. Specter: And, as a result of what President Kennedy said to him, did he instruct you to observe that Presidential admonition? Hill: Yes, sir. Specter: How, if at all, did that instruction of President Ken-

114   2 H 136-137.

nedy affect your action and – your action in safeguarding him on this trip to Dallas? Hill: We did not ride on the rear portions of the automobile. I did on those four occasions because the motorcycles had to drop back and there was no protection on the left-hand side of the car."

However, keeping in mind what Boring told this reviewer, the ARRB's Doug Horne – by request of this author – interviewed Mr. Boring regarding this matter on 9/18/96. Horne wrote: "Mr. Boring was asked to read pages 136–137 of Clint Hill's Warren Commission testimony, in which Clint Hill recounted that Floyd Boring had told him just days prior to the assassination that during the President's Tampa trip on Monday, November 18, 1963, JFK had requested that agents not ride on the rear steps of the limousine, and that Boring had also so informed other agents of the White House detail, and that as a result, agents in Dallas (except Clint Hill, on brief occasions) did not ride on the rear steps of the limousine. Mr. Boring affirmed that he did make these statements to Clint Hill, but stated that he was not relaying a policy change, but rather simply telling an anecdote about the President's kindness and consideration in Tampa in not wanting agents to have to ride on the rear of the Lincoln limousine when it was not necessary to do so because of a lack of crowds along the street." SS Agent Clint Hill rides on the rear of the Presidential limousine during the Dallas motorcade, November 22, 1963. This reviewer finds this admission startling, especially because the one agent who decided to ride on the rear of the limousine in Dallas anyway – and on at least four different occasions – was none other than Clint Hill himself. Returning to Hill's book, Hill writes on pages 276-277: "What was most useful, from the Secret Service standpoint, were the special handles on the trunk and the steps on the rear bumper area where two additional agents could ride, and have immediate access to the occupants, should the need arise." Then, in an awkward sentence, Hill continues: "But, as I'd been told the day before, the president did not want us there, on the back of the car." Lisa McCubbin was also the co-author of Gerald Blaine's *The Kennedy Detail*: boy, does this stuff sound familiar---the mantra of JFK-is-to-blame.

After noting that President Kennedy trusted Kellerman "completely" (page 274) and wrongly noting that the SS-100-X was in service since March 1961 (page 276; it was actually in service since June 1961, 3 months later), Hill totally gleans over the infamous drinking incident of 11/21-11/22/63 involving nine agents of the Secret Service, including Clint Hill himself, Paul Landis, Glen Bennett, and Jack Ready! Interestingly, they were all from Shift Leader Emory Roberts' particular shift.

Significantly, none of the agents from the V.P. LBJ detail were involved in the drinking incident. Regarding the issue of the bubbletop, although Hill states (on page 284) that agent Lawson conveyed to Sam Kinney, the driver of the follow-up car, that the bubbletop was to be removed in Dallas, Sam told this reviewer on 10/19/92 and, again, on 3/4/94 and 4/15/94: "It was my fault the top was off [the limousine in Dallas] – I am the sole responsibility of that." In addition, Kinney's oft-ignored report dated November 30, 1963 confirms this fact[115], as does the former agent's recently-released February 26, 1978 HSCA interview: "... SA Kinney indicated that he felt that his was the responsibility for making the final decision about whether to use the bubble-top."[116] Hill, in his zeal to show how "normal" it was for JFK not to use the bubbletop, makes an error, as well as many omissions- he writes: "It was the same whether he was in Berlin, Dublin [wrong-JFK used the top on part of this trip, in bad *and* good weather!], Honolulu, Tampa, San Antonio, or San Jose, Costa Rica." What Hill omits are the many times JFK used a *partial* top (just the front and back with the middle open) *or* the *full* top (New York Spring 1963, several motorcades in D.C., Venezuela, and many other trips). On page 286, Hill states that Bill Greer, the driver of JFK's car, was "a Catholic," yet his own son Richard told me on two occasions that his father was a Methodist. (When asked, "What did your father think of JFK?," Richard did not respond the first time. When this author asked him a second time, Greer responded: "Well, we're Methodists ... and JFK was Catholic.")! In addition, Hill states that Greer "spoke with a bit of a brogue," something not in evidence on his lengthy 1970 interview available on my YouTube Channel.

On page 287, Hill describes the makeup of the follow-up car and writes: "Glen Bennett from the Protective Research Section, handling intelligence." Oh, really? Thanks for the confirmation, Clint. Officially-speaking, he was NOT acting as an active PRS agent that day ... well, at least according to your own colleagues who spoke to me. For his part, former WHD agent J. Walter Coughlin, who assisted fellow agent Dennis R. Halterman on the advance for the San Antonio part of the Texas trip (November 21, 1963), wrote the author: "I can only add the following – I was not in Dallas, so my knowledge is hearsay from good friends who were there." Glen Bennett was on all these trips [second New York, Florida, and Texas] not as a member of PRS but as a temporary shift agent in

115   18 H 730.
116   RIF#180–10078–10493.

that so many of us (shift agents) were out on advance. "This I do know to be a fact and read nothing more into it." Furthermore, the author must have touched a nerve in Coughlin. Winston Lawson wrote the author: "I understand from my friend Walt Coughlin that you wondered why Glen Bennett from PRS was on the trip [note: the author did not tell Coughlin, who lives in Texas, about the author's contact with Lawson, who lives in Virginia, regarding this or any other question]. Nothing sinister about it and had nothing to do with threats or intelligence. There were so many trips, MD and FL, just prior to TX and so many stops in TX that the small WH Detail was decimated supplying advance people. A number of temporarily assigned agents were on all 3 shifts in TX ... I believe Walt had been on an advance before he went to his stop in TX." Clearly, we have a conflict: the written record, my research, and Clint Hill's account versus Walt Coughlin's and Win Lawson's statements to myself. Was PRS Agent Glen Bennett monitoring mortal threats to JFK's life, made in the month of November, and was this covered up afterwards? Is this the reason for the conflicting accounts – and the timing – of Bennett's participation in the second New York trip, the Florida trip, and the Texas trip? Did Bennett ride in the follow-up car and participate on these trips for this purpose? I strongly believe this to be the case. Thanks again, Clint, for the confirmation.

On pages 288-289, Hill mentions that JFK looked back at him on two different occasions during the fateful Dallas motorcade – when Hill briefly rode on the rear of the car on Main St, as depicted in the photo on page 289 – yet did not say anything. JFK not saying anything speaks volumes, in and of itself. Mainly, that he did not care, one way or the other, if the agents were there doing their duty or not. But what is most troubling is the fact that no films or photos this author has ever seen reveal JFK allegedly turning to look at Hill in the first place! Hmmm.... Just to reiterate the point of SAIC Behn's absence from the Texas trip and its importance further, Hill writes (on page 297): "Jerry Behn ... was with the president all the time, just like I was with Mrs. Kennedy. They had a great relationship. The president loved him, trusted him ... Jerry decided to take a week off.... His first annual leave in three years." Kind of convenient.

On pages 290, 291, 305, and 306, Clint Hill states firmly, as he has many times in the past[117], that the *back* of JFK's head was gone, thus indicating that President Kennedy was shot from the front, as entrance

117   Hill's November 30, 1963, report: 18 H 740–5. WC testimony: 2 H 141, 143 (See also the 2004 National Geographic documentary, *Inside the U.S. Secret Service*). See also "The Kennedy Detail," pages 216-217, 266+ media appearances.

wounds leave small holes, while exit wounds leave large holes. Page 290: "...blood, brain matter, and bone fragments exploded from the back of the president's head. The president's blood, parts of his skull, bits of his brain were splattered all over me---on my face, my clothes, in my hair." Page 291: "His eyes were fixed, and I could see inside the back of his head. I could see inside the back of the president's head." Page 305: (at the autopsy) "the wound in the upper-right rear of the head." Page 306: "It looked like somebody had flipped open the back of his head, stuck in an ice-cream scoop and removed a portion of the brain..."

Unlike *The Kennedy Detail*, Clint Hill has written (again, with Lisa Mc-Cubbin) a fine book. That said, it is best to take some of his pre-assassi-nation "reenactments" of statements made by others ("faction"?) with a huge grain of salt, while also noting – with interest – those assassination and post-assassination revelations and statements that do ring true and are of interest to all.

POSTSCRIPT

It was announced that the first book Clint Hill was involved with, Lisa McCubbin's and Gerald Blaine's *The Kennedy Detail*, going to be made into a movie, set for release in 2013, the 50th anniversary of the assassi-nation. Fortunately, thanks to my efforts, the movie was scrapped. The movie should have been about Abe Bolden. That is a great story and a truthful one.

According to Ch. 8 of the ARRB's *Final Report* (1998): Congress passed the JFK Act of 1992. One month later, the Secret Service began its compliance efforts. However, in January 1995, the Secret Service destroyed presidential protection survey reports for some of President Kennedy's trips in the fall of 1963. The Review Board learned of the destruction approximately one week after the Secret Service destroyed them, when the Board was drafting its request for additional information. The Board believed that the Secret Service files on the President's trav-el in the weeks preceding his murder would be relevant. As the ARRB's Doug Horne wrote in a memo dated April 16, 1996: "The 'final decision' to approve the Texas trip made 'late Tuesday night' indicates that decision came on September 24, 1963 ... the Secret Service Protective Survey Re-ports ... which were destroyed in 1995 commence with trip files starting on this same date: September 24, 1963." In addition, the ARRB's Joan Zimmerman noted in a May 1, 1997, Memorandum to File: "Thus far, the US Secret Service collection is in 6 gray archive boxes for documents, 7 large, flat gray boxes with newspapers and clippings, and 1 small box with a tape cassette.... In Box 5 there are three folders marked "trip file." All are empty." The chairman of the ARRB, Judge Jack Tunheim, stated: "The Secret Service destroyed records after we were on the job and working. They claimed it was a mistake that it was just by the normal progression of records destruction."[118] More important are the Florida/Chicago Secret Service Advance reports that the Secret Service intentionally destroyed after being asked for them by the ARRB, and that, according to *The Kennedy Detail*, Gerald Blaine has copies of and preserved.[119] The largest number of known destroyed JFK documents for the U.S. Secret Service was implemented by James Mastrovito, publicly recorded in the ARRB Collection, Joan Zimmerman Correspondence File, Created 04/01/97 CALL REPORT/PUBLIC. USSS Records. Mastrovito destroyed a vial containing a portion of JFK's brain, along with 5 or 6 file cabinets of material, according to the two-page document. James Mastrovito went on to a career in the CIA and he was a former member of JFK's White House Detail!

118   *CBS News*, December 13, 1999.
119   E-mail from researcher Bill Kelly 4/18/12.

CHAPTER THREE

THE DISCOVERY CHANNEL
DOCUMENTARY *THE KENNEDY DETAIL*
(BASED ON THE 2010 GERALD BLAINE BOOK)

B
efore I even begin to discuss this two-hour program, it is necessary for one to have read my lengthy review of the book of the same name, *The Kennedy Detail*. This Discovery Channel documentary originally aired – twice – on 12/2/10 and, again, on 12/4/10 (It was originally supposed to debut on the 47th anniversary of the assassination on 11/22/10 but, for some reason or reasons unknown, the show aired a week and a half later. Like the release of the book on 11/2/10, Election Day, the marketing strategy of Blaine's work was a tad suspect, in my opinion, but I digress). As one who has interviewed and corresponded with most of the Secret Service agents who served under JFK, I was most looking forward to this documentary, as there can be an appeal to an audio/visual format of one's point-of-view that can get lost in translation in strict black and white writings. That said, as with the book of the same

name, there are some things to commend in *The Kennedy Detail* television special, while there are also several noteworthy items to condemn or, at the very least, tread cautiously on.

I must give credit where credit is due: I was most impressed with many of the visuals – the many sundry films and photographs used – in this documentary. In addition, I was also heartened to see then-and – now photographs of the agents and some of their wives, as well. For the record, the JFK Secret Service agents involved in the production were (naturally) Gerald Blaine (in Austin on 11/22/63), Clint Hill (in Dallas on 11/22/63), Paul Landis (same), Winston Lawson (same), David Grant (same, albeit at the Trade Mart), Ron Pontius (the 11/21/63 Houston lead advance agent), Tom Wells, and, oddly enough, Toby Chandler (attending Secret Service school in Washington, D.C. on 11/22/63). The non-assassination aspects of this program where, by and large, entertaining and somewhat riveting at times; in this regard, I don't have much of a problem with these areas of the production, per se, except with the almost too saccharine "Camelot" portrayal of the Kennedys and the "choir-boy," near angelic image that was portrayed of the agents themselves, traits also to be found in the book, as well. Then again, regarding the latter image portrayal, one would think it would be in Blaine's best interest to put the best foot forward, so to speak, and present the agents in the finest light possible, especially considering their miserable failings on 11/22/63, the day President Kennedy was assassinated under their watch.

There is an old saying: "The devil is in the details." It is with this in mind that a look at some of those details, mentioned in the program or avoided, as they pertain to the Secret Service and the assassination of JFK, is in order now.

In a curious and ironic program note, the 2009 Discovery Channel documentary *Secrets of the Secret Service* aired right before both initial airings of *The Kennedy Detail* program and, in this show, an official Secret Service documentary, the narrator, as well as a couple former agents, Joseph Funk and Joe Petro, briefly mention the mistakes the agents made with regard to the assassination that go directly against what is being espoused in the Blaine production; quite a noticeable contrast, to say the least, and one many people, myself included, noticed immediately ! In general, the "blame-the-victim" (JFK) notion that is such part and parcel of both the Blaine book and the documentary is largely replaced by rightfully noting the mistakes made by the agency (taking the president through Dealey Plaza, in particular), as well as the equally false "blame-the-staff" idea, a notion Blaine does not even mention in his book and is, for the record, like blaming JFK for the security deficiencies, false. Specifically, the most alarming contrast with *The Kennedy Detail* program is what *The Secrets of the Secret Service* decided TO deal with that the Blaine show strangely avoided (although it is mentioned in his book): the infamous WFAA/ABC black and white video of an agent being recalled at Love Field during the start of the motorcade in Dallas. This program "buys into" my notion of what is being depicted hook, line, and sinker, which is quite an endorsement, considering that, once again, this is an official Secret Service documentary, made with agency input (as mentioned in my review of the book, many other people "bought into" my notion of what is being shown in this footage, including, notably, former JFK agent Larry Newman, the Rybka family, and countless authors and researchers who have viewed the video, not to mention the 3 million plus people who have viewed this controversial video, popularized by myself, on You Tube). It is strange that Blaine chose not to show this footage, even to debunk it. Equally disturbing is the contrast between his views, as espoused only in his book, and my views, as displayed on the very same network on the very same night of Blaine's documentary!

To his "credit," Blaine and Hill both endorse their book point-of-view regarding the Love Field agent recall video during their joint appearance on C-SPAN on 11/28/10. Ironically, I was discussed by the agents and host Brian Lamb on the show (I was also noted in a major review of the book in the *Vancouver Sun* but, again, I digress)! For her part, co-author Lisa McCubbin posted the following on 11/24/10 on the official Facebook edition of *The Kennedy Detail*: "Contrary to Vince Palamara's claims, the book was absolutely NOT written to counteract his letter to Clint Hill. Mr. Hill never read Palamara's letter – it went straight into the trash. Gerald Blaine wrote this book on his volition, and Mr. Hill contributed after much deliberation." For his part, Hill told Brian Lamb on the C-SPAN program four days later: "I recall receiving a letter which I sent back to him. I didn't bother with it … he called me and I said" Hello" but that was about it. But he alleges that because he sent me a letter 22 pages in length apparently, and that I discussed that with Jerry. I forgot that I ever got a 22-page letter from this particular individual until I heard him say it on TV and I never discussed it with Jerry or anybody else because it wasn't important to me." Yet, in the biggest contradiction of all, Blaine *quoted from my letter to Hill* when I spoke to him on 6/10/05 and mentioned his deep friendship with Hill, as well, extending back to the late 1950's! For the record, I received Hill's signed receipt for the letter, and it was *never* returned to me, either. For his part, Blaine stated on the very same C-SPAN program: "I have never talked to any author of a book," another blatant falsehood that went unchallenged – Blaine was interviewed on 5/12/65 for Manchester's massive best-selling *The Death of a President* (Blaine is also thanked in Manchester's *One Brief Shining Moment*, to boot) and he was interviewed 2/7/04 and 6/10/05, not to mention e-mail correspondence, by myself for my book *Survivor's Guilt: The Secret Service & The Failure To Protect President Kennedy*.

Bear with this seeming digression just a tad more, for it does indeed bear directly on both Blaine's book and on the documentary under specific discussion herein. On the C-SPAN appearance with Hill, regarding myself, Blaine stated: "I am familiar with him, I don't know him… My assessment of Mr. Palamara is that he called probably all of the agents [true], and what agent who answers a phone is going to answer a question "Was President Kennedy easy to protect?" [many of them did, and, like Blaine, told me that JFK was a very nice man, never interfered with the actions of the Secret Service at all, nor did President Kennedy ever order the agents off his limousine] Well, probably he was too easy to protect because he was assassinated [what?]. But the fact that the agents aren't going to tell him anything [many told me information of much value, Blaine included] and he alludes to the fact that when I wrote the book, most of these people were dead. Well, I worked with these people, I knew them like brothers, and I knew exactly what was going on and always respected Jim Rowley because he stood up to the issue and said" Look, we can't say the President invited himself to be killed so let's squash this." So that was the word throughout the Secret Service and he – Mr. Palamara is – there are a number of things that had happened [sic] that he has no credibility [your opinion, Mr. Blaine], he is a self-described expert in his area which I don't know what it is, he was born after the assassination [as was your co-author, Lisa McCubbin!] and he keeps creating solutions to the assassination until they are proven wrong [again, your opinion, Mr. Blaine]." But Blaine wasn't finished with me just yet: "The Zapruder film, when the Zapruder film was run at normal speed, another theme that Palamara throws out is that Bill Greer stopped the car, when it's run at its normal speed, you will notice the car absolutely does not stop at all. This happened in less than six seconds after the President was hit in the throat and moving along." Oh, so you agree with my "solutions" that JFK was shot in the neck from the front, do you, Mr. Blaine? And there were close to 70 witnesses to the limousine slowing or stopping, including seven Secret Service agents and Jacqueline Kennedy – not my "theme" or theory, just the facts. Returning directly to *The Kennedy Detail* documentary, Ron Pontius specifically refers to one of my articles (also a part of a chapter in my book) without naming me. As the narrator, Martin Sheen, notes: "The most painful theories point fingers at the agents themselves." To his credit, Pontius mentioned earlier in the program how the threats to Kennedy's life increased dramatically over those directed toward Eisenhower when JFK took office. That said, the same narrator later mentioned that "Dallas worried the men on the detail," a notion seemingly not made manifest in the security preparations for the fateful Dallas trip.

Keeping all these points into focus, as with the book itself, it is the fraudulent allegations that JFK ordered the agents off the limousine in Tampa, Florida on 11/18/63, which allegedly were made into standing orders for Kennedy's trip to Texas four days later, that is given a spotlight herein. Blaine's words are simply incredible (literally, not credible) and deserve to be quoted, verbatim, here: "President Kennedy made a decision, and he politely told everybody, 'You know, we're starting the campaign now, and the people are my asset,'" said agent Jerry Blaine. "And so, we all of a sudden understood. It left a firm command to stay off the back of the car." Huh? "Everybody"? *That* alleged statement "left a firm command"? As I stated in the review for Blaine's book, not only do many films and photos depict the agents (still) riding on (or walking/ jogging very near) the rear of the limousine in Tampa , including a few shown in this documentary, Congressman Sam Gibbons, who actually rode a mere foot away in the car with JFK, wrote to me in a letter dated 1/15/04: ""I rode with Kennedy every time he rode. I heard no such order. As I remember it the agents rode on the rear bumper all the way. Kennedy was very happy during his visit to Tampa. Sam Gibbons." Also, photographer Tony Zappone, then a 16-year-old witness to the motorcade in Tampa (one of whose photos for this motorcade was ironically used in *The Kennedy Detail*!), told me that the agents were "definitely on the back of the car for most of the day until they started back for MacDill AFB at the end of the day." Agent Hill fibs and blames the entering of the freeway via Dealey Plaza as the reason agents weren't on the back of the car during the shooting, neglecting to mention the fact that, during prior trips, the agents rode on the rear of the car at fast highway speeds, including *in Tampa* four days before, as well as in Berlin and Bogota, Columbia, to name just a couple others. Again, please see my detailed review of *The Kennedy Detail* book for much more on this.

While it is nice to see Toby Chandler and David Grant talk about JFK, they add little or nothing to the assassination debate itself (and neither Grant nor Hill mention the fact that Grant is Clint Hill's brother in law, a fact revealed to myself when I spoke to Gerald Blaine on 6/10/05). For his part, Paul Landis lambastes researchers for "having a field day" with conspiracy theories yet doesn't mention that HE himself tremendously helped these "theorists" via his reports (plural) describing a shot to JFK from the front. Hill further confirms that the back of JFK's head was gone. Finally, Agent Lawson says that there were only three shots, yet fails to mention that, around the very same time as the filming of this documentary, he also stated that he "saw a huge hole in the back of the president's head."

Is it any wonder, then, why I refer to *The Kennedy Detail* Discovery Channel documentary as being slick propaganda, designed to blame President Kennedy for his own assassination by falsely stating that he ordered the agents off his limousine, as well as propagating the whole Oswald-acted-alone mantra? Viewer beware.

CHAPTER FOUR

Former Kennedy Secret Service Agent Paul Landis book *The Final Witness*

PAUL LANDIS

I personally find 88-year-old former JFK Secret Service Agent Paul Landis a bit of an enigma: very credible in some respects, not so credible in others. Landis, who's October 2023 book *The Final Witness* made big headlines in early September 2023 on CNN, NBC, The BBC, TMZ, *Vanity Fair*, *The New York Times*, *People Magazine*, and other media outlets, was largely an unknown commodity to the public at large other than to JFK assassination researchers, as he is one of the eight Secret Service follow-up car agents who rode mere feet away from President Kennedy's limousine when the assassination occurred on 11/22/63

(Sadly, Landis was also one of the 9 agents who drank the morning of the assassination[120]). The specific book excerpt that has caused such an uproar is the claim that Landis found a whole intact bullet on the top of the back seat of the presidential limousine-specifically, above the president's seat where the bubble top would normally attach.

This was an explosive claim. If true, the whole Warren Commission single bullet theory would fall down like a house of cards and, thus, a conspiracy of (at least) two shooters would be readily apparent to all, as the so-called "magic bullet" (also known as Commission Exhibit CE399) could not have been the one to go on to allegedly strike Texas Governor John Connally in the back and cause all of his wounds. The bullet Landis claims to have found apparently did not even travel through JFK's back but came back out of the wound as some sort of "short charge." As everyone knows, accused assassin Lee Harvey Oswald only had enough time to fire three bullets during the assassination with the ill-equipped bolt action Mannlicher Carcano rifle: one shot missed, one shot was the "magic bullet" that allegedly went thru Kennedy and on to Connally, and then there was the fatal head shot. Any more bullets and the Warren Commission was wrong- simple as that. Even President Kennedy's nephew, the son of Robert Kennedy, commented as much:

Robert F. Kennedy Jr ✓
@RobertKennedyJr
⋯

The magic bullet theory is now dead. This preposterous construction has served as the mainstay of the theory that a single shooter murdered President Kennedy since the Warren Commission advanced it 60 years ago under the direction of the former CIA Director Allen Dulles whom my uncle fired. The recent revelations by JFK's Secret Service protector Paul Landis have prompted even the New York Times-among the last lonely defenders of the Warren Report-to finally acknowledge its absurdity.

🔵 nytimes.com/2023/09/09/us/…

9:51 PM · Sep 9, 2023 · **31.8K** Views

So why is Landis an enigma? Because he appears to straddle the fence on the key issues of the case:

On the one hand, he says he now "has his doubts," yet, on the other hand, he also states that he believes Oswald was the lone shooter. In addi-

---

120   18 H 687.

tion, Landis wrote not one but two Secret Service reports shortly after the assassination that both indicate that a shot came from the front[121]:

> My reaction at this time was that the shot came from somewhere towards the front, but I did not see anyone on the overpass, and looked along the right-hand side of the road. By this time we were almost at the overpass, and the only person I recall seeing was a negro male in light green slacks and a beige colored shirt running across a grassy section towards some concrete steps and what appeared to be a low stone wall. He was in a bent over position, and I did not notice anything in his hands.
>
> By now both the President's car and the follow-up car were traveling at a high rate of speed. As we passed under the overpass, I was looking back and saw a motorcycle policeman stopping approximately where I saw the negro running. I do not recall hearing a third shot.
>
> Paul E. Landis, Jr.
> Special Agent
> November 27, 1963

Page Five of Statement of Special Agent Paul K. Landis, Jr., dated Nov. 30, 1963:

> I had drawn my gun, but I am not sure exactly when I did this. I did leave my suit coat unbuttoned all during the motorcade movement, thinking at the time that I could get to my gun faster this way, if I had to.
>
> I glanced towards the President and he still appeared to be fairly upright in his seat, leaning slightly toward Mrs. Kennedy with his head tilted slightly back. I think Mrs. Kennedy had her right arm around the President's shoulders at this time. I also remember Special Agent Clinton Hill attempting to climb onto the back of the President's car.
>
> It was at this moment that I heard a second report and it appeared that the President's head split open with a muffled exploding sound. I can best describe the sound as I heard it, as the sound you would get by shooting a high powered bullet into a five gallon can of water or shooting into a mellon. I saw pieces of flesh and blood flying through the air and the President slumped out of sight towards Mrs. Kennedy.
>
> The time lapse between the first and second report must have been about four or five seconds.
>
> My immediate thought was that the President could not possibly be alive after being hit like he was. I still was not certain from which direction the second shot came, but my reaction at this time was that the shot came from somewhere towards the front, right-hand side of the road.

If that wasn't enough, Landis even verified their contents almost 16 years later when the House Select Committee on Assassinations (or HSCA) did an outside contact report involving Landis[122]:

> (164) JFK Exhibit 647 (V HSCA–JFK hearings, 519). Landis confirmed to the committee the accuracy of his statement to the Warren Commission. Outside contact report with Paul Landis, February 17, 1979, House Select Committee on Assassinations (JFK document 014571).
> (165) Ibid.

That said, when Paul Landis was interviewed for Secret Service Agent Gerald Blaine's 2010 book *The Kennedy Detail*, he changed his tune[123]:

121   18 H 758-759; 18 H 751-757.
122   HSCA REPORT, pages 89 and 606.
123   *The Kennedy Detail* by Gerald Blaine (2010), page 353.

It had taken Paul Landis a long time to get over the trauma of what he'd seen. And it wasn't until many years later that he was able to admit to himself that what he thought he heard and what he thought he saw in the chaos of those tragic moments had very simple explanations. He had said that one of the shots he heard seemed to have come from somewhere toward the front, but when he thought back with a rational mind, he believed it must have been an echo. It wasn't a shot from the front: it was the shot fired from behind him, echoing off the overpass directly ahead.

The initial Landis book hype via Amazon.Com gives one the impression that the former agent will debunk conspiracy claims. From the Amazon.Com book page:

By mid-1964, the nightmares from Dallas remain, and he resigns. It isn't until the fiftieth anniversary that he begins to talk about it, and he reads his first books on the assassination. **Landis learns about the raging conspiracy theories—and realizes where they all go wrong.**

PAUL LANDIS LEARNS ABOUT THE RAGING CONSPIRACY THEORIES—AND REALIZES WHERE THEY ALL GO WRONG.

And yet, the September 2023 media blitz left the opposite impression: this was a book that would scream that there was something rotten in Denmark and there indeed was a conspiracy (the bullet business).

Landis book states that he is "the final witness," yet this is not true: fellow author[124] and Secret Service agent Clint Hill (on the opposite running board of the follow-up car), as well as Mary Moorman, the Newman Family, Tina Towner (also an author[125]), Milton Wright, Rosemary and Linda Willis, and others who witnessed the assassination are still with us. In addition, Landis book claims he is finally "breaking his silence," yet nothing could be further from the truth: in addition to his two Secret Service reports in the Warren Commission volumes (the second a lengthy seven pages of details), Landis had the aforementioned 1979 HSCA contact, an interview for a 1983 newspaper article,[126] an interview for a 1988

124   Author of the books *Mrs. Kennedy & Me* (2012), *Five Days in November* (2013), *Five Presidents* (2016), and *My Travels with Mrs. Kennedy* (2022). In addition, Hill wrote the Foreword and contributed significantly to the Gerald Blaine book *The Kennedy Detail* (2010).
125   *Tina Towner: My Story as the Youngest Photographer at the Kennedy Assassination* (2012).
126   *The Coshocton (Ohio) Tribune,* 11/20/83; *Greenfield (Ohio) Daily Times,* 11/22/83.

newspaper article[127], a 2003 interview for the A&E program *All The President's Kids* (also a DVD), interviews for both the 2010 book *The Kennedy Detail* and the television documentary of the same name (also a DVD), a 2014 *Vanity Fair* article[128], a 2016 Sixth Floor Museum videotaped oral history, a 2016 Cleveland.Com interview, as well as several You Tube videos depicting local Ohio programs that Landis participated in.

In the 2016 Cleveland.Com interview, Landis came out against the Warren Commission's single bullet theory that is essential in having Oswald as the lone assassin:

In fact, 2016 was something of a banner year for Secret Service revelations, as Clint Hill came out in his book *Five Presidents* also denouncing the single bullet theory[129]:

He sounds almost proud of not having read the Warren Report, and said they got it right about no conspiracy and that Oswald as the lone actor, but blew it with the single-bullet theory. That theory holds that a single shot struck the President and also wounded Governor John Connally.

As with the Connallys before them, it is as if former agents Landis and Hill cannot comprehend the ramifications of not believing the single bullet theory.

I was satisfied with the commission's conclusion that Oswald acted alone, and to this day, I believe that to be the case—there has never been any factual evidence to prove otherwise. The one conclusion with which I disagree is the "Magic Bullet Theory"—the notion that the first shot which passed through President Kennedy's neck then entered Governor Connally's body. Governor and Mrs. Connally and I were all of the same opinion—having been up-close witnesses—that the governor's wounds were caused by the second shot, the one that did not hit President Kennedy.

Staying on Clint Hill for a moment, the former agent has been on the record for decades stating that the fatal wound to JFK involved the right rear of his head, indicating (although he would never admit on the record) a shot from the front, as entrance wounds make small wounds and exit wounds make larger wounds:

127 *The Columbus (Ohio) Dispatch*, 11/20/88.
128 Could the Secret Service Have Saved J.F.K.? | Vanity Fair. (https://www.vanityfair.com/news/politics/2014/10/secret-service-jfk-assassination)
129 *Five Presidents* by Clint Hill (2016), page 178.

Excerpts from Hill's 11/30/63 report[130]:

> As I lay over the top of the back seat I noticed a portion of the President's head on the right rear side was missing and he was bleeding profusely. Part of his brain was gone. I saw a part of his skull with hair on it lying in the seat. The time of the shooting was approximately 12:30 p.m., Dallas time. I looked forward to the jump seats and noticed Governor Connally's chest was covered with blood and he was slumped to his left and partially covered up by his wife. I had not realized until this point that the Governor had been shot.

> At approximately 2:45 a.m., November 23, I was requested by ASAIC Kellerman to come to the morgue to once again view the body. When I arrived the autopsy had been completed and ASAIC Kellerman, SA Greer, General McHugh and I viewed the wounds. I observed a wound about six inches down from the neckline on the back just to the right of the spinal column. I observed another wound on

> the right rear portion of the skull. Attendants of the Joseph Gawler Mortuary were at this time preparing the body for placement in the casket. A new casket had been obtained from Gawler Mortuary in which the body was to be placed.

An excerpt from Hill's 3/9/64 Warren Commission testimony[131]:

> Mr. Specter. What did you observe as to President Kennedy's condition on arrival at the hospital?
> ⇨ Mr. Hill. The right rear portion of his head was missing. It was lying in the rear seat of the car. His brain was exposed. There was blood and bits of brain all over the entire rear portion of the car. Mrs. Kennedy was completely covered with blood. There was so much blood you could not tell if there had been any other wound or not, except for the one large gaping wound in the right rear portion of the head. ⇧

One of several examples from *The Kennedy Detail*[132]:

> tered around the car like vile confetti. A pool of blood covered the floor. And slumped across the seat, President Kennedy lay unmoving, a bloody, gaping, fist-sized hole clearly visible in the back of his head. ⇦

An excerpt from Hill's first book *Mrs. Kennedy & Me*[133]:

> As I peered into the backseat of the car, I saw the president's head, in her lap. His eyes were fixed, and I could see inside the back of his head. I could see inside the back of the president's head. ⇧

An excerpt from Hill's second book *Five Days in November*[134]:

> IN NOVEMBER
> | 139
> The doctor points to a wound on the right rear of the head. This, he says, was the fatal wound. He lifts up a piece of the scalp, with skin and hair still attached, which reveals a hole in the skull, and an area in which a good portion of the brain matter is gone. I close my eyes for a moment, wincing, as the doctor keeps talking.

---

130   18 H 740-745.
131   2 H 141.
132   *The Kennedy Detail*, page 217.
133   *Mrs. Kennedy & Me*, page 291.
134   *Five Days in November*, page 139.

An excerpt from Hill's third book *Five Presidents*[135]:

FIVE PRESIDENTS | 155

and skull fragments. The president's head was in Mrs. Kennedy's lap, his
... fixed, and a gaping hole in the back of his skull.

And, perhaps most dramatically, Hill demonstrating the JFK head wound
on the television documentary *JFK: The Final Hours* in 2013 (also a DVD):

In a September 2023 discovery by this author, it turns out that Paul
Landis mirrored Hill's location for the JFK head wound during his 2016
Sixth Floor Museum oral history[136]:

135   *Five Presidents*, page 155.
136   Paul Landis on location of JFK head wound: blockbuster. (https://www.youtube.com/

Hill and Landis were colleagues and friends for many years. Here is a 2010 photo of them (with Hill's future wife and four-time co-author Lisa McCubbin) during the filming of *The Kennedy Detail* documentary in Dealey Plaza:

However, Hill came out against Landis book after he made the following announcement on his Twitter account:

Clint Hill ✓
@ClintHill_SS

I will be on NBC Nightly News tonight with my response to the New York Times article about Paul Landis' book.
@SecretService
@nytimes
@peterbakernyt

4:09 PM · Sep 10, 2023 · **1,042** Views

4 Reposts   **37** Likes

Sure enough, Hill denounced Landis book on *NBC Nightly News* on 9/10/23. His thoughts were outlined in the Vanity Fair article referenced above:

watch?v=zITNoi2U3II)

"I didn't want to talk about it," Mr. Landis said. "I was afraid. I started to think, did I do something wrong? There was a fear that I might have done something wrong and I shouldn't talk about it."

Indeed, his partner, Clint Hill, the legendary Secret Service agent who clambered onto the back of the speeding limousine in a futile effort to save Kennedy, discouraged Mr. Landis from speaking out. "Many ramifications," Mr. Hill warned in a 2014 email that Mr. Landis saved and shared last month.

Mr. Hill, who has set out his own account of what happened in multiple books and interviews, cast doubt on Mr. Landis's version on Friday. "I believe it raises concerns when the story he is telling now, 60 years after the fact, is different than the statements he wrote in the days following the tragedy" and told in subsequent years, Mr. Hill said in an email. "In my mind, there are serious inconsistencies in his various statements/stories."

The crux of the matter seems to be, for both Clint Hill and certain members of the JFK assassination research community (this current author included), the fact that Landis is previously on record a whopping three different times[137] in stating that what he now in 2023 calls a whole bullet, which he placed on JFK's stretcher in the emergency room, was then merely a bullet "fragment" which he "gave to somebody." Here is what he said in 1983[138]:

> **Landis said that when he got to the Kennedy limousine outside the hospital, the president had already been taken inside, but he helped Mrs. Kennedy out. He said there was a bullet fragment on the top of the back seat that he picked up and gave to somebody.**

Here is what Landis said in 1988[139]:

---

137   Although, importantly, not in either of his 1963 reports.
138   *The Coshocton (Ohio) Tribune*, 11/20/83; *Greenfield (Ohio) Daily Times*, 11/22/83.
139   *The Columbus (Ohio) Dispatch*, 11/20/88.

he remembers "going by the president's convertible and seeing the blood on the seat." And then he saw something else. "I distinctly remember there was a bullet fragment on the seat which I picked up and handed to somebody." He doesn't remember to whom, but he does recall hesitating beforehand, wondering, "Should I grab it, or should I leave it where it is in the car?"

And here is what Landis conveyed in *The Kennedy Detail* from 2010[140]:

> When Agent Paul Landis helped Mrs. Kennedy out of the car he saw a bullet fragment in the back where the top would be secured. He picked it up and put it on the seat, thinking that if the car were moved, it might be blown off. And then he saw a bloody Zippo lighter with the presidential seal on it. He picked it up and put it in his pocket. He picked up her hat and purse and brought them inside.

Landis claimed in the Blaine book that he put the fragment on the seat, rather than giving it to somebody as he previously stated in both 1983 and 1988. If all this weren't enough, Landis makes no mention of finding a bullet or bullet fragments in his 2016 Sixth Floor Museum oral history[141].

In Landis own 9/12/23 NBC interview, separate from the one Hill did, he reports three gunshots (which in 2016 he said were fired in "5 to 6 seconds," with the second and third fired rapidly one after the other[142]) and didn't address the discrepancy with his initial 2-shot reports from decades ago. He also never mentioned stating (again in two different reports) that one of the shots came from the front. Incongruously, he still seemed to favor an Oswald-did-it scenario and that there was no grassy knoll shot, despite his initial two reports stating that a shot came from the front.

What's more, according to fellow follow-up car Secret Service agent Sam Kinney's neighbor Gary Loucks[143] (reported publicly for the first time in 2013), Kinney admitted to Loucks in 1986 to finding an extra bullet and putting it on a stretcher, a story eerily like Landis claims a

---

140   *The Kennedy Detail*, page 225.
141   Paul Landis - no mention of bullets or fragments in 2016 interview plus bad memory. (https://www.youtube.com/watch?v=L7ZDZC89Y3Y)
142   Paul Landis - fast shots that sounded different but fails to mention frontal shots from HIS reports.(https://www.youtube.com/watch?v=TJD0CdAgIgk)
143   Loucks died on 2/23/23. Gary Lee Loucks (1946-2023) - Find a Grave Memorial.(https://www.findagrave.com/memorial/249979212/gary-lee-loucks)

decade later. One wonders if Landis read the articles about Loucks and Kinney or saw the video[144]? Likewise, Parkland Hospital Nurse Phyllis Hall[145] came out in the same year, 2013, to state that she saw a mystery bullet at Parkland.[146] One also wonders if Landis saw the articles or the videos about her story. Interestingly, Hall's 2013 story surfaced yet again in September 2023 to corroborate Landis tale.[147]

Possible corroboration for Landis 2023 story (or something he may have viewed previously)[148] comes from HSCA attorney Belford V. Lawson, in charge of the Secret Service area of the "investigation," the author of a memo regarding an interview with Nathan Pool conducted on 1/10/77 and headlined "POOL's CO-DISCOVERY OF THE 'TOMLINSON' BULLET." In the memo, Pool mentions the fact that two Secret Service agents were by the elevator, one of which " remained there throughout most or all of Pool's stay." Before we can catch our breath, a third Secret Service agent enters the picture; although all these men were in the immediate vicinity of the discovery of the bullet, one agent "was within 10 feet when Pool recognized the bullet." According to Pool, the bullet was pointed, and he added that it "didn't look like it had hit anything and didn't look like it had been in anything."

Lawson felt that further development of Pool's testimony may reveal the following:

QUOTE: "A SECRET SERVICE AGENT WAS FOR A SIGNIFICANT PERIOD OF TIME CLOSE ENOUGH TO THE ELEVATOR TO PLANT A BULLET; MAY LEAD TO AN IDENTIFICATION OF THAT AGENT..."[149]

In addition, author Jim DiEugenio wrote the author: "During the last days of the public hearings of the House Select Committee, Congressman, now Senator Chris Dodd, gave the most important revelation. He stood up or sat up and asked Professor G. Robert Blakey to answer one

144   JFK Secret Service Agent Sam Kinney's neighbor's (Gary Loucks) revelations(https://www.youtube.com/watch?v=ZaW6k0N6Zzl)
145   Hall died on 4/18/23. Obituary | Phyllis J. Hall of Irving, Texas | Donnelly's Colonial Funeral Home) https://www.colonialofirvingfuneral.com/obituary/phyllis-hall)
146   Nurse claims JFK had another bullet lodged in body after assassination – New York Daily News (https://www.nydailynews.com/2013/11/10/nurse-claims-jfk-had-another-bullet-lodged-in-body-after-assassination/)
147   JFK assassination nurse says she SAW the 'pristine bullet' Secret Service agent Paul Landis now claims he retrieved from limo and placed on stretcher - upending the 'magic bullet' theory | Daily Mail Online (https://www.dailymail.co.uk/news/article-12509921/JFK-assassination-nurse-Phyllis-Hall-Paul-Landis.html?ito=amp_twitter_share-top)
148   As referenced in my books and prevalent online.
149   https://ia601206.us.archive.org/31/items/nsia-PoolNathan/nsia-PoolNathan/Pool%20Nathan%2001.pdf

question. And he said, Mr. Blakey, will you please explain to me about the bullet that was found in the President's limousine that cannot be ballistically matched to the Oswald weapon? Congressman Dodd never received an answer to this day."

Finally, in yet another story prevalent online that predates Landis 2023 bullet story, Captain James Young[150] story of a bullet – a spent, misshapen, but otherwise intact, bullet – that Young, a Navy doctor, said was found late at night, on the floor, in the back of Kennedy's limousine. He inspected it himself. The bullet was found by two chief petty officers who, during the autopsy, were sent to retrieve any skull fragments they could find in the limousine. They came back with three pieces of bone, and the bullet. The skull fragments were reported – but not the bullet.

Writer Ed Curtin thoughtfully wonders if Paul Landis book is merely a "limited hangout."[151] The man seen with Landis during several televised interviews and the author of the new *Vanity Fair* article, Cleveland-based attorney James Robenalt, helped Landis to "process his memories," a strange choice of words, indeed.[152]

The more I investigate this whole thing, the more skeptical I become of Landis 2023 statements. Just as Jean Hill embellished her account in her book *The Lady in Red*, perhaps to sell books and make her account more dramatic, I believe such is the case here. And, just like Jean Hill, the "good news" is that the core of their story is true- Jean Hill was there and indicated a shot came from the knoll. Landis wrote in two reports that a shot came from the front, he verified their contents when the HSCA contacted him in early 1979 as they were writing the final report, and I want to believe his denouncement of the single bullet theory in 2016 (echoing Clint Hills own denouncement in the same year in his book *Five Presidents*) and his stating/demonstrating that the back of JFK's head was missing (also in 2016, again echoing Clint Hill) are both true.

As for these 2023-vintage statements about the bullet – I don't believe it. I wanted to at first, but it falls apart upon deeper scrutiny.

This whole thing almost reminds me of the Roscoe White story that broke out in August 1990: everyone was so excited as Ricky White made the media rounds. Oh, my Lord – there is a photo of his wife with Ruby!

150   White House Physician, Autopsy Eyewitness, questions President Ford about Missing Bullet - ASSASSINATION ARCHIVES.(https://aarclibrary.org/white-house-physician-autopsy-eye-witness-questions-president-ford-about-missing-bullet/)
151   Another Magical JFK Assassination Pseudo-Debate and Limited Hangout | Dissident Voice.(https://dissidentvoice.org/2023/09/another-magical-jfk-assassination-pseudo-debate-and-limited-hangout/)
152   James Robenalt - Wikipedia,(https://en.wikipedia.org/wiki/James_Robenalt)

Wow- he was a Dallas police officer trainee. What?! He had the third back-yard photo...

But then, upon further scrutiny, the main part of his story fell to pieces-his father was the grassy knoll shooter as "proven" by a diary that no longer existed. Beverly Oliver said she saw Roscoe White on the knoll (yeah, right); Gerry Patrick Hemming said he knew Roscoe (sure he did) ...

Then Ricky disappeared and that was that.

Will Paul Landis likewise disappear and avoid the tough questions? We shall see.

Well, the book was due out October 10, 2023, yet my pre-ordered hardcover was delayed until the end of the month. Being impatient, I decided to get the readily available Kindle edition.[153] Having devoured the entire book in one day, I must say that I was disappointed, both for what Landis says and for what he does not say. Quite frankly, if it wasn't for the massive advance hype, I think his book would have sunk without a trace with meager sales, to boot (when I originally posted about his upcoming book, very few people seemed to care until the huge media hype came along). In fact, judging by the early mixed reviews on Amazon, Landis should be lucky that he has garnered a lot of advance sales because word of mouth from this point on will not be favorable.

Comically, right from the start, the Acknowledgments section of the book mentions Clint Hill: "I appreciate your support for my book." Yet, as we know, Hill came out against his book on NBC and, if that wasn't enough, Landis was not invited to a get-together of all surviving Kennedy Detail Secret Service agents at the residence of Hill and his wife (and co-author) Lisa McCubbin Hill.[154] Ron Pontius, Gerry Blaine, Ken Giannoules, Tom Wells, and Rad Jones came to the Hill's residence, as well as another mutual friend, former Secret Service Director Joseph Clancy, yet Landis (who was Hill's friend for decades and participated in both *The Kennedy Detail* book and documentary) was not invited and not present.

From the Introduction, we learn that Landis was given the Josiah Thompson book *Six Seconds in Dallas* in 2014 and that he "actively avoided reading any books about the events of November 22, 1963," although he does acknowledge reading *The Kennedy Detail* to which, as already noted, he participated in both the book and documentary.

---

153   With this in mind, all references are to the Kindle edition.
154   Clint Hill Facebook 9/24/23. Hill noted: "There were messages from former USSS director Lew Merletti and Secretary of State Tony Blinken and his wife Evan Ryan, the granddaughter of James J. Rowley, my first boss at the White House."

The bulk of the book will have little interest to all but the most ardent Kennedy fanatics and Secret Service buffs, but I will note some items along the way of getting to the more "meat and potato" points about the bullet and so forth.

From Chapter One we learn that fellow Kennedy agents Richard Johnsen (the future keeper of CE399) and David Grant (future co-advance agent with Win Lawson in Dallas and Clint Hill's brother-in-law) were roommates of Landis during his Secret Service career.

From Chapter Two Landis notes the influence that fellow Ohio native Robert Foster had on his Secret Service career-Landis began his time in the agency in 1959, ending in 1964[155] (Foster would go on to be a member of the Kiddie Detail during the JFK years: the agents who looked after Caroline and John, Jr.).

Chapter 3 mentions Landis' study of the 700-page Secret Service manual (this is only of interest for those who like to criticize Colonel Fletcher Prouty's claim that there was indeed a Secret Service manual. Landis mentions having to study it during his training).

Chapter 4 duly notes Landis time on the President Eisenhower grandchildren detail at Gettysburg, PA in 1960. Future JFK agents (and then-Ike White House Detail agents) Gerald Behn, Floyd Boring, Tom Wells, Stu Stout, Harry Gibbs, Sam Kinney, Bill Greer, Ernie Olsson, Ken Wiesman and John Campion are mentioned. Interestingly, Landis states that he is "proud" to have "planted the seed" for the Secret Service going on to use the AR-15 rifle, which became an official weapon of the agency. For his part, Landis became an official member of President Kennedy's White House Detail within days of the inauguration: 1/23/61, to be exact.

In Chapter 5, after mentioning the Secret Service manual once again, Landis fondly notes his positive interaction with JFK and how the President knew his name and the names of the other agents on the detail.

Chapter 6 chronicles Landis' time at Hyannis port as part of his 14-month time on the Kennedy Kiddie Detail along with fellow agents Tom Wells and Lynn Meredith. Landis, code name *Debut*, was the second youngest agent on the Kennedy Detail at 26, with fellow agent Ken Giannoules, also 26, beating him by a mere few months as the youngest one. The 12/19/61 Joseph P. Kennedy Sr. stroke is noted, as is a cute story about how Landis brought Caroline and her pony Macaroni into the actual Oval Office itself, much to JFK's bemusement.

---

155   The same time span as agent Gerald Blaine.

Chapters 7-9 reminds one heavily of Clint Hill's first book *Mrs. Kennedy & Me*, as Landis chronicles his time as a member of the First Lady Detail assisting Clint Hill in Ravello, Italy (along with fellow agents Toby Chandler and Paul Rundle), during the Cuban Missile Crisis of October 1962 (Landis formally joined the First Lady Detail during this time), the loss of Patrick Kennedy in August 1963, and Jackie Kennedy's trip to Greece and Morocco in October 1963. Upon their return to Washington, D.C., Landis playfully wore a fez- while still sitting on the plane, President Kennedy (after greeting Jackie) shook his head from side to side and told Landis "Off with the fez, Mr. Landis."

Chapter Ten, titled "Texas," mentions the October weekend trip Jackie made to Camp David, along with Clint Hill, the Kiddie Detail, Caroline, John Junior and the children's nanny Maude Shaw. Interestingly, as with Hill's four books and Blaine's book *The Kennedy Detail*, Landis makes no mention whatsoever of the death of Secret Service agent Tom Shipman at Camp David on 10/14/63.[156] Landis mentions that the agents received a briefing about the upcoming Texas trip on 11/20/63 and that Dallas was known as the "City of Hate," as Dallas was known for the attack on UN Ambassador Adlai Stevenson, the foul JFK as traitor notion, and the idiotic idea that the UN was a communist front. As Landis notes, there was "reason to be on alert."

After mentioning the trips to San Antonio and Houston (mentioning fellow agents Emory Roberts, Jack Ready, Don Lawton, William McIntire, Glen Bennett, Jim Goodenough, Andy Berger and "Muggsy" O'Leary), the Fort Worth trip of 11/21-11/22/63 is briefly chronicled. The infamous drinking incident involving nine agents, four of which rode on the follow-up car (Hill, Ready, Bennett and Landis himself), which occurred at both the Fort Worth Press Club and The Cellar is conveniently glossed over, as Landis denies that anyone was either drunk or misbehaving, although he does concede that he stayed until the early morning hours and got no sleep whatsoever. The bubble top decision is mentioned, yet no one is specifically mentioned as being the culprit for leaving the top off in Dallas (as I have noted in my books, Secret Service agent Sam Kinney was adamant to me on three occasions that he-Sam-was solely responsible for the top's removal and that JFK had nothing to do with it).[157]

---

156   See the authors books *Survivor's Guilt: The Secret Service & The Failure to Protect President Kennedy, The Not-So-Secret Service, Who's Who in the Secret Service* and *Honest Answers About the Murder of President John F. Kennedy.*
157   The JFK bubble top: Sam Kinney's decision + all the times it was used (1/3 of all motorcades)(https://www.youtube.com/watch?v=QbBH_ZYBlKg)

Secret Service agent Bill Duncan is noted as the advance agent for Fort Worth, while Winston Lawson is noted as being the lead advance agent for Dallas. Fellow agent Larry Newman told me that he was concerned that Kennedy aides Dave Powers and Ken O'Donnell rode in the follow-up car, as he did not think they belonged there,[158] and Paul Landis voices the same concern, even noting that they were unexpected and uninvited guests.

Interestingly, Landis remembered agent Don Lawton throwing up his arms "as if in frustration" at Love Field as the motorcade started to move out (something this reviewer noted over thirty years ago and popularized in his books, online blogs, conference presentations and television appearances[159]). Landis thought it was because of uninvited guests Powers and O'Donnell, yet he notes that "I have since read that he was left behind to help secure the area for our departure later that afternoon." However, Landis states that "I personally find this difficult to believe, because Love Field was already secured for our arrival. We were already short of agents and needed all of the on-site coverage we could get." As with the omission of any word about agent Thomas Shipman's death, Landis makes no mention of agent Henry Rybka, the other agent (along with Don Lawton) recalled and left behind and Love Field.

Landis, after duly noting fellow follow-up car agents Sam Kinney (the driver), Emory Roberts, George Hickey (manning the AR-15), Clint Hill, Tim McIntire, Jack Ready, Glen Bennett and himself, also mentions that agent Glen Bennett was "our protective research agent," yet, officially, he was merely an extra agent added to the somewhat depleted detail of agents. That said, Landis' comment corroborates both Clint Hill's statement in his book and my own research that agent Bennett was there as an unofficial covert monitor of threats to Kennedy's life and the true nature of his reason for riding in the follow-up car was hidden for decades after the assassination.[160]

Landis notes that the Dallas motorcade was ten miles long (in contrast, the Tampa, Florida motorcade of 11/18/63, which entailed agents on the rear of the limo and infinitely better overall security, was a whopping 28 miles long). Landis rightly notes that Clint Hill got on the rear of the presidential limousine several times and that the motorcade, travelling at "30-35 mph" before they got to Main Street, had driver Sam Kinney hugging the rear bumper of JFK's limo, maintaining a 3-5 foot distance between

---

158   Interview with Larry Newman.
159   See, for example, the author on *A Coup in Camelot*.
160   See the author's book *The Plot to Kill Kennedy in Chicago* (2024).

the cars the whole time (although there would be a markedly wider distance between the two cars on Elm Street when the assassination began). Landis notes that they were barely moving at a snail's pace around the sharp, almost hairpin turn from Houston Street onto Elm Street.

When the assassination started, Landis states that "everything happened so fast" and that the shooting occurred within "5-6 seconds." Landis does state that the second shot "sounded louder than the first one" and that it "had a different feeling, a different reverberation." From Landis' description of the 3 shots, he says he heard, it sounds like there were more than three shots, for he states that the *second* one occurred as "Hill was starting to pull himself up onto the limo" and that the *third* shot was the head shot! Landis states that the head wound was "massive," yet does not state exactly where it was, unlike his 2016 Sixth Floor Museum oral history, in which he demonstrates that it was located at the "right rear" of the head.

Disappointingly, perhaps influenced by his participation in *The Kennedy Detail*, Landis, with no first-hand knowledge (he admits that this was his first motorcade), states that the agents were not on the rear of the limo because JFK did not want them there, a notion the author has adamantly debunked. Landis does admit that Shift Leader Emory Roberts instructed the agents to cover Vice President LBJ as soon as the follow-up car stopped at Parkland Hospital, quite a switch in allegiance from Kennedy to Johnson.

Chapter 11, titled "Parkland," begins with Landis noticing "a crack in the windshield" of the presidential limousine and further adding that Texas Governor John Connally was "probably (hit) by the second bullet"; that he "saw two brass bullet fragments sitting in a pool of bright red blood" on the rear limousine seat; and that he also "saw a bullet on top of the tufted black leather cushioning" and that it was "a completely intact bullet," yet he does not state the obvious contradictions these observations would have to the official government Warren Commission single bullet theory, an absolutely essential component to having Lee Harvey Oswald acting as the sole shooter. In fact, the official photo of CE399, the magic bullet, is shown with the caption that this was "the bullet that Special Agent Paul Landis found in the limousine"!

Landis wonders where the agents were when he discovered the intact bullet, yet Sam Kinney (one of the ones he mentions as missing) was indeed still there, as many photos and films prove. Landis claims he held the bullet in his hand, placed it in his suit pocket, and (not long afterward) placed it on the examination table next to JFK's left shoe, none of which he ever stated before when (as noted in part one) he was interviewed in 1983, 1988 or 2010.

Landis goes on to mention that Texas law forbids the president's body from leaving Texas, yet, as we know, the agents forcibly removed JFK's body at gunpoint on their way to Love Field and Air Force One. Landis also notes fellow agent Glen Bennett taking notes aboard Air Force One. Interestingly, Landis also states that agent Roy Kellerman, nominally in charge of the Texas trip, persisted and insisted that Landis watch the swearing in ceremony, fodder for those who believe something happened to Kennedy's body while the ceremony was taking place.

Chapter 12 has a few items of interest. After noting that roommate and fellow agent David Grant (Hill's brother-in-law and advance agent for the Trade Mart) stayed in Dallas to assist the police in their investigation, he notes that some of the agents thought that LBJ had something to do with the assassination! Also of interest: Landis states that, not only were all the agents in Dallas told to write reports, but they were all told to watch the Zapruder film: "all agents were required to view the film and sign off that they had seen it. It was mandatory." Landis refused to do so and heard nothing more about it.

Remarkably, Landis claims to have purchased a Mannlicher-Carcano like Oswald's from *American Rifleman* magazine back in March 1958 and that he brought his rifle to the White House to show his fellow agents on the morning of 11/25/63, Kennedy's funeral. Of note, Landis does not mention Gerald Blaine's alleged "meeting" from this same morning wherein the agents supposedly talked of suppressing the "fact" that Kennedy told them to stay off the limo so as not to blame the president.

Chapter 13 takes note of Landis' PTSD and how he would play the assassination over and over in his mind which led to his eventually leaving the Secret Service on 8/15/64, three days after his 29th birthday.

The Epilogue has Landis finally admitting that he read the Warren Report, albeit in 2018. Surprisingly, Landis admits that he was indeed contacted by the HSCA in 1979, yet he omits what he conveyed: *that he stands behind his two reports!* In fact, perhaps the most glaring omission of all: *Landis does not mention that he stated in BOTH of his reports that a shot came from the front!* I find these omissions very troubling, to put it mildly. Landis 'forgets' to mention the fact that he wrote something in *two* reports that goes against official history *and* he doesn't bother to mention the bullet he allegedly found: bizarre and suspicious.

Quite frankly, I find the entire book a real "bait and switch" scenario: hype the book about the bullet Landis found while it racks up best-selling sales in pre-order, only to deliver a pamphlet's worth of interesting and new information. And, as noted above, there are glaring omissions and the whole bullet business leaves one wondering if this was added to sell books (as he wrote nothing about it in 1963 or said nothing about it in 1983, 1988 or 2010 when given the chance) and, perplexingly, Landis does not go into any detail about the significance of this alleged find and how it debunks official history (if true). Seasoned researchers know about the significance of a whole bullet found where it was in Landis' scenario, but I can imagine the public being quite confused (and totally in the dark about Landis' two reports that stated a shot came from the front, as well as his demonstration of a right rear head wound in 2016).

But, hey- Landis has a runaway best-seller (in advance sales) for his children and grandchildren to enjoy…

CHAPTER FIVE

FORMER KENNEDY SECRET SERVICE AGENT CLINT HILL'S BOOK
FIVE PRESIDENTS

O n the second to last page, Hill/McCubbin write: "As with our previous two books, our overriding concern was to present a factual account to preserve history, while also abiding by the Secret Service pledge to be worthy of trust and confidence." I would say it is the latter part of that statement that has guided McCubbin, Hill and Blaine through all five books.

Oh, what I hath wrought to the world. I am thoroughly convinced that it was my 22-page letter to Clint Hill in 2005 that awoke a sleeping giant. Hill, then 73 and with zero want or desire to write a book (a sort of badge of honor that he carried for decades), was angered by my letter, a "cliff notes" version of the basics from my then self-published first book critical of the JFK-era Secret Service entitled *Survivor's Guilt*. It is important to emphasize the fact that Hill had an unlisted address and phone number at the time; it was only through the good fortune of an unsolicited bit of help via a colleague of Hill's, former agent Lynn Meredith, that I was able to obtain this then highly sought bit of information. As I discovered during my June 2005 conversation with Gerald Blaine, Clint shared the contents of my private letter to his fellow former agent, a man who, I soon found out, was his best friend for many years and who was, by any measurable standard, an obscure agent of the Secret Service who was on the Texas trip (but not in Dallas), having served a meager five years with the agency.

Perhaps you can figure out where this is headed to.

As fate would have it, it was during this same summer of 2005 that two things happened: Gerald Blaine began writing his book and Clint Hill, writer of the Foreword to the book (and participant in the book tour and numerous television programs), destroyed his personal notes he had in his possession for decades. It was also during this very same time that Lisa McCubbin, an obscure former television reporter who lived in Qatar in the Middle East for six years as a freelance journalist[161], began helping Blaine with the writing of his book. McCubbin was born after the assassination and was friends with the Blaine family; in fact, she had dated Blaine's son. In an unexpected turn of events, McCubbin (born in 1964) would start a romantic relationship with Hill (born in 1932), although Hill is still married. This partnership, professional and otherwise, would reap many benefits: *The Kennedy Detail* in 2010 and the accompanying Emmy-nominated Discovery documentary of the same name, *Mrs. Kennedy and Me* in 2012; *Five Days In November* in 2013[162]; *Five Presidents* in 2016, and *My Travels With Mrs. Kennedy* in 2022, all of which would go on to become *New York Times* best-sellers, having the distinct advantage of being published by the biggest publishing house in the world, Simon and Schuster, who can guarantee instant articles on Yahoo, *People* magazine exposes, and coverage on Fox, CNN, and NBC. McCubbin even brags on her website that "she is widely respected within the U.S. Secret Service for her responsible and accurate writing about this highly secretive agency."

And, yet, as I have written at length about in both my book *Survivor's Guilt*, my other book *The Not-So-Secret Service*, and on countless blogs and posts online, her work cannot be trusted with anything controversial. Sure, you can take it to the bank when she writes about harmless historical items such as Hill's many interactions with Jackie Kennedy and other *Red-*

---

161   Bio - Lisa McCubbin Hill. (https://lisamccubbin.com/bio/)

162   A mostly repetitive photo book that appears to have been a cash grab for the 50th anniversary. Since this book is basically a shortened version of *Mrs. Kennedy and Me* with glossy photos, I chose not to formally review it. Likewise, Hill's 2022 book *My Travels with Mrs. Kennedy* is another mostly repetitive photo book, so I didn't feel it necessary to formally review it, either. All Hill's books (and the one Blaine book) were co-written with Lisa McCubbin, Hill's (current) wife.

book/Reader's Digest type moments, but her work should be viewed with a jaundiced eye when the Kennedy assassination is mentioned.

Hill, Blaine and McCubbin are very aware of my work, no delusions of grandeur here. Apart from my aforementioned 22-page letter that opened Pandora's box, Hill and Blaine have discussed my work on C-SPAN with CEO Brian Lamb (in Hill's case, twice); Blaine sarcastically names me as a Secret Service "expert" on pages 359-360 of his book (and quite a few other pages are a direct response to my work); I am credited at the end of a 2013 television program in which Hill briefly addresses my "allegations" (McCubbin also participated as well[163]); Blaine had his attorney send me a threatening letter; McCubbin, who contacted me about my blog, gave my first book a one star on *Good Reads* and has even admitted on C-SPAN of finding information that contradicted Blaine (almost certainly my work); Blaine added my book as an item "to read" on *Good Reads*; Blaine and Hill friend (and former agent) Chuck Zboril, much aware of my blog, gave my first book a one-star review on Amazon; former agent Ron Pontius mentions one of my articles without naming me on the television documentary; and I have been treated to petty harassment by several other personal friends of Blaine, both at home and at my former place of employment.

With all of this in proper focus, it is time to examine the latest offering from the Hill/McCubbin partnership, *Five Presidents*.

While serving five different presidents is somewhat noteworthy, Hill is hardly the first or only one to have served five or more presidents or to have written books about their service. SAIC Edmund Starling (author of the 1946 book *Starling of the White House*), SAIC/ Assistant Director Rufus Youngblood (author of the 1973 book *Twenty Years in the Secret Service: My Life With Five Presidents*), Chief/Director (and former SAIC) James Rowley, SAIC Gerald Behn, ASAIC Floyd Boring (who contributed to David McCullough's 1993 book *Truman* and the 2005 Stephen Hunter book *American Gunfight*), ASAIC Roy Kellerman, Art Godfrey, Chuck Zboril (misspelled "Zobril" on page 451), Winston Lawson, Emory Roberts, Vince Mroz, Howard Anderson, Morgan Gies, SAIC of PRS Bob Bouck, John Campion, Ron Pontius, Stu Stout, Hill's brother-in-law David Grant, Director Stu Knight, and others served five or more presidents (the number is quite large if one were to include agents from field offices and/or on temporary assignments, as it was not unusual for an agent from the FDR-Ike era to serve for many years on the White House detail,

163   *JFK: The Final Hours* 2013, National Geographic (also a DVD).

76

later known as the Presidential Protective Division, or in the Washington field office, among many other field offices around the country and, indeed, the world. The number is even larger if one was also to include those agents who also protected former presidents or vice presidents who later became president such as Truman, Nixon, LBJ, Ford, and Bush 41).

Part 1 of the book, encompassing the first seven chapters, details Hill's time protecting President Eisenhower. After learning that Hill served in Army Counter Intelligence from 1954-1956 (pages 8-10), serving duty at Fort Holabird (where Richard Case Nagell and fellow agent Win Lawson also served), Hill makes a troubling error, claiming that James Rowley was the Special Agent in Charge of the White House detail since the FDR days (page 14) when, in actual fact, he became SAIC on 5/3/46 during the Truman era, replacing George Drescher.[164] In yet another contradiction to the writing of Gerald Blaine and Lisa McCubbin found on page 398 of *The Kennedy Detail*, wherein they state that Ike usually rode in a closed car, there are seven photos of Eisenhower in a motorcade and every photo depicts him in an open vehicle. This is in addition to various times in the actual text where Hill mentions Ike riding in an open car (this reviewer has found dozens and dozens more photos online of President Eisenhower in an open-topped vehicle. In fact, one is hard pressed to find any photos of Ike in a closed car).

In the coup de grace, Hill (and, presumably, McCubbin) writes on page 44, not realizing the stark contradiction, "[the canvas roof] really bothered Ike, who liked seeing the crowds, but more important, wanted them to have the opportunity to see him ... President Eisenhower preferred to use the car as an open convertible whenever possible so he could stand up and be even more visible to people viewing the motorcade."

On pages 40 and 46 the heavy use of well-armed military guards on Ike's foreign trips paints a picture in sharp contrast to Dallas circa 11/22/63. On page 48, there is a minor contradiction: Hill states that Ike's eleven-nation tour was his first time out of the United States, yet, on page 24, he writes of an earlier one-day trip to Canada with Ike.

On pages 53-55, Hill describes working with Harvey Henderson, a controversial and racist agent from Mississippi who harassed fellow agent Abraham Bolden to no end.[165] While Hill describes Henderson as "a good old Southern boy," he was more forthcoming to author Maurice Butler: "Now there were certain individuals in the service, I won't deny

164   George Drescher oral history, Herbert Hoover Library.
165   *Survivor's Guilt* (2013), pages 174-175, 403, 407-408.

that who were very, very bigoted. Most of them came from Mississippi or Alabama or somewhere in the South. Sometimes we had problems with them. They didn't want to work with a black agent."[166] Fellow agent Walt Coughlin told me, "Harvey Henderson he [Bolden] is probably rite (sic) about."[167] Yet *The Kennedy Detail's* Gerald Blaine, in typical fashion, wrote this reviewer on 6/12/05: "I don't remember anybody on the detail that was racist. Merit was perceived by a person's actions, their demeanor, reliability, dependability and professional credibility – not race! Harvey was not even on the shift that Bolden was during his thirty days stay. Even though Harvey Henderson was from Mississippi, I never heard of him discriminating nor demeaning anyone because of race." Can the reader see why I have major problems with history as seen through the Blaine and McCubbin prism? There's a real tendency to whitewash and omit crucial information. They know better ... and they know I know better, but they are hoping you do not, if that makes any sense. But I digress a tad.

Also on page 55, Hill notes that local police helped secure buildings and routes of travel, as well as checking out the local medical facilities (which he further notes on page 81). Yet, again, when President Kennedy goes to Dallas, officially speaking, no buildings were secured, the motorcade route was woefully short staffed, and they allegedly did not know that Parkland Hospital was the closest hospital in case of emergency.

Overall, I would assess Part 1 of the book-the Ike era- as a decent perspective of an agent's time protecting the former World War II hero. Although glimpses of Eisenhower come through, I was left more with Hill's outlook on trying to do his job than any deep analysis of Ike.

Part 2 covers the Kennedy era and encompasses chapters 8-19 and much of it will be familiar to anyone who has read the three previous Lisa McCubbin co-authored books; lots of repetition here. That said, there are some items of interest. On page 112, it is noted that the 27-mile motorcade route in Caracas, Venezuela was massively guarded by the host country's heavily armed military, involving more than 30,000 soldiers and 5,000 police officers. The bubbletop was used, despite the nice weather, and agents rode on the rear of the limousine.[168]

On page 133, while discussing President Kennedy's European tour (in an obvious allusion to the upcoming Dallas trip several months later), Hill writes: "There was no way to check every building or every rooftop,"

---

166   *Out From the Shadow: The Story of Charles L Gittens Who Broke The Color Barrier In The United States Secret Service* by Maurice Butler, KY: Xlibris, 2012, pp. 125-126.
167   *Survivor's Guilt* (2013), page 408.
168   See photo in *Survivor's Guilt*.

yet that is precisely what they were able to do on past trips, at least those involving multi-story buildings.[169] Chapters 16 and 17 (pages 141-160) cover the Texas trip and the assassination. On page 142 McCubbin, as she did with Blaine in *The Kennedy Detail* and in the prior two books with Hill, mentions once again the alleged "order" from President Kennedy, via Floyd Boring, to not have the agents on the back of the car. I have written at length on this specific topic, as I am extremely skeptical of the veracity and timing of this situation. My first reaction when reading this section was "McCubbin HAD to put that one in there again.» On page 152, not realizing the huge contradiction, Hill/ McCubbin write: "I knew the president didn't want us on the back of the car, but I had a job to do." Hill jumped off and on the back of the limousine four different times on Main Street. So much for the president's "order.» No other agent attempted to get on the back of the car.

Hill deals with the infamous drinking incident at Kirkwood's the night before JFK's death in a very dismissive fashion on page 147. Hill was one of nine agents who drank the early morning of the assassination. Hill was also one of the four agents who drank alcohol who would go on to work the follow-up car in Dallas (the others were Paul Landis, Jack Ready and Glen Bennett).

On pages 153-154, Hill writes of the shooting sequence and, as he has done in the past (echoing the same thoughts as Dave Powers and Governor Connally on the matter), Hill states that all three shots made their mark and there was no missed shot: the first shot hit JFK, the second hit Connally, and the third was the fatal head shot. Again, he does not realize the grave contradiction to official history. In this regard, he once again repeats what he has written (and said) many times before: JFK had "a gaping hole in the back of his skull" (page 155).

Once again, as was noted in their prior works (and as I was the first to note in my own work):" Normally [SAIC Gerald] Behn would be on the [Texas] trip, but as fate would have it, he had decided to take a few days off-his first vacation in years..." (page 156). "As fate would have it." huh? On page 178, Hill states his disagreement with the "magic bullet theory," stating that Governor Connally and his wife Nellie agreed with him. Hill cannot seem to understand you cannot have your cake and eat it, too: either there was a "magic bullet" or there were two assassins. Still, it is nice to have him on the record about this vital issue. And he seems unaware that as authors like Joe McBride have shown, Connally disagreed with

169   See *Survivor's Guilt, The Not-So-Secret Service* and *The Plot to Kill Kennedy in Chicago.*

the entire thesis of the Warren Report. (McBride, *Into the Nightmare*, p. 418)

Overall, I would assess Part 2 of the book-the Kennedy years- as largely repetitive from his and McCubbin's past books, which all seem to tout the same recurring agenda in two parts: his adamant stand that there was only one assassin (despite his contradictory views as expressed by his statements about the wounds and the shooting sequence), and that the agents did the best they could, despite their feelings of failure (and making sure to put that false blame-the-victim nugget in there again for good measure). That said, there were some new tidbits of information about prior trips and, to be fair, the Kennedys shine through in a positive way in this section.

Part 3, the LBJ section, encompasses chapters 20-29 and is arguably the best part of the book- Hill really captures Johnson and the so-called "Johnson treatment" quite well. Even before the formal Johnson section of the book begins, the JFK section ends with Hill's auspicious first greeting to LBJ in October 1964 when the President visited Jackie Kennedy in New York. Hill extended his hand to Johnson and said "Hello, Mr. President, I am Agent Clint Hill." LBJ simply ignored him, reached into his back pocket, pulled out a handkerchief, and blew his nose. Hill said the experience, witnessed by the agents of the White House detail who were guarding LBJ, was "humiliating."

Another minor error occurs on page 227 when Hill states that the Kennedys visited Mexico in 1961-it was 1962, as is correctly noted on page 114.

What I think makes the LBJ section such a winner is not just that it is the longest section of the book, but that the "safe" button was switched to off and Hill is telling the true stories with the bark off, so to speak.

Hill succeeds the best here when he vividly describes Johnson's interactions with himself and others, as well as the impromptu nature of the brusque Texan. Like the travels of Ike and JFK, the many travels, domestic and foreign, of Johnson are noted and Hill (and McCubbin) do an admirable job describing the interaction the president had with the hosts and with the spectators, as well as with the agents themselves. When the McCubbin "team" (either with Blaine or Hill) aren't treading into controversial waters, they succeed with some well-written stories and presidential anecdotes. Perhaps this is why I liked *Mrs. Kennedy and Me* the most- other than a couple pages, it was harmless fun about the elegant First Lady and a touch of Camelot, albeit a tad maudlin and trite in places.

In this regard, I believe *Five Presidents* is a very close second to that work, with *Five Days in November* being disposable and forgettable and *The Kennedy Detail* as the worst by a country mile for its deceit and deception. In fact, one could argue that *Five Presidents*, despite the Kennedy-era repetition and one page (page 142, to be exact) of controversy, is the best of the lot, but I digress.

It is a shame, for history's sake, that an agenda pervaded two of the three earlier books (and a very small part of the other two, this one included) because, again, when McCubbin and Hill just tell the tales, I find myself begrudgingly admiring the vivid pictures of the presidents they draw. In hindsight, perhaps it was Blaine as the true culprit in all of this and Hill merely thought it was good to have in-house symmetry when a touch of the blame-the-victim (JFK) mantra was repeated in his books-- less readers would be left to wonder why he appeared to disagree with his adamant colleague. Paradoxically, when it comes to Ike, Hill is diametrically opposed to Blaine (the above-mentioned open car versus Blaine's claim of an Eisenhower preference for a closed car).

Funny enough, there is also fodder for the LBJ-did-it crowd on page 235: Hill, describing Johnson's 1966 trip to Australia, wrote that the president "crouched down in the backseat ... it was the only time I ever saw a president duck down in the rear seat of a car to avoid being seen." Roger Stone and Phil Nelson, take note.

On pages 236-237, Hill describes the Melbourne, Australia trip, wherein angry Vietnam War protestors threw balloons filled with paint at the presidential limousine and, by extension, several of the agents surrounding the car. Hill again makes a minor error, stating that agents Rufus Youngblood and Lem Johns rode on the rear of the car when, in fact, it was Youngblood and Jerry Kivett, as several clear films and photos of the motorcade incident demonstrate, although Johns was indeed there and was also splattered with paint, albeit in his position walking by the automobile.

The travels and tribulations for LBJ continue through 1967 and 1968, as Hill does a good job of documenting the activities of President Johnson in relation to the monumental events of this two-year period. In particular, the assassinations of MLK (pages 278-286) and RFK (287-295), as well as the turbulent 1968 Democratic convention (pages 303-306), are remarkably described in the context of Hill's and LBJ's reaction to them. Interestingly, although Hill's brother-in-law, fellow agent David Grant, is mentioned on one page (page 303), once again, as he did in his previous two books, Hill does not mention their family connection (al-though Blaine did so in *The Kennedy Detail* and in a conversation with myself in 2005, although nothing was mentioned when Grant and Hill appeared, separately, on the television documentary of the same name). As I describe in my forthcoming book *The Not-So-Secret Service*, I believe there was bad blood between the two near the end of Grant's life, hav-ing something to do with his writing partner, among other things (Grant passed away 12/28/2013). Hill's wife Gwen is mentioned in his obitu-ary, but Clint is not. As mentioned above, Hill is still legally married to Gwen[170]).

Part 4 covers Hill's involvement in the protection of Presidents Nixon and Ford and encompasses chapters 30-38. Although quite interesting. Hill was off the front lines of presidential protection and relegated to, first, the SAIC of the vice president's detail for Spiro Agnew and, shortly there-after, to Secret Service headquarters. He was first Deputy Assistant Direc-tor of Protective Forces, then later Assistant Director of the Presidential Protective Division (PPD). So, the intimacy and interaction with both President Nixon and Ford pales in comparison to the prior three presi-dents, especially LBJ. That said, it is what it is; Hill was where he was in those moments in history. Still, there are several items of special interest. On page 367, after describing how fellow agent (since the Kennedy days) Hamilton Brown was angered by President Nixon's disregard for security protocol by visiting anti-war demonstrators at the Lincoln Memorial on 5/9/70, Hill writes: "all of us were disgusted with the attitude of the pres-ident for placing himself in such a vulnerable position."[171]

On page 376, Hill reveals that he was "one of very few people who knew about the [Nixon] taping system, and, as with all types of similar privileged information, it was kept very private, limited to people on a need-to-know basis." After learning on page 381 that then-Secretary of the Treasury John Connally was instrumental in promoting Hill to his highest position in the Secret Service (the Assistant Director of PPD), Hill describes the inner turmoil he felt in having to witness multiple view-ings of the Zapruder film of the JFK assassination during Secret Service training classes.

On pages 388-391, Hill totally whitewashes the Bob Newbrand-as-in-formant matter. Agent Newbrand was used as a plant by Nixon and his henchmen to try to obtain information of a derogatory nature against Ted

DAVID GRANT Obituary (2013) - Fairfax, VA - The Washington Post. (https://www.legacy.com/us/obituaries/washingtonpost/name/david-grant-obituary?id=6023836)
171 See my book *Survivor's Guilt*, especially chapters 1 and 10.

Kennedy.[172] Interestingly, Hill was in contact with Alexander Butterfield and James McCord (and agent Al Wong), principal people in the Watergate mess.

While the dismissal of agents Bob Taylor, the SAIC of PPD, and his assistant, Bill Duncan, by the Nixon/ Haldeman gang is relatively old news for those like me who study these things (page 403), Hill adds that agent Art Godfrey was also a victim of the purge. To my knowledge, there is no evidence that Godfrey, whom I spoke to and corresponded with, was removed by Nixon's hand (Director Rowley retired in October 1973). While Deputy Directors Rufus Youngblood and Lem Johns were ousted by the Haldeman gang a few years earlier. In fact, Godfrey was a favorite of Nixon, belonged to the February Group (die-hard Nixon loyalists), watched the Grand Prix with Nixon after the president's fall from grace, and was even asked by Nixon's best friend Bebe Rebozo to work for him.[173] Further, it is a matter of record that Godfrey retired in 1974, a year after this all took place, as ASAIC of PPD, not from some field office.[174] Godfrey served on PPD protecting Presidents Truman, Ike, JFK, LBJ and Nixon. I am skeptical of Hill's assertion. Perhaps Hill is simply mistaken.

Chapters 37, 38 and the Epilogue contain some fascinating personal details of Hill's final days as an agent and the troubled aftermath, as Hill has had trouble coping with his failure on 11/22/63. He goes into detail about his appearance on *60 Minutes* in November 1975 (which aired the next month). Hill states that Mike Wallace's interview was the first time, other than his Warren Commission testimony, that he had ever spoken to anyone about the assassination (pages 429 and 430). This is wrong; Hill was interviewed by William Manchester for his massive best-seller *The Death of a President* (on 11/18/64 and 5/20/65, to be exact). Manchester also talked to *The Kennedy Detail's* Gerald Blaine, Gerald Behn, Bill Greer, Roy Kellerman, Lem Johns, and a host of other agents. However, to be fair to Hill, Blaine also denies ever talking to any author (including Manchester) before he wrote his book. In addition, Hill also spoke about the assassination for *60 Minutes* once again (November 1993), The History Channel's *The Secret Service* (1995; also, a home video), The Discovery Channel's *Inside the Secret Service* (1995; also, a home video), and National Geographic's *Inside The U.S. Secret Service* (2004; also a DVD still available).

---

172   See *The Not-So-Secret Service.*
173   *The Arrogance of Power: The Secret World of Richard Nixon* (2000) by Anthony Summers, pages 247 and 262.
174   *Survivor's Guilt*, chapter 13.

On the second to last page, Hill/McCubbin write: "As with our previous two books[175], our overriding concern was to present a factual account to preserve history, while also abiding by the Secret Service pledge to be worthy of trust and confidence." I would say it is the latter part of that statement that has guided McCubbin, Hill and Blaine through all four books. Sometimes to extremes - don't embarrass the agency (what J. Edgar Hoover would call "the bureau") and protect reputations as they would protectees.

Nevertheless, with all the points and previous disclaimers in mind, *Five Presidents* must be considered a worthy addition to anyone's library. The first was the worst…they saved the best for last.

---

175   By both definition and book order release, this statement omits *The Kennedy Detail*.

CHAPTER SIX

AUTHOR CAROL LEONNIG'S SECRET SERVICE BOOK *ZERO FAIL*

A s someone who has written extensively about the Secret Service, especially the Kennedy years, I was looking forward to 3-time Pulitzer Prize winning author Carol Leonnig's hyped book *Zero Fail*. While this is not a review of her book, per se, it is a tale of disappointment and how I was once again the victim of some sophisticated and sinister hacking, which directly affected my books and my work. This is something I went through back in 2010, when former Secret Service agent Gerald Blaine's book *The Kennedy Detail* was in the news and again when my own book *Survivor's Guilt: The Secret Service & The Failure to Protect President Kennedy* was coming out.

In the short days before Leonnig's book was due to be released (5/18/21), I was admittedly quite excited about reading the book, even having it on pre-order from Amazon in anticipation. The author is a very respected journalist who had previously co-authored the number one best-selling anti-Trump book *A Very Stable Genius*. I had high hopes that, when Leonnig tackled the Kennedy era she would put on her investigative reporter hat and do some digging to find the real truth on the matter of Kennedy's Secret Service protection, or lack thereof, in Dallas.

Then, the flood of articles and media appearances began, and my heart sank. Leonnig merely bought into the old canard that JFK ordered the agents off his limo and was reckless with his own security – the old blame-the-victim mantra – no doubt enhanced by personal interviews with former agent/authors Clint Hill and Gerald Blaine. I kept thinking to myself "surely this acclaimed author has to know of my work; she has to know there is a huge dissenting view on this matter."[176] But, alas, Leonnig chose the lazy way out and didn't do her own thinking on the subject.

That was the first part of my disappointment ... then came the real shocker.

On the eve of her book being released, I went to my Amazon author page, and, to my horror, I discovered that *ALL FIVE OF MY BOOKS WERE GONE*...gone! I immediately went to my bookmarks and found that the individual URLs were still there, but the books were gone from my author page. It gets worse. When I did a search in Amazon using the terms "Vince Palamara," "Vincent Palamara," "Palamara," "JFK assassination," "Kennedy assassination" or "Secret Service," none of my books – which were normally at or near the very top of these search terms, especially my latest *Honest Answers About the Murder of President John F. Kennedy* – were missing. Nothing was there!

By removing my books from my author page, they were essentially invisible to the potential buyer. Then I checked out Josiah Thompson's popular new book *Last Second in Dallas*. Same thing: his book was gone too! I also checked a few other very recent pro-conspiracy books ... same fate. I let author Larry Hancock know of this alarming situation and he became an instant student of this hack and the ramifications of the disappearance of his books from Amazon. I also alerted Josiah to this drastic situation via a mutual friend, writer Matt Douthit. First and foremost, I fired off some edgy messages to Amazon's support staff. It took about 6 hours or so, but

---

176   She does indeed: she references my fourth book *Who's Who in the Secret Service* on page 504 of her book, as well as citing a video on my You Tube page.

the books slowly came back. But, and it's a big but: *There was no explanation from Amazon regarding how or why this happened!* As someone told me: they wouldn't hack their own products and "kill their own," so to speak; they want the money and sales. This had to have been a nefarious hack with a purpose (for the record, no lone-nut books were harmed in the making of this hack. Also, older titles were not touched, either).

I cannot help but think that someone – knowing Leonnig's red hot volume was due for release, and seeing all the hype articles and television appearances and the positive effect this would have on curious minds wishing to check out books related to the Secret Service and the Kennedy assassination like mine, Josiah's, Larry's and a couple others – somehow did a malicious hack to erase them from searches. With Amazon offering no explanation and realizing how highly unusual this was, what else was one to think? Since 2013, when my first book came out, and ever since, this has never happened before[177] and I make this statement as someone who admittedly checks out my books a few times daily to monitor for positive comments, negative comments, sales, and any potential mischief, so any other past hack would have been known to me.

This feeling is further enhanced due to this fact: I am the victim of previous harassment due to my work.

As readers of my detailed review of *The Kennedy Detail* well know, I am firmly convinced that Gerald Blaine's book was written to counter my work on the Secret Service. In fact, both Gerald Blaine and Clint Hill took to C-SPAN to address some of my criticisms, even showing a You Tube video of myself speaking about their book (Hill wrote the Foreword to Blaine's book, contributed to its contents, did the book and media tours, and ended up in a romantic relationship with co-author Lisa McCubbin which led to four books: *Mrs. Kennedy & Me, Five Days In November*[178], *Five Presidents* and *My Travels with Mrs. Kennedy*). Keep in mind-this was all before my first book was published, although it was a self-published affair at the time with a link on my blog as part of my heavy online presence (I will return to this later).

I went on to write a critical review of Blaine's book on Amazon which was deleted with no explanation, despite many "likes" and positive comments. Then it began: my blog was hacked, and I temporarily could not add to it or see it online. The same thing happened to my You Tube channel. It

---

177   Technically, a much smaller hack had happened on Amazon just to myself on one form of my first book before. I will get to this shortly.
178   Not reviewed by me because it was basically a rehash of his first book with many photos related to those five days in November 1963.

took several days to get them back. But this was only the beginning. In the middle of 2013, I suddenly saw a drastic reduction in my online presence. All my many blogs and sites were still up, nothing had changed on my end, yet Google acted like most of my work didn't exist, despite a heavy search-term presence from 1998 to mid-2013. Someone told me I was most likely the victim of algorithms and hidden HTML coding which made a lot of my work disappear despite still technically being online. When one did searches for "Clint Hill," "Gerald Blaine," "The Kennedy Detail" or (especially) "JFK Secret Service," my work came up for years in commanding fashion with little or no competition. But 2013 was the 50th anniversary of the assassination, when the media was truly working overtime to close dissent on the case and wrap it all up as "Oswald did it-get a life."

But this was only *the start* of my troubles.

My first book *Survivor's Guilt* was due out in October of 2013. Gerald Blaine marked my book as "to read" on *Good Reads*; Lisa McCubbin gave it a one-star rating on *Good Reads* before it even came out; and former JFK Secret Service agent Chuck Zboril gave my book a one-star review on Amazon when it did come out, which prompted a specific friend of Blaine's (whom I will not name for legal reasons and to give him any notoriety), a person formerly in military intelligence who had also worked for the United States Post Office, to begin bothering me online with many nasty comments on both Amazon and my blogs. What was truly bizarre about this individual was that he seemed to be able to track my every moment online and know when I was at work!

Which relates to this, not once but twice I was called to a private conference room at work, as a woman from Human Resources (HR) alerted me to the fact that the same above noted individual wrote to the CEO of my company attempting to get me fired for:

a) my unpatriotic attacks on Blaine and

b) doing these things during company time.

Neither of these had any merit. My reviews of Blaine's book never crossed the line into libel, and I only wrote my criticisms at home, not on the clock at work. In any event, the lady from HR informed me that (luckily) the CEO never sees his mail first, as they always screen it and, more importantly, they sided with me: nothing I did went against company policy, it was under the First Amendment protection. In fact, they added that they would seek legal remedies against him if he ever wrote again!

I also had the kindle version of my first book disappear for a couple days from Amazon. I had to fight to get it back: no explanation was forthcoming. In addition, all my hundreds of reviews on Amazon were wiped out – the excuse being that someone – I wonder who – reported my reviews as "biased" (!). So, they all went away. I am no longer able to write reviews for books; I can only edit my book page, because I am an author of five books.

In the interest of transparency, there may have been a specific reason why I became the target of this harassment. I wrote an e-mail to Stephen Gyllenhaal, the director of Gerald Blaine and Clint Hill's upcoming Hollywood movie *The Kennedy Detail* (based on Blaine's book). I alerted the director of my criticisms of Blaine's book in no uncertain terms. The letter, while G-rated and professional, seems to have had an impact. Not long after, Blaine's proposed movie sank without a trace and the once impressive website they had for the movie-in-progress (with several Academy Award winning production people included) likewise disappeared.

Which leads us to the present day. *Zero Fail* may be an epic professional failure when it comes to its Kennedy-era chapter. But it achieved its goal: the whole blame-the-victim mantra is once again alive and well (Leonnig's book is another massive number one best-seller). I must say that I am heartened by a few Amazon reviews of her book which note the truth about my work:

> *The media hype for this book is all wrong! With all due respect, the Kennedy Detail agents are on record many years ago debunking the notion that President Kennedy had asked them to get away from the limo or order the bubble top off or reduce the number of motorcycles. What's more, the Secret Service was the only boss the president of the United States truly has, to quote from Presidents Truman, Johnson, and Clinton. Author Vincent Palamara has proven this in multiple books he has written.*
>
> *How can you take this book seriously when she gets the part about JFK so wrong. The notion that JFK told the SSA not to ride the limo in Dallas has long been disproved. He never interfered with the SSAs and what they wanted to do. There are numerous SSA agents who have stated this on the record. You can see them on YouTube – or read their written statements. The notion that JFK interfered was promoted by a select few SSA's to deflect blame from the agency for their MASSIVE failure that day in Dallas. The salacious press of the day ate it up and fiction became fact – for a while – until it was debunked. The fact that this author is oblivious to this and still repeats those old canards causes me to question the rest of her "investigatory" prowess.*

Renowned author Vince Palamara, via his many interviews with many of the Secret Service agents who guarded JFK, as well as sundry White House aides, has demonstrated overwhelmingly that President Kennedy did not order the agents off his limousine or even interfere with the agent's actions at all. Special Agent in Charge of the White House Detail Gerald Behn (who outranks anyone Leonnig interviewed in extreme old age if at all) told Palamara that President Kennedy never ordered the agents off his car. Agents Floyd Boring, Sam Sulliman, Robert Lilley, and many others said the same thing. What's more, presidential aide Dave Powers and Florida Congressman Sam Gibbons (who rode with Kennedy during the entire 28-mile Tampa motorcade) said the same thing.

The moral to this story – my story – is this: if one thinks that the Kennedy assassination is not a current event in some respects, you are wrong. There are still those who will do anything they can to tamp down on dissent.

CHAPTER SEVEN

THE MYSTERY OF JFK'S MOTORCYCLE ESCORT AND RELATED MATTERS

"The Secret Service men were not pleased because they were in a "hot" city and would have preferred to have two men ride the bumper of the President's car with two motorcycle policemen between him (JFK)…"[179]

– DPD motorcycle officer Marrion L. Baker

To the Warren Commission[180]

    Mr. Baker: At this particular day in the office up there before we went out, I was, my partner and I, we received instructions to ride right beside the President's car.

    Mr. Belin: About when was this that you received these instructions?

    Mr. Baker: Let's see, I believe we went to work early that day, somewhere around 8 o'clock.

179   *The Day Kennedy Was Shot* by Jim Bishop, p. 134 (1992 edition).
180   3 H 244.

Mr. Belin: And from whom did you receive your original instructions to ride by the side of the President's car?

Mr. Baker: Our sergeant is the one who gave us the instructions. This is all made up in the captain's office, I believe.[so far, so good]

Mr. Belin: All right.

Mr. Dulles: Captain Curry?

Mr. Baker: Chief Curry; our captain is Captain Lawrence.

Mr. Belin: Were these instructions ever changed?

Mr. Baker: Yes, sir. When we got to the airport, our sergeant instructed me that therewouldn't be anybody riding beside the President's car.[the change at Love Field]

Mr. Belin: Did he tell you why or why not?

Mr. Baker: No, sir. [important to remember: nothing about JFK or even who told the unnamed sergeant to make this change] We had several occasions where we were assigned there and we were moved by request.

Mr. Belin: On that day, you mean?

Mr. Baker: Well, that day and several other occasions when I have escorted them. ["them" is probably hyperbole for President's Kennedy AND Johnson: see "C" below. Baker only escorted JFK once: 11/22/63]

Mr. Belin: On that day when did you ride or where were you supposed to ride after this assignment was changed?

Mr. Baker: They just--the sergeant told us just to fall in beyond it, I believe he called it the press, behind the car.

Mr. Belin: Beyond the press?

Mr. Baker: Yes, sir.

Mr. Belin: Did he tell you this after the President's plane arrived at the airport or was it before?

Mr. Baker: It seemed like it was after he arrived out there.

Mr. Belin: Had you already seen him get out of the plane?

Mr. Baker:Yes, sir.

Mr. Belin: About what time was it before the motorcade left that you were advised of this, was it just before or 5 or 10 minutes before, or what?

Mr. Baker: It was 5 or 10 minutes before.

Mr. Belin: All right. Then the motorcade left and you rode along on a motorcycle in the motorcade?

Mr. Baker: Yes, sir.

B. To the HSCA[181]: JFK did it---

---

181   11 HSCA 528, 536-537, regarding Baker's 1/17/78 interview with the staff of the HSCA (JFK document No. 014899).

"Baker...stated to the committee that it was at the President's request that they made no effort to stay in close formation immediately to the rear of the Presidential limousine...[Baker] asserted that the President was responsible for [his] position near the press bus."

C. The truth comes out[182]:"I think that morning we were already assigned locations when we arrived at headquarters. They didn't want anyone around the Presidential car, so they told us to follow in behind the news media. We didn't know whose instructions those were; it might have been from the Secret Service. I know [Pres.] Johnson didn't want anyone around him, especially a motorcycle officer."

D. To Vince Palamara[183]:

Palamara: "Are you aware of any orders not to have the motorcycles ride right beside JFK's limousine?"

Baker*: "Yes."

II. DPD motorcycle officer Billy Joe Martin----

A. To the Warren Commission[184]:

Mr. Ball: Did you at any time come abreast of the President's car in the motorcade?

Mr. Martin: No, sir.

Mr. Ball: Were you under certain instructions as to how far behind the car you were to keep?

Mr. Martin: Yes, sir.

Mr. Ball: What were those instructions?

Mr. Martin: They [plural=Secret Service]instructed us that they didn't want anyone riding past the President's car and that we were to ride to the rear, to the rear of his car, about the rear bumper.

Mr. Ball: I think that's all, Officer. [?!]

B. Amazing admission[185]:

Martin "said that at morning muster the four [Presidential motorcycle officers] were ordered that under no circumstances were they to leave their positions "regardless of what happened.""

C. To the HSCA-

JFK did it[186]:

---

182   *No More Silence* by Larry Sneed (1998), p. 123.
183   10/98 letter to Vince Palamara.
184   6 H 293.
185   *Murder From Within* by Fred Newcomb & Perry Adams (1974), p.33.
186   11 HSCA 528, 536, regarding Martin's 1/17/78 interview with the HSCA staff, done on

"…Martin stated to the committee that it was at the President's request that they made no effort to stay in close formation immediately to the rear of the Presidential limousine … Martin confirms the Presidential objection to the close positioning of motorcycles."

D. From Martin's paramour, assassination eyewitness Jean Hill[187]:

Hill, quoting Martin: "…they told us out at Love Field right after Kennedy's plane landed.… Well, while Kennedy was busy shaking hands with all the well-wishers at the airport, Johnson's Secret Service people came over to the motorcycle cops and gave us a bunch of instructions.… They also ordered us into the darndest escort formation I've ever seen. Ordinarily, you bracket the car with four motorcycles, one on each fender. But this time, they told the four of us [Martin, Hargis, Chaney, & Jackson] assigned to the President's car there'd be no forward escorts. We were to stay well to the back and not let ourselves get ahead of the car's rear wheels under any circumstances. I'd never heard of a formation like that, much less ridden in one, but they said they wanted to let the crowds have an unrestricted view of the president. Well, I guess somebody got an 'unrestricted view' of him, all right."

III. DPD motorcycle officer H.B. McLain[188]:

"The escort route had been picked out for him [JFK] by the Tactical Group. Normally we had done our own scheduling, but they took it upon themselves this time. It was rather unusual because they had people working in positions they didn't normally work. We usually rode side by side with the senior man riding on the left and the junior man on the right. In this case, they had it reversed."

IV. DPD motorcycle officer James W. Courson[189]:

"We were given our assignments that morning through our sergeant [unnamed] which had been coordinated between the Secret Service and the police department."

V. DPD motorcycle officer Bobby Joe Dale[190]:

"Two or three days prior to the President's visit we'd ridden with the Secret Service checking to see where the turns and problem areas might be. We had three possible routes, but we didn't know which one we were

---

the same day as Baker's, above (JFK document no. 014372).

187   *JFK: The Last Dissenting Witness* (1992), pp. 112-114.

188   *No More Silence* by Larry Sneed (1998), p. 162.

189   *No More Silence* by Larry Sneed (1998), p. 127.

190   *No More Silence* by Larry Sneed (1998), pp. 132-133.

THE MYSTERY OF JFK'S MOTORCYCLE ESCORT AND RELATED MATTERS

going to take, and we were not briefed on it. But by riding during the week, I kept hearing the phrase "escape routes," which dawned on me later that should something happen to any part of the motorcade we had an escape route to either Baylor or Parkland Hospitals...Once we were assembled and the President was ready to go, we started the motorcade by going out a gate at the far end. At that time, we didn't know which route we were taking; we had three: right, straight, or left. As we were leaving, the word came over the radio that we would use the particular route that went left."

B. Corroboration for Dale[191]:

"From an administrative standpoint, (DPD's Charles) Batchelor** believed that the failure of the Secret Service to inform the police adequately in advance of the exact route to be taken by the president prevented them from adequately organizing their men and taking the necessary security precautions."

VI. DPD Sergeant Samuel Q. Bellah[192]:

"On the night before his assignment, Bellah reviewed the planned route with his captain. The route was not the original that was to go straight through Dealey Plaza, but a revised route. The original plan would have skirted the Texas Book Depository building by a block, but the altered plan turned to pass directly in front of the building."

VII. DPD motorcycle office Clyde A. Haygood[193]:

"Clyde A. Haygood … [was] assigned to the right rear of the Presidential limousine. The activity of [Haygood] indicated again a departure from standard maximum-security protection. Haygood, for example, admitted that although he was stationed to the right rear of Kennedy's car, he was generally riding several cars back and offered no explanation for this. Haygood … was on Main Street at the time of the shooting... Haygood and Baker were too far from the Presidential limousine to afford Kennedy any protection."

VIII. DPD motorcycle officer (Sergeant) Stavis Ellis[194]:

"I was in charge of the actual escort of the President's car. All the other officers had their assignments, but some were just assigned to us as surplus. At the airport, Chief Curry told me, "Look, you see that double-deck

---

191   HSCA RIF# 180-10109-10411: WC document, Griffin to Rankin, 4/2/64.
192   *Fairfield (TX) Recorder*, 11/17/88: based off interview with Bellah (photo inc.) provided to the author by Bellah.
193   11 HSCA 528-529; see also 6 H 297.
194   *No More Silence* by Larry Sneed (1998), pp. 143-144.

bus up there [one of the Press Busses]? That's full of news media. Now they've got to get to the Mart out there where the President is going to talk, but we don't want them messing up this motorcade. Just give them one of your men back there and tell him to escort them there on time but to keep them out of the motorcade and not to mess with us." So I got M.L. Baker*and told him exactly what the chief had told me. That put him behind us quite a bit."

IX. DPD Captain Perdue W. Lawrence[195]:

> Mr. Griffin: At the time of your first meeting with Chief Batchelor were you given any special instructions about the protection of the President?
>
> Captain Lawrence: None.
>
> Mr. Griffin: When was the next time you received some instructions from one of your superiors?Captain Lawrence: The next time was, to the best of my knowledge, the motorcade assignments--possibly 2 days before the President arrived – I asked how we would escort this motorcade.
>
> Mr. Griffin: And with whom did you discuss that?
>
> Captain Lawrence: Chief Lunday and Chief Batchelor.
>
> Mr. Griffin: Was anybody from the Secret Service present at that time? Captain Lawrence: Not at that time no. [important to keep in mind]
>
> Mr. Griffin: What were you told about the purpose of the officers that were being provided, if anything?
>
> Captain Lawrence: I was told that there would be these lead motorcycle officers, and that we would also have these other officers alongside [not to the rear of]the President's car and the Vice President's car, and some of the others that would be in the motorcade, and approximately how many officers would be needed for the escort, and at that time I had prepared a list of 18 solo motorcycle officers, this included three solo sergeants.
>
> I was also instructed that about this motorcade--that when it reached Stemmons Expressway, Chief Batchelor told me that he wanted a solo motorcycle officer in each traffic lane, each of the five traffic lanes waiting for the motorcade, so that no vehicles, on Stemmons Expressway would pass the motorcade at all and he wanted these solo motorcycle officers to pull away from the escort and get up there on Stemmons Freeway and block the traffic, and some of

these officers, he stated, would pull past the Presidential car.

[…]

Mr. Griffin: When did that conversation take place?

Captain Lawrence: That conversation took place about the 20th of November – 2 days before.

Mr. Griffin: Now, did you receive another set of instructions or orders after that?

Captain Lawrence: Yes, on the evening of November 21, this was the first time that I had attended any security meeting at all in regards to this motorcade. At approximately 5 P.M. I was told to report to the conference room on the third floor, and when I arrived at the conference room the deputy chiefs were in there, there were members of the Secret Service – Mr. Sorrels, Captain Gannaway, Captain Souter of radio patrol, and Capt. Glen King, deputy chiefs, assistant chiefs, and Chief Curry, and one gentleman, who I assume was in charge of the security for the Secret Service. This was the first time I had attended any conferences in regard to the security of this escort, and I listened in on most of the discussion and I heard one of the Secret Service men say that President Kennedy did not desire any motorcycle officer directly on each side of him, between him and the crowd, but he would want the officers to the rear. This conversation I overheard as Chief Batchelor was using a blackboard showing how he planned to handle this – how plans had been made to cover the escort.[…]

Mr. Griffin: Was there ever any discussion that you heard about taking precautions designed to prevent some sort of assault on the President that would be more severe than simply placards, picketing, and people throwing rotten eggs and vegetables, and things like that?

Captain Lawrence: Not to my knowledge, other than the fact that the Secret Service man in there--when it was mentioned about these motorcycle officers alongside the Presidents car, he said, "No, these officers should be back and if any people started a rush toward the car, if there was any movement at all where the President was endangered in any way, these officers would be in a position to gun their motors and get between them and the Presidential car," and he mentioned, of course, the security and safety of the President and those words were mentioned.

[…]

Mr. Griffin: Let's go back a little bit and let me ask you--when did you first give instructions to the men who were actually stationed along the route as to what they should do?

Captain Lawrence: I gave them those instructions on the morning of November 22 and I had with me at the time--I had the detail with me and some notes that I had written...

X. Asst. Chief of DPD Charles Batchelor**, Deputy Chief George L. Lumpkin, & Deputy Chief M.W. Stevenson---

A. 11/30/63 report to Chief Curry[196]:

"[DPD Captain Perdue] Lawrence then said there would be four (4) motorcycles on either side of the motorcade immediately to the rear of the President's vehicle [as borne out by his 11/21/63 report***]. MR. LAWSON [OF THE SECRET SERVICE] STATED THAT THIS WAS TOO MANY, that HE [Lawson]thought two (2) motorcycles on either side would be sufficient, about even with the rear fender of the President's car."

B. ***DPD Captain Perdue Lawrence Exhibit re: motorcycle distribution DATED NOVEMBER 21, 1963, the day before the assassination[197]:

In addition to DPD motorcycles officers B.W. Hargis and B.J. Martin, H.B. MCLAIN AND J.W. COURSON WERE SLATED TO RIDE ON THE LEFT SIDE OF JFK'S LIMOUSINE. Also, in addition to DPD motorcycle officers D.L. Jackson and J.M. Chaney, C.A. HAYGOOD AND M.L. BAKER WERE SLATED TO RIDE ON THE RIGHT SIDE OF JFK'S LIMOUSINE!

XI. DPD Chief Jesse Curry---A. To the Warren Commission[198]:

(included in the actual transcript is a bizarre error involving a seemingly deliberate edit)

Mr. Curry: In the planning of this motorcade, we had had more motorcycles lined up to be with the President's car, but the Secret Service didn't want that many.

Mr. Rankin: Did they tell you why?

Mr. Curry: We actually had two on each side but we wanted four on each side and they asked us to drop out some of them and back down the motorcade, along the motorcade, which we did. [this does not answer the question and is repeated verbatim below]

---

196   21 H 571.
197   Handwritten comments from 7/24/64; 20 H 489; same as HSCA JFK Exhibit F-679.
198   4 H 171.

Mr. Rankin: How many motorcycles did you have?

Mr. Curry: I think we had four on each side of him.

Mr. Rankin: How many did you want to have?

[Here it is, repeated. Notice that even this does not answer this particular question!]

Mr. Curry: We actually had two on each side but we wanted four on each side and they asked us to drop out some of them and back down the motorcade, along the motorcade, which we did.

Mr. Rankin: So that you in fact only had two on each side of his car?

Mr. Curry: Two on each side and they asked them to remain at the rear fender so if the crowd moved in on him they could move in to protect him from the crowd.

Mr. Rankin: Who asked him to stay at the rear fender?

Mr. Curry: I believe Mr. Lawson.

Mr. Rankin: The Secret Service man?

Mr. Curry: Yes, sir.

XII. Secret Service Agent Winston G. Lawson ---

A. To the Warren Commission[199]:

DULLES: "…do you recall that any orders were given by or on behalf of the President with regard to the location of those motorcycles that were particularly attached to his car?'

LAWSON: "Not specifically at this instance orders from him."

[Lawson would go on to say "it was my understanding that he did not like a lot of motorcycles surrounding the car," something not borne out by very recent prior motorcades from 11/18-11/22/63]

HSCA conclusion 200: "The Secret Service's alteration of the original Dallas Police Department motorcycle deployment plan prevented the use of maximum possible security precautions...Surprisingly, the security measure used in the prior motorcades during the same Texas visit (11/21/63) shows that the deployment of motorcycles in Dallas by the Secret Service may have been uniquely insecure.... The Secret Service knew more than a day before November 22 that the President did not want motorcycles riding alongside or parallel to the Presidential vehicle…"

---

199   4 H 338.
200   HSCA Volume 11, page 529.

Yet at least 6 motorcycles surrounded JFK's limousine (inc. 1-2 directly beside him) on 3/23/63 in Chicago, on the European tour of June-July 1963 (encompassing Germany, Italy, & Ireland), the 11/18/63 Florida trip, and, most importantly, in San Antonio on 11/21/63, Houston on 11/21/63, and Fort Worth on the morning of 11/22/63. [see addendum, below, for more on Lawson and the motorcycle issue]

Also:

Dallas Morning News reporter Tom Dillard[201]: "We lost our position at the airport. I understood we were to have been quite a bit closer. We were assigned as the prime photographic car which, as you probably know, NORMALLY A TRUCK PRECEDES THE PRESIDENT ON THESE THINGS [MOTORCADES] AND CERTAIN REPRESENTATIVES OF THE PHOTOGRAPHIC PRESS RIDE WITH THE TRUCK. In this case, as you know, we didn't have any and this car That I was in was to take photographs which was of spot-news nature." Dillard forcefully said the same thing on C-Span on 11/20/93, telling the TV audience that the flatbed truck was "canceled at the last minute" and they were put in Chevrolet convertibles "which totally put us out of the picture." [all previous trips, inc. Florida, has press/ photographers very close in front and behind JFK's limousine, inc. WH photographer Cecil Stoughton, who rode in the SS follow-up car from July 1963 until 11/21/638]

Henry Burroughs, AP photographer (rode in Camera Car #2)[202]: "I was a member of the White House pool aboard Air Force One when we arrived with JFK in Dallas on that fateful day. We, the pool, were dismayed to find our pool car shoved back to about #11 position in the motorcade. We protested, but it was too late."

"The ninth car was a Chevrolet convertible for White House motion picture photographers. It was impossible to take pictures in a position so remote from the President. Behind it were two more automobiles with photographers."[203]

"The press was displeased with its place in the parade. Some felt they could have reported a better story watching the motorcade from any of the buildings downtown. Even their wire representatives- AP, UPI, and American Broadcasting- sitting forward in a special car, were six hundred feet behind the Kennedys and could see little except the Mayor of Dallas directly ahead."[204]

201   6 H 163.
202   1998 letter to the author.
203   Jim Bishop's *The Day Kennedy Was Shot* (1992 edition): p. 133.
204   Jim Bishop's *The Day Kennedy Was Shot* (1992 edition): p. 133-134.

"Dr. George Burkley ... felt that he should be close to the President at all times.... Dr. Burkley was unhappy ... this time the admiral protested. He could be of no assistance to the President if a doctor was needed quickly."[205]

Seth Kantor's notes[206]: "Will Fritz's men called off nite (sic) before by SS. Had planned to ride closed car w/ machine guns in car behind Pres." [which could mean someplace behind JFK's car, as was the case in Chicago, IL, on 3/23/63[10] & New York on 11/15/63]

Milton Wright, Texas Highway Patrolman (driver of Mayor Cabell's car)[207]: "As I recall, prior to the President arriving at the airport we were already staged on the tarmac. I do not recall what position I was in at that time, but it was not #1[the number taped to his car's windshield]. At the last minute there was a lot of shuffling, and I ended up in the 5th vehicle. My vehicle was the last to leave downtown after the shooting because the police set up a roadblock behind my car."

General Godfrey McHugh (rode in VIP car): McHugh was asked to sit in a car farther back in the motorcade, rather than "normally, what I would do between the driver and Secret Service agent in charge of trip"[208] – he admitted this was "unusual."[209] "Ordinarily McHugh rode in the Presidential limousine in the front seat. This was the first time he was instructed not to ride in the car so that all attention would be focused on the President to accentuate full exposure."[210]

And, as regards the Dallas Police, in keeping with all prior motorcades in 1963, DPD Captain Glen King stated that the Secret Service was primarily responsible for the President's security, while the role of the DPD was a supportive one.[211]

ASAIC Roy Kellerman, to FBI agents' Sibert & O'Neil on the night of the murder: "the advanced security arrangements made for this specific trip were the most stringent and thorough ever employed by the Secret Service for the visit of a President to an American city."[212]

---

205   Jim Bishop's *The Day Kennedy Was Shot* (1992 edition): p. 109-110, 134.

206   20 H 391; see also 4 H 171-172 (Curry); 11 HSCA 530.

207   9/3/98 e-mail to the author.

208   For example, McHugh rode here in Tampa on 11/18/63: RIF#154-10002-10423.

209   CFTR radio (Canada) interview 1976.

210   5/11/78 interview with the HSCA's Mark Flanagan (RIF#180-10078-10465 [see also 7 HSCA 14]).

211   20 H 453, 463-465; see also Curry, p. 9.

212   FBI RIF#124-10012-10239; Kellerman would go on to deny ever saying such a thing: 18 H 707-708.

JFK, to San Antonio Congressman Henry Gonzalez on 11/21/63: "The Secret Service told me that they had taken care of everything - there's nothing to worry about."[213]

President Kennedy, to a concerned advance man, Marty Underwood on 11/21/63: "Marty, You worry about me too much" [*Evening Magazine* CBS video 11/22/88; interview with Marty Underwood 10/9/92].

DPD Chief Curry, *Dallas Morning News*, 10/26/63[214]: "LARGE POLICE GUARD PLANNED FOR KENNEDY-Signs Friday pointed to the greatest concentration of Dallas police ever for the protection of a high-ranking dignitary when President Kennedy visits Dallas next month.... The deployment of the special force, he said, is yet to be worked out with the U.S. Secret Service."

---

213   *High Treason*, page 127.
214   22 H 626.

CHAPTER EIGHT

MY LETTER TO CLINT HILL (AND HOW IT AWOKE A SLEEPING GIANT)

I have had many, many people ask me over the years about my bold letter to Clint Hill I sent which awakened a sleeping giant and caused both him and Gerald Blaine to write their books. Without further ado, here it is. The beauty of this letter is that it is essentially a "cliff notes" version of my Secret Service research. I have not edited or corrected the letter in any way, shape or form. This is exactly how Hill received and read it. I think you will find it highly intriguing, to say the least. The genesis of what was to come from Hill, Blaine and I spawned from this letter, as well.

Read on.

THE INFAMOUS LETTER:

On 6/2/05, the author mailed this lengthy, 22-page letter to former WHD agent Clinton J. Hill (Certified, Return Receipt Requested with a S.A.S.E. to boot).

> "Mr. Clinton J. Hill 6/1/05
>
> SUBJECT: Lynn Meredith (and colleagues) and PROOF that you are 100% NOT to blame for the actions and inactions of 11/22/63 ... a couple others must share the burden instead.
>
> "Dear Mr. Hill,
> How are you, sir? It is a very great honor to get in touch with you

(of all the former agents of the USSS, you and Robert L. "Bobby D" DeProspero are arguably the most respected). Mr. Lynn S. Meredith, an esteemed colleague of yours from bygone days, gave me your address (and your number, although I thought it best to write to respect your privacy as much as possible). Mr. Meredith kindly volunteered to provide this information without my asking because, quote, "If you really want to receive a very definite and accurate statement about [subject detailed shortly], I strongly recommend that you try to contact former agent Clint Hill. He was a good friend of mine and we were assigned together with the Kennedy family for the better part of four years, but I have had no contact with him since I retired twenty-one years ago. "

As for myself, I am a 38-year-old student of history with a tremendous interest in the history of the United States Secret Service, especially during the period from FDR to Reagan, with a special emphasis on the JFK/ LBJ years (as an aside, I was born 6/25/66 while you were protecting LBJ [Floyd Boring was born 6/25/15, but I digress]). In that regard, since 1991, I have spoken to and/ or corresponded with over 60 former agents, something of a world record (the Warren Commission spoke to 12 agents and officials, including yourself. The old record breaker, the HSCA in the 1970's, spoke to 44, albeit with subpoena power and a 6-million-dollar budget from Congress). I am NOT a journalist---just an amateur with a sincere interest in (the history of) the USSS. I consider myself to be "the civilian Mike Sampson, Archivist." (one other interesting item: I worked for 9 years at the Federal Reserve Bank in Pittsburgh: Mr. Jerry Bechtle was the head of security for the reserve banks – he came to the site a few times – and is also apparently the regional director for your AFAUSSS meetings!) In addition, I have done much document research, as well as collecting quite a trove of books, videos, and DVDs relating to the USSS (I have your appearances on *60 Minutes* from 1975 and 1993, as well as your appearances on the 1995 History Channel documentary *The Secret Service*, the 1995 Discovery Channel documentary *Inside The Secret Service*, and the 2004 National Geographic documentary *Inside The U.S. Secret Service*).

My interest in the agency was sparked by, of all things, the '60's television classic *The Wild, Wild West* (about the Secret Service of the 1860's!), which led me to pursue non-controversial aspects of the agency, so to speak. However, all this was to change, quite by accident, on 9/27/92: the day I spoke – on three different occasions – to Jerry Behn, the former SAIC of the WHD from Sept. 1961 to

Jan. 1965. Before these conversations, I had taken it as gospel that President Kennedy was difficult to protect and had even ordered the agents off his limousine before, especially during the Tampa, Florida trip of 11/18/63. In fact, on 4/22/64, exactly 6 months to the day after those tragic events in Dallas, the Warren Commission had Chief Rowley obtain reports from five of his agents, including Gerald A. Behn, Floyd M. Boring, Emory P. Roberts, John D. Ready, and yourself. Taking them at face value and at first glance, one gets the natural impression that JFK did indeed impose this order. However, this is at first glance…seems no one bothered to take a second look, so to speak. This is where the story gets very, very interesting, indeed (*Please* bear with this and read the fruits of my labor in full: the following *proves* you are 100% not to blame for anything that did or did not transpire on 11/22/63. I only wish this information would have been provided to you many years ago – before your 1990 trek to Dallas from the nearby AFAUSSS convention- for your peace of mind).

Although Behn, not on the Texas trip (this will become important in a moment), stated unequivocally in his report that JFK "told me that he did not want agents riding on the back of his car," this was in the context of two 1961 trips, one of which was the funeral of Sam Rayburn, a non-motorcade affair. That said, on 9/27/92, Behn told me quite emphatically in a raspy voice I will remember forever: "I don't remember Kennedy ever saying that he didn't want anybody on the back of his car." Before I could catch my breath, he added: "I think if you watch the newsreel pictures, you'll find agents on there from time to time," an understatement after seeing newsreels of the trips to Germany, Italy, Ireland, Hawaii, Chicago, etc. from 1963 alone. Importantly, Mr. Behn ended his 1964 report by stating: "As late as November 18 [1963] …he [JFK] told ASAIC Boring the same thing [or so Boring claimed]."

Assistant Special Agent in Charge (ASAIC) Floyd M. Boring, also not on the Texas trip, dealt primarily with the 11/18/63 Tampa, Florida trip in his report, while also mentioning the 7/2/63 Italy trip, alleging that President Kennedy made this request for both stops. Boring made the Florida trip in place of Mr. Behn. That said, in yet another alarming contradiction that caught me totally off guard, Boring exclaimed: "No, no, no-that's not true… [JFK] was a very easy-going guy … he didn't interfere with our actions at all," thus also contradicting his report (more on Mr. Boring in a moment).

Assistant To the Special Agent in Charge (ATSAIC) Emory P. Roberts (on the Florida and Texas trips), the shift leader/commander of the Secret Service follow-up car – the late Mr. Roberts deals exclusively with the 11/18/63 Tampa, Florida trip in his report: Boring was Roberts sole source, via radio transmission from the limousine ahead of his follow-up vehicle, for JFK's alleged request.

Special Agent (SA) John David "Jack" Ready (on the Texas trip) – Ready's very brief report deals exclusively with the 11/18/63 Tampa, Florida trip. However, Mr. Ready was not on this specific trip: Mr. Boring was, once again, his sole source for JFK's alleged request. Ready would not respond to written inquiries from myself.

Finally, your report deals with the 11/18/63 Tampa, Florida trip and Boring second-hand, as well: like Ready, you were not on this trip, either (more on your report – as it is a very honest, important piece of history – in a moment).

So, of the five Secret Service reports, four have as their primary source for JFK's alleged request Agent Boring, including one by Boring himself, while the remaining report, written by Mr. Behn, mentions the same 11/18/63 trip with Mr. Boring as the others do. Both Behn and Boring totally contradicted the contents of their reports at different times, independent of each other, to me. In addition, agents did ride on the rear of the limousine on 7/2/63 and 11/18/63 anyway, despite these alleged Presidential requests, as the film and photo record prove. With Boring joining Behn in refuting the substance of their reports, the official Secret Service 'explanation' falls like a house of cards. Behn's report, Boring's report, and your report are not even on any Secret Service or Treasury Dept. stationery, just blank sheets of paper. In fact, your report is the only one of the five that is undated, a telling error to make in an official government report written by request of the head of the Secret Service … or was it really an error, per se?

(William Manchester reported in his acclaimed massive best-seller *The Death of a President*: "Kennedy grew weary of seeing bodyguards roosting behind him every time he turned around [indicating the frequency of the event], and in Tampa on November 18 [1963], just four days before his death, he dryly asked Agent Floyd Boring to 'keep those Ivy League charlatans off the back of the car.' Boring wasn't offended. There had been no animosity in the remark." Incredibly, Boring told me: "I never told him [Manchester] that." As for the merit of the quote itself, as previously mentioned, Boring said: "No, no, no-that's not true," thus contradicting his own report in the process. Incredibly, *Boring was not even interviewed for manchester's book!*)

In fact, the devastating effect these reports had can be

best summed up by Treasury Secretary C. Douglas Dillon's Memorandum for Chief Justice Earl Warren dated 12/18/63: "...the President had [allegedly] frequently stated that he did not wish to have the agents riding on these steps [on rear of limousine] during a motorcade and had repeated this wish only a few days previously to agents assigned to him in Tampa [Florida, 11/18/63]. (In Dallas SA Hill, who had been assigned to Mrs. Kennedy and had not been in Tampa with the President, occasionally rode on the left rear step. Agent Ready, who was aware that the President had specifically stated his objection to agents' riding on the steps, did not ride the step in Dallas)."

Now, to your report (the keystone): "I... never personally was requested by President John F. Kennedy not to ride on the rear of the Presidential automobile. I did receive information passed verbally from the administrative offices of the White House Detail of the Secret Service to Agents assigned to that Detail that President Kennedy had made such requests. I do not know from whom I received this information.... No written instructions regarding this were ever distributed ... (I) received this information after the Presidents return to Washington, D. C. This would have been between November 19, 1963 and November 21, 1963 [note the time frame!]. I do not know specifically who advised me of this request by the President."

Your undated report was presumably written in April 1964, as the other four reports were written at that time. Why you could not "remember" the specific name of the agent who gave you JFK's alleged desires is very troubling, but through NO fault of your own ... in fact, you revealed the name on 3/9/64, presumably before your report was written, in (obviously pre-rehearsed) testimony under oath to the future Senator Arlen Specter, then a lawyer with the Warren Commission:

Specter: "Did you have any other occasion en route from Love Field to downtown Dallas to leave the follow-up car and mount that portion of the President's car [rear portion of limousine]?"

Hill: "I did the same thing approximately four times."

Specter: "What are the standard regulations and practices, if any, governing such an action on your part?"

Hill: "It is left to the agent's discretion more or less to move to that particular position when he feels that there is a danger to the President: to place himself as close to the President or the First Lady as my case was, as possible, which I did."

Specter:"Are those practices specified in any written documents of the Secret Service?"

Hill: "No, they are not."

Specter: "Now, had there been any instruction or comment about your performance of that type of a duty with respect to anything President Kennedy himself had said in the period immediately preceding the trip to Texas?"

Hill: "Yes, sir; there was. The preceding Monday, the President was on a trip to Tampa, Florida, and he requested that the agents not ride on either of those two steps."

Specter: "And to whom did the President make that request?"

Hill: "Assistant Special Agent in Charge Boring."

Specter: "Was Assistant Special Agent in Charge Boring the individual in charge of that trip to Florida?"

Hill: "He was riding in the Presidential automobile on that trip in Florida, and I presume that he was. I was not along."

Specter: "Well, on that occasion would he have been in a position comparable to that occupied by Special Agent Kellerman on this trip to Texas?"

Hill: "Yes sir; the same position."

Specter: "And Special Agent Boring informed you of that instruction by President Kennedy?"

Hill:"Yes sir, he did."

Specter: "Did he make it a point to inform other special agents of that same instruction?"

Hill: "I believe that he did, sir."

Specter: "And, as a result of what President Kennedy said to him, did he instruct you to observe that Presidential admonition?"

Hill: "Yes, sir."

Specter: "How, if at all, did that instruction of President Kennedy affect your action and – your action in safeguarding him on this trip to Dallas?"

Hill:"We did not ride on the rear portions of the automobile. I did on those four occasions because the motorcycles had to drop back and there was no protection on the left-hand side of the car."

(Yet, during Chief Rowley's Warren Commission testimony, he was asked the following:

Mr. Rankin: "Chief Rowley, I should like to have you state for the record, for the Commission, whether the action of President Kennedy in making these statements was understood by you or properly could have been understood by the agents as relieving them of any responsibility about the protection of the President."

Mr. Rowley: "No; I would not so construe that, Mr. Rankin. The agents would respond regardless of what the President said if the situation indicated a potential danger. The facilities were available to them. They had the rear steps; they would be there as a part of the screen. And immediately in the event of any emergency they would have used them." Rowley even added: "Now, if the thing gets too sticky, you put the agent right in the back seat, which I have done many times with past Presidents.")

Furthermore, on 9/18/96, by my request, the Assassination Records Review Board's Doug Horne interviewed Mr. Boring regarding this matter. Horne wrote: "Mr. Boring was asked to read pages 136-137 of Clint Hill's Warren Commission testimony, in which Clint Hill recounted that Floyd Boring had told him just days prior to the assassination that during the President's Tampa trip on Monday, 11/18/63, JFK had requested that agents not ride on the rear steps of the limousine, and that Boring had also so informed other agents of the White House detail, and that as a result, agents in Dallas (except Clint Hill, on brief occasions) did not ride on the rear steps of the limousine. *Mr. Boring affirmed that he did make these statements to Clint Hill, but stated that he was not relaying a policy change, but rather simply telling an anecdote about the president's kindness and consideration in Tampa in not wanting agents to have to ride on the rear of the Lincoln limousine when it was not necessary to do so because of a lack of crowds along the street.*"

I find this admission startling, especially because the one agent who decided to ride on the rear of the limousine in Dallas anyway – and on at least 4 different occasions – was none other than yourself!

This also does not address what the agents were to do when the crowds were heavier, or even what exactly constituted a "crowd," as *agents did ride on the rear steps of the limousine in Tampa on November 18, 1963, anyway* (agents Donald J. Lawton, Glen E. Bennett, & Charles T. Zboril, to be exact)!

Furthermore, as noted above, both your written report and your testimony sure convey a stricter approach than one stemming from an alleged "kind anecdote." In fact, as mentioned above, you twice stated in your report that you *did not recall* who the agent was who told you, and the other agents, not to ride on the rear of the limousine, yet you named him under oath to Counsel Specter: Floyd Boring.

The deathblow to the Tampa tale: I wrote to former Florida Congressman Samuel Melville Gibbons on 1/7/04 and asked him if he had heard President Kennedy order the agents off the rear of the limousine. Gibbons rode in the rear seat with JFK and Senator George Smathers on the Tampa trip of 11/18/63. Gibbons' response in full, dated 1/15/04: "I rode with Kennedy every time he rode. I heard no such order. As I remember it the agents rode on the rear bumper all the way. Kennedy was very happy during his visit to Tampa. Sam Gibbons."

Furthermore, an amazing document was released in the 1990's concerning, among many other related topics, the issue of the agents' presence (or lack thereof) on the limousine. This is a 28-page "Sensitive" memorandum from Belford Lawson, the attorney in charge of the Secret Service area for the HSCA, addressed to Gary Cornwell & Ken Klein dated 5/31/77 and revised 8/15/77. Apparently, Attorney Lawson was suspicious of Mr. Boring, for he wrote on the final page of this lengthy memorandum: "Subject: Florida Motorcades in November 1963…Was Floyd Boring, the Senior SS Agent on the White House detail, lying to SS Agent Hill when he told Hill that JFK had said in Tampa … that he wanted no agents riding upright on the rear bumper step of the JFK limousine? Did JFK actually say this? Did Boring know when he told this to Hill that Hill would be riding outboard on the JFK follow-up car in Dallas on November 22, 1963? Did Boring say this to Ready or Roberts?"

***Floyd M. Boring, Emory P. Roberts, & William R. Greer bear *the* burden for the security lapses in Dallas; no one else (more on Roberts & Greer later) ***

The Washington Post reported on 5/14/98: "During private meetings, sources said, [Then-Secret Service Director Lewis C.] Merletti told officials from [Kenneth] Starr's office [investigating the President Clinton/Monica Lewinsky matter] and the Treasury and Justice departments that trust and proximity to a president are crucial to protecting him … the service ran through the history of assassination attempts, showing instances where they succeeded or failed, possibly depending on how close agents were to an intended victim. Sources said they produced rare photographs of John F. Kennedy's fateful 1963 motorcade through Dallas, where agents were not standing on running boards on the back of his exposed automobile when shots rang out because the president several days before had ordered them not to … Merletti indicated to the court that the assassination in a moving limousine of President John F. Kennedy "might have been thwarted had agents been stationed on the car's running boards." To drive the point home even further, here is an excerpt from Director Merletti's testimony, as reported in "The Washington Post" from 5/20/98: "I have attached, as Exhibit A to this Declaration, photographs of President John F. Kennedy's visit to Tampa, Florida on November 18, 1963. We use these photographs, and the ones attached as Exhibit B, in our training exercises. Exhibit A demonstrates the lengths to which protective personnel have been forced to go to try to maintain proximity to the President. In the photographs contained in Exhibit A, agents are kneeling on the running board of the Presidential limousine, while the vehicle was traveling at a high rate of speed [note: a contradiction---according to prior official agency mythology, the agents shouldn't even be there at all!]. I can attest that this requires extraordinary physical exertion. Nevertheless, they performed this duty in an attempt to maintain close physical proximity to the President. Exhibit B, by contrast, scarcely needs any introduction. It is a series of photographs of the Presidential limousine, taken just four days later, on November 22, 1963, in Dallas, Texas. As can be seen at the instruction of the President, Secret Service agents had been ordered off of the limousine's running boards. An analysis of the ensuing assassination (including the trajectory of the bullets which struck the President) indicates that it might have been thwarted had agents been stationed on the car's running boards. In other words, had they been able to maintain close proximity to the President during the motorcade, the assassination of John F. Kennedy might have been averted. Exhibit C contains a series of photographs taken during the actual assassination that demonstrate how critical and tragic the absence of proximity to the protectee can be."

Furthermore, actor John Malkovich repeated the myth of JFK's alleged orders to millions of theater patrons in the Secret Service "sponsored" blockbuster 1993 Clint Eastwood movie *In the Line of Fire*: "You wanted to station agents on his bumpers and sideboards-he refused. And do you know why I think he refused? I think he refused because he had a death wish." For his part, Jerry Parr, a major consultant to the *In the Line of Fire* movie, told Larry King on 7/14/98: "The critical factor [in Dallas] ... was the fact that he ordered the two agents off the car...which made him very vulnerable to Lee Oswald's attack."

Just a random sampling of comments from just some of your colleagues on the matter:

Rufus W. Youngblood, ASAIC of LBJ Detail: On 10/22/92, Youngblood confirmed: "There was not a standing order" from JFK to restrict agents from the back of the limousine – the agents had "assigned posts and positions" on the back of the President's car. On 2/8/94, Youngblood added: "President Kennedy wasn't a hard ass ... he never said anything like that [re: removing agents from limo and the like]. As a historian, he [Manchester] flunked the course – don't read Manchester." Youngblood knows of what he speaks: he was interviewed by Manchester on 11/17/64.

Robert I. Bouck, SAIC of PRS: On 9/27/92, Bouck confirmed that having agents on the back of the limousine depended on factors independent of any alleged Presidential "requests": "Many times there were agents on his car." On 4/30/96, the ARRB's Doug Horne questioned Bouck: "Did you ever hear the President personally say that he didn't want agents to stand on the running boards on his car, or did you hear that from other agents?" Bouck: "I never heard the President say that personally. I heard that from other agents." The former agent also told the ARRB that JFK was the "most congenial" of all the presidents he had observed (Bouck served from FDR to LBJ).

DNC Advance man Martin E. "Marty" Underwood - He could not believe that Mr. Behn wrote in his report that JFK desired to have the agents off the car (later repudiated by Mr. Behn, of course), citing Clint Hill's actions on 11/22/63 as just one of "many times" that agents were posted on the back of the JFK limousine. During this 10/9/92 interview, Underwood confirmed that JFK never ordered the agents off the rear of the car.

Aide David F. Powers (rode in the follow-up car on 11/22/63) & Jacqueline Kennedy (rode with President Kennedy in the limousine)- In a personal letter dated 9/10/93, Mr. Powers wrote: "Unless they were 'running' along beside the limo, the Secret Service rode in a car behind the President, so, no, they never had to be told to "get off" the limousine." This comment rivals Behn's shocking statements to myself due to the source: President Kennedy's longtime friend and aide and a man who was on countless trips with the President. For the record, Agent Bob Lilley endorsed Mr. Powers view: "Dave would give you factual answers." In addition, the ARRB's Tom Samoluk told me that, during an interview he conducted with Powers in 1996, the former JFK aide and friend agreed with my take on the Secret Service!

For her part, Jackie "played the events over and over in her mind.... She did not want to accept Jack's death as a freak accident, for that meant his life could have been spared – if only the driver in the front seat of the presidential limousine [Agent William R. Greer] had reacted more quickly and stepped on the gas ... if only the Secret Service had stationed agents on the rear bumper..."

Winston G. Lawson, WHD (lead) advance agent for the Dallas trip: In a stunning letter dated 1/12/04, Lawson wrote: "I do not know of any standing orders for the agents to stay off the back of the car. After all, foot holds and handholds were built into that particular vehicle. I am sure it would have been on a "case by case" basis depending on event, intelligence, threats, etc. Jerry Behn as Special Agent in Charge of the White House Detail ... would have been privy to that type of info more than I [see above]. However, it never came to my attention as such. I am certain agents were on the back on certain occasions." The agent should be certain of that last understatement---he rode on the back of the limousine on the 7/2/63 Italy trip. Coming from one of the chief architects of security planning in Dallas, this is very important, to say the least.

Robert E. Lilley, WHD agent with JFK from election night until Oct. 1963: transferred to Boston Office – When I told Lilley what Mr. Behn said in September 1992, that Kennedy never said a thing about having the agents removed from the limousine (thus repudiating his own report), Lilley responded: "Oh, I'm sure he [JFK] didn't [order agents off his car, agreeing with Behn]. He was very cooperative with us once he became President. He was extremely cooperative. Basically, 'whatever you guys want is the way it will be.'" Lilley later reiterated this on two different occasions (9/21/93 and 6/7/96, respectively). Lilley also refuted the Bishop and Manchester accounts, adding that, as an example, on a trip with JFK in Caracas, Venezuela, he and "Roy Kellerman rode on the back of the limousine all the way to the Presidential palace" at speeds reaching "50 miles per hour." Furthermore, Lilley did the advance work for JFK's trip to Naples, Italy in the summer of 1963: again, agents rode on the rear of the limousine.

Arthur L. Godfrey, ATSAIC of WHD – The former agent told me on 5/30/96, regarding the notion that JFK ordered the agents not to do certain things which included removing themselves from the rear of the limousine: "That's a bunch of baloney; that's not true. He never ordered us to do anything. He was a very nice man...cooperative." Godfrey reiterated this on 6/7/96. Asked if whether aide Ken O'Donnell did any similar ordering, Godfrey said emphatically: "He did not order anyone around." As just one example, Godfrey was on the Italy trip mentioned in Boring's report above and agents frequently rode on the rear of the limousine- one of the agents was none other than Winston G. Lawson. In a letter dated 11/24/97, Godfrey stated the following: "All I can speak for is myself. When I was working [with] President Kennedy, he never ask [ed] me to have my shift leave the limo when we [were] working it," thus confirming what he had also told me telephonically on two prior occasions.

Samuel A. Kinney, WHD – The affable former agent told me on 3/5/94, regarding the "official" notion of history that President Kennedy ordered the agents off the rear of the limousine and the like: "That is absolutely, positively false ... no, no, no: he had nothing to do with that [ordering agents off the rear of the limousine].... No, never-the agents say, 'O.K., men, fall back on your posts'...President Kennedy was one of the easiest presidents to ever protect; Harry S. Truman was a jewel just like John F. Kennedy was ... 99% of the agents would agree ... (JFK) was one of the best presidents ever to control-he trusted every one of us." Regarding the infamous quote from William Manchester, Kinney said, "That is false. I talked to William Manchester; he called me on the book ... for the record of history that is false - Kennedy never ordered us to do anything. I am aware of what is being said but that is false." Finally, just to nail down this issue, I asked Kinney if an exception was made on 11/22/63: "Not this particular time, no. Not in this case." Kinney also told me that Ken O'Donnell did not interfere with the agents: "Nobody ordered anyone around."

Donald J. Lawton, WHD; rode on rear of limousine 3/23/63 (Chicago) & 11/18/63 (Tampa); relegated to airport duty 11/22/63---When I told Lawton on 11/15/95 what fellow agent Kinney said, namely, that JFK never ordered the agents off the rear of the limousine, he said: "It's the way Sam said, yes" (Meaning, he agrees with Kinney, it happened the way Kinney said). Asked to explain how he dismounted the rear of the limousine in Tampa, Lawton said: " I didn't hear the President say it, no. The word was relayed to us – I forget who told us now---you know, 'come back to the follow-up car.'" This would have been Boring, by radio, to Roberts, then finally to the agents – Lawton, Zboril, and Berger---on the limousine. According to Lawton, JFK was "very personable...very warm." Asked about the tragedy in Dallas, Lawton said, "Everyone felt bad. It was our job to protect the President. You still have regrets, remorse. Who knows, if they had left guys on the back of the car...you can hindsight yourself to death." Paradoxically, when I asked Lawton if JFK really made the statement to Boring mentioned above, Lawton said: "The President told him [Boring], I think he said, 'get the college kids off the back of the car.'" (See Blaine & Newman, below.) That said, in a letter dated, ironically, 11/22/97, Lawton wrote: "Since I am currently employed by the Secret Service [?] I do not believe it appropriate that I comment on former or current protectees of the Service. If you spoke with Bob Lilley as you stated then you can take whatever information he passed on to you as gospel [see Lilley's comments, above]."

Secret Service Chiefs James J. Rowley and Urbanus E. "U.E." Baughman – Rowley told the Warren Commission: "No President will tell the Secret Service what they can or cannot do." Apparently, Rowley thought the agents DID ride on the rear of the limousine throughout the motorcade, for he added: "...the men at some point came back to this [follow-up] car." In fact, Rowley's predecessor, former Chief U.E. Baughman, who had served under JFK from Election Night 1960 until Sept. 1961, had written in his 1962 book *Secret Service Chief*: "Now the Chief of the Secret Service is legally empowered to countermand a decision made by anybody in this country if it might endanger the life or limb of the Chief Executive. This means I could veto a decision of the President himself if I decided it would be dangerous not to. The President of course knew this fact." Indeed, an AP story from 11/15/63 stated: "The (Secret) Service can overrule even the President where his personal security is involved. "

To the point, when Baughman was asked by U.S. News & World report on 12/23/63 about the Service's protective efforts in Dallas, he said: "I can't understand why Mrs. Kennedy had to climb over the back of the car, as she did, to get help ... [this matter] should be resolved." Apparently, Baughman was puzzled by the lack of agents on or near the rear of the limousine.

Press Secretary Pierre Salinger: JFK had a good relationship with the Secret Service and, more importantly, did NOT argue with their security measures. This was based on my correspondence with noted journalist Roger Peterson from 2/99 (from Peterson's very recent conversations with Salinger).

Cecil Stoughton, WH photographer---Stoughton wrote: "I did see a lot of the activity surrounding the various trips of the President, and in many cases, I did see the agents in question riding on the rear of the President's car. In fact, I have ridden there a number of times myself during trips...I would jump on the step on the rear of the [Lincoln] Continental until the next stop. I have made photos while hanging on with one hand... in Tampa [11/18/63], for example. As for the [alleged] edict of not riding there by order of the President- I can't give you any proof of first-hand knowledge." Stoughton went on to write: "I am bothered by your interest in these matters." In a later letter, Stoughton merely corroborated his prior written statements: "I would just jump on and off [the limo] quickly- no routine, and Jackie had no further remarks to me." It should be explained that, according to Stoughton's book, Jackie had told him to stay close to the limo in July 1963, and he did up to and including the Houston, TX trip of 11/21/63 (There are photos that Stoughton made from the follow-up car that day, as well). Then, for some unknown reason, Stoughton was relegated to a position further away from JFK on 11/22/63.

Charles T. Zboril, WHD, Lawton's partner on the rear of the limo in Tampa on 11/18/63 – Former Agent Zboril curiously did not give me a straight answer on this issue when interviewed on 11/15/95. Zboril said: "Well, Don Lawton and I are just sub-notes [sic] because somebody else testified on behalf of us about what happened in Tampa"- this was Clint Hill, testifying to Arlen Specter about why agents were not on the rear of the car during the assassination. When asked if it was true that JFK had ordered the agents off the limousine four days before Dallas, which I already knew not to be true, Zboril got emotional: "Where did you read that? I... If-if you read it in the Warren Report, that's what happened...Do you want me commenting officially? I'm pretty sure it's there [in the Warren Report] ... I'm talking to someone I don't know. I'm talking to you as frank as I can...If you read it in there [the Warren Report], it happened ... I gave you more than I would give someone else." The agent also added: "There is an old adage that we used in the Secret Service: 'Don't believe anything you read and only half of what you see,'" the identical sentiment used by Jean and Jerry Behn. Zboril then gave me his home address and requested that the author send him anything on this matter, promising to respond back. He never did. Included in the package the author sent was a video of Agent Lawton being recalled at Love Field by Agent Roberts (more on this in a moment).

FBI Director J. Edgar Hoover to President Lyndon B. Johnson, 1:40 P.M., 11/29/63: "You see, there was no Secret Service man standing on the back of the car. Usually, the presidential car in the past has had steps on the back, next to the bumpers, and there's usually been one [agent] on either side standing on these steps... [ellipsis in text] ...Whether the President asked that that not be done, we don't know." So, as of 11/29/63, a week after the murder, the myth hadn't been set in motion yet. From Hoover's Memorandum for Messrs. Tolson, Belmont, & Mohr, November 29, 1963: "...there was no Secret Service Agent on the back of the car; that in the past they have added steps on the back of the car and usually had an agent on either side standing on the bumper; that I did not know why this was not done - that the President may have requested it..."

Newsmen: ABC's Ron Gardner, ABC's Jim Haggerty (former Eisenhower Press Secretary), & UPI's Robert J. Serling: Shortly after the assassination on 11/22/63 before a television audience of many millions of people, Gardner reported: "Secret Service agents normally walk directly beside the car. We can't see any in these pictures." Also, on the very same day before an enormous television audience, Haggerty maintained that agents normally walked or jogged near the rear of the president's car, adding that he had a hand in planning many motorcades (as did his successor, Pierre Salinger). For his part, Serling wrote on 11/23/63: "There are two absolute rules for motorcade protection: The agent running or riding at the President's shoulder must never leave that position unless relieved. The other is to turn out the manpower in all Secret Service cars the moment trouble arises and get secret service bodies around the President."

Samuel E. Sulliman, WHD (On Texas trip, in Dallas, at the Trade Mart): Sulliman told me on 2/11/04 that agents were on the back of the limousine a lot; in fact, he remembered riding there on the trips to Ireland and Germany. When told of Art Godfrey's comments on the matter (see above), the former agent agreed with his colleague and said twice, regarding the notion that JFK ordered the agents off the car, "I don't think so." Sulliman also said that JFK was "easy to get along with." As for who exactly was responsible for the decision to remove the agents from the rear area of the limousine, Sulliman said: "I can't tell you who made the decision." I took this to mean that he honestly did not know, rather than the notion that he was hiding the true answer.

Frank G. Stoner, PRS: During an interview conducted on 1/17/04, former agent Stoner, who served in the Secret Service from January 1945 until 1969, said that Manchester was "probably trying to sell books" when he suggested that Kennedy ordered the agents off the back of the limousine. In fact, the 84-year-old former agent laughed at the mere suggestion. Stoner also agreed with several of his colleagues that JFK was "very personable": "He was an old Navy man. He understood security. He wouldn't have ordered them off the car."

Gerald W. "Jerry" O'Rourke, WHD (on Texas trip but not the Dallas stop; on WHD from Eisenhower to LBJ/1964) – In a letter dated 1/15/04, O'Rourke wrote: "Did President Kennedy order us (agents) off the steps of the limo? To my knowledge President Kennedy never ordered us to leave the limo." The agent added: "President Kennedy was easy to protect as he completely trusted the agents of the Secret Service. We always had to be entirely honest with him and up front so we did not lose his trust."

Vincent P. Mroz, WHD (Truman, Eisenhower, and part-time with JFK, LBJ [9 months], and Nixon): During an interview conducted on 2/7/04, the former agent said that President Kennedy was "friendly, congenial---he was really easy to get along with … just like Truman." When asked, point blank, if JFK had ever ordered the agents off the car, Mroz said forcefully: "No, no – that's not true." When asked a second time, the former agent responded with equal conviction: "He did not order anybody off the car."

J. Walter Coughlin, WHD (on Texas trip but not the Dallas stop): I e-mailed the former agent, asking him: "How often did agents ride on the rear of the limousine during JFK's time (and/or walk, jog, or run nearby)? Coughlin responded: "In almost all parade situations that I was involved with we rode or walked the limo." Also, in the same message, I asked Coughlin: "What was President Kennedy like? Was he easy to protect?" The former agent responded in the same reply: "Very funny and very friendly. Knew all the agents by first name." (Regarding LBJ, Coughlin wrote: "Didn't like anyone and could be very surly. Hard to protect - did not like to take advice.") Coughlin later wrote: "The rear steps [of the limousine] were very adequate for safety." Finally, to clarify this matter further, I asked Coughlin: "So far, combing the literature, books, interviews, etc., I've found that Behn, Boring, Blaine, Mroz, Godfrey, Lawson, and Dave Powers said that President Kennedy did not order the agents off his limousine – do you think William Manchester and others took "poetic license" on this matter?" Coughlin responded: "Yes I do."

Gerald S. Blaine, WHD (on Texas trip but not the Dallas stop): Blaine told me on 2/7/04 that President Kennedy was "very cooperative. He didn't interfere with our actions. President Kennedy was very likeable – he never had a harsh word for anyone. He never interfered with our actions." When I asked Blaine how often the agents rode on the back of JFK's limousine, the former agent said it was a "fairly common" occurrence that depended on the crowd and the speed of the cars. In fact, just as one example, Blaine rode on the rear of JFK's limousine in Germany in June 1963, along with fellow Texas trip veterans Paul A. Burns and Samuel E. Sulliman. Blaine added, in specific reference to the agents on the follow-up car in Dallas: "You have to remember, they were fairly young agents," seeming to imply that their youth was a disadvantage, or perhaps this was seen as an excuse for their performance on 11/22/63. Surprisingly, Blaine, the WHD advance agent for the Tampa trip of 11/18/63, said that JFK did make the comment "I don't need Ivy League charlatans back there," but emphasized this was a "low-key remark" said "kiddingly" and demonstrating Kennedy's "Irish sense of humor." However, according to the "official" story, President Kennedy allegedly made these remarks only to Boring while traveling in the presidential limousine in Tampa: Blaine was nowhere near the vehicle at the time, so Boring had to be HIS source for this story! In addition to Emory Roberts, one now wonders if Blaine was a source (or perhaps the source) for Manchester's exaggerated 'quote' attributed to Boring, as Agent Blaine was also interviewed by Manchester (see above). [Note: since this letter was sent, the author phoned Blaine on 6/10/05 (In fact, Blaine had just spoken to Hill on 6/9/05, shortly after---unbeknownst to Blaine – the author had contacted Hill via Registered Mail. Blaine is close to Hill – he attended Hill's son's wedding, along with fellow former agent Bill Livingood). The former agent said the remark "Ivy League charlatans" came "from the guys … I can't remember who [said it] …I can't remember." Thus, Blaine confirms that he did not hear the remark from JFK (When asked if agents rode on the rear of the limousine on the Italy trip in 1963, Blaine said forcefully: "Oh yeah, oh yeah." It turns out he was one of the agents) Blaine also added that the lack of agents on the rear of the car "had no impact," adding: "Well, maybe a hesitation." That is all it took. The former agent also said: "Don't be too hard on Emory Roberts. He was a double, even a triple checker. He probably took Jack Ready's life into consideration." If only he would have taken Jack Kennedy's life with the same degree of concern.]

Larry Newman, WHD (October 1961 to October 1963, then Washington Field Office): In a friendly if somewhat contentious interview conducted on 2/7/04, Newman told me that there was "no policy" regarding the use of agents on the rear of Kennedy's car, further adding that the question was "hard to answer: it depends on the crowd, the threat assessment, and so forth. There was not a consistent rule of thumb." This comment will become important later. In addition, regarding the controversial "Ivy League Charlatan" remark first mentioned in Manchester's book and noted by Lawton and Blaine (above), Newman said: "When Kennedy went to Florida [11/18/63], supposedly, I didn't hear this directly, Kennedy said to Boring 'Get the Ivy League charlatans off the back of the car.'" The former agent added that Manchester's work, while with some merit, became "part of myth, part of truth." I couldn't agree more. Regarding Boring, Newman said: "Boring will only tell you the company line. I'm no friend of Boring's." What Boring told me went against the "company line" he espoused back in 1964. And, from the latter comment, Newman obviously has no love lost for his former boss on the WHD. The former agent said that both Behn and Boring were "extremely loyal to JFK," adding: "Boring told you Kennedy didn't want any agents on the car; then again, he's been a proponent that JFK wasn't a womanizer." Both comments are true-Boring did indeed convey both sentiments.

Newman phoned me unexpectedly on 2/12/04 to say that "there was not a directive, per se" from President Kennedy to remove the agents from their positions on the back of his limousine. The former agent seemed troubled by my research into the matter. Newman did ridicule former Director Merletti's testimony in 1998 (see above). Regarding Roberts' order not to move and his conduct, in general, Newman said: "They were probably afraid to hit the street at that speed." When told that the cars were traveling quite slowly, including the limousine's decelerating speed from a meager 11.2 mph, he had nothing to say in response. When asked if Tim McIntyre may shed more light on the matter (knowing full well that he said as much to me on 2/7/04), Newman now said he is "hiding out" and "probably, he wouldn't talk to you anyway." Fair enough. Newman seemed concerned yet strangely helpful in conversation. He reiterated that he has no good feelings for Boring (in contrast to his warm feelings for Kellerman) and – describing himself – said: "I'm not a good guy." (!) Finally, Newman said: "You need to get inside the nuts and bolts." That is what I am attempting to do.

J. Frank Yeager, WHD (on Texas trip but not the Dallas stop): In a letter dated 12/29/03, Yeager wrote: "I did not think that President Kennedy was particularly "difficult" to protect. In fact, I thought that his personality made it easier than some because he was easy to get along with..." Regarding my question, "Did President Kennedy ever order the agents off the rear of his limousine," Yeager responded: "I know of no "order" directly from President Kennedy ... I don't know what form or detail that this request was made ... I also do not know who actually made the final decision, but we did not have agents on the rear of the President's car in Dallas."

ASAIC Floyd M. Boring – Perhaps even more startling than the comments of Behn, Powers, and Lawson, Floyd Boring told me, in reference to JFK's alleged "desires" mentioned by Mr. Bishop, Manchester ("quoting" Boring), and himself in his own report: "He actually – No, I told them.... He didn't tell them anything.; He just – I looked at the back and I seen these fellahs were hanging on the limousine – I told them to return to the car...[JFK] was a very easy-going guy ... he didn't interfere with our actions at all"! I reiterated the point – Mr. Boring was still adamant that

JFK never issued any orders to the agents; he even refuted Manchester's book (see above). Remember, Boring is admitting it came from him, and not JFK! Regarding exactly who makes the decision regarding the agents' proximity to the President, Agent Jerry Parr told Larry King: "I would say it was the agent in charge who makes that decision." When asked, point blank, if JFK had ever ordered the agents off the rear of the limousine, including in Tampa on 11/18/63, Boring told me again: "Well that's not true. That's not true. He was a very nice man; he never interfered with us at all." In a letter received on, of all dates, 11/22/97, Boring confirmed what he had previously told me on two previous occasions (9/22/93 and 3/4/94, respectively) when he wrote: "President Kennedy was a very congenial man knowing most agents by their first name. He was very co-operative with the Secret Service, and well liked and admired by all of us." Not only does Boring NOT mention anything about JFK's alleged "desires" to restrict security during his two lengthy oral histories, but the agent also stated: "...of all the administrations I worked with, the president and the people surrounding the president were very gracious and were very cooperative. As a matter of fact, you can't do this type of security work without cooperation of the people surrounding the president..."

Author Jim Bishop revealed the seemingly unknown fact that Floyd Boring was the number one agent involved in the Dallas trip back in the 1960's in his book *The Day Kennedy Was Shot*: ".. [LBJ] called Secret Service Chief James Rowley. 'Rufe [Youngblood] did a brave thing today,' he said. 'He jumped on me and kept me down. I want you to do whatever you can, the best that can be done, for that boy.'" He hung up [this was 11/22/63]. It had not occurred to him that Rowley, too, was lonely. If there was any blame, any official laxness, it didn't matter that the planning of the Texas trip had been in the capable hands of Floyd Boring."

And, to the JFK Library in the 1970's, Boring said: "Part of my job at the White House during the entire President Kennedy administration was to be in charge of the advance work. I used to assign people to do the advance work, and most of the overseas trips I did myself in conjunction with other people on the detail."

To the Truman Library in the 1980's, Boring added: "I was on all the advance work out of there. I was assigned all the advance work, sort of an administrator.... I was second in charge [behind Special Agent in Charge Jerry Behn]."

Finally, fellow former agent Sam Kinney told me, regarding SAIC Gerald A. "Jerry" Behn's absence from the Texas trip, leaving ASAIC (#2)

Floyd M. Boring to be the agent in charge of the Texas trip: "Here's the story on that. We got, as agents, federal employees, thirty days a year annual leave. We lose it, because they can't let us go ... there was only " x " amount of agents back then in the whole wide world ... they could not let us off...Jerry Behn had probably worked three years without any annual leave at all and this particular time, he could get some time off and he didn't go to Dallas. Roy Kellerman was third in charge, so he took the thing (sic), which is, you know-he's qualified. Floyd Boring stayed home-he could get his time off and he could still handle whatever came about from his house; there was very little correspondence between [the agents in Dallas] because Win Lawson had the advance."

The 1996 ARRB interview of Boring: "Boring independently recalled that he was the person who assigned Winston Lawson as the S.S. advance agent for the Dallas leg of the Texas trip but could not recall why or how "Win" Lawson was given that assignment." Agent David Grant, who worked hand in glove with Boring on the controversial 11/18/63 Florida trip, assisted Lawson in the advance preparations in Dallas. Boring was also involved in the pre-11/22/63 checks of the Protective Research Section's (PRS) files of any potential threats to JFK reported in Dallas which, incredibly, yielded nothing, a matter fellow ASAIC Roy Kellerman found unusual, as did fellow agent Abraham Bolden, as common sense would seem to dictate (interestingly, according to his Truman Library oral history, Boring worked for PRS back in the 1940's!). Yet Boring had begun his ARRB interview exclaiming: "I didn't have anything to do with it, and I don't know anything," a similar sentiment he first gave to me before probing further into the mystery. I later asked Boring: "Were you involved in any of the planning of the Texas trip?" Then, the agent finally admitted: "Well, no, I sent-ah, yeah, I was involved in that, yeah."

Indeed, Mr. Boring IS interesting, to say the least. He bears the brunt of the burden.

Second would be ATSAIC Emory P. Roberts (albeit following orders via Boring): When you testified to Mr. Specter "We did not ride on the rear portions of the automobile," you probably meant agent John Ready, who was recalled by Agent Emory Roberts to the follow-up car when he started to react to the gunfire on 11/22/63. Mr. Roberts had ordered the men not to move even after recognizing the first shot as a shot, while a host of others thought the noise was a mere firecracker or motorcycle backfire. Mr. Roberts was the SAIC of the follow-up car who attempted, along with Ready, to defend his strange actions and inactions by noting the speed of the limousine, which was actually decelerating from an already slow speed of 11.2 miles per hour, not the "15-20" or 20-25" mph noted in Ready & Robert's reports, as well as the distance between his car and the limousine, which was merely a scant five feet at the most when the shooting began, not the "20-25 " & "25-30" feet noted in their reports. (Even Inspector Thomas Kelley got into the act, later testifying: "The agents, of course, in the follow-up car were some distance away from the action.") If that wasn't enough, Ready's first report stated the follow-up car slowed. His next report stated it was JFK's limo that slowed instead (actually, both vehicles slowed down).

Regarding Roberts' disturbing order not to move, agent Sam Kinney, the driver of the follow-up car, told me that this was "exactly right." SA Ready was the agent who was assigned to JFK's side of the limousine, as you were assigned to Jackie's side. Roberts came to Ready's rescue in yet another report: "SA Ready would have done the same thing [as Agent Hill did] if motorcycle was not at President's corner of car"(!) Strange, but this posed no problem at all for Agent Donald J. Lawton on November 18, 1963, in Tampa (but unfortunately, like Agent Henry Rybka, Lawton was left at Love Field and was not in the motorcade detail). Even Chief Rowley got in on the act – he told the Warren Commission: "Mr. Hill, who was on the left side, responded immediately – as he looked toward the Presidential car, being on the left side, he scanned from left to right, and when he saw there was something happening to the President following a noise, he immediately jumped from his position to get aboard from his side. Mr. Ready scanned to the right, so he was looking away from the President, because he was looking around from the right side. Consequently, he wasn't aware of what was happening in the front. The car was also going on a turn at that time." The car was heading straight to the overpass at the time.

If that weren't enough, as I discovered back in 1991 when viewing slow motion black and white video footage of the Love Field departure, one can see agent Donald J. Lawton jogging to the rear of the limousine on JFK's side only to be recalled by none other than Emory P. Roberts, who rises in his seat in the follow-up car and, using his voice and several hand-gestures, orders Lawton to cease and desist ! As the ARRB's Doug Horne wrote in a memo dated 4/16/96, based on viewing the video shown during my presentation at a 1995 research conference (later to be shown during my brief appearance on the History Channel in 2003): "The bafflement of the agent who is twice waved off of the limousine is clearly evident. This unambiguous and clearly observed behavior would seem to be corroboration that the change in security procedure which was passed to SA Clint Hill earlier in the week by ASAIC Floyd Boring of the Secret Service White House Detail was very recent, ran contrary to standing procedure, and that not everyone on the White House Detail involved in Presidential protection had been informed of this change." (With regard to the Love Field video, former agent Larry Newman told me that he "never saw that before" and, when questioned on the matter, said he didn't know all the particulars and that Tim McIntyre would be a good source on this. To date, I have been unable to obtain commentary from McIntyre – or Ready, or Landis – on this matter.)

All of this begs the question: were Henry Rybka and Donald Lawton the two agents who were supposed to have ridden on the rear of the limousine in Dallas?

It appears that Mr. Hill – thankfully, for Mrs. Kennedy's sake – disobeyed Mr. Roberts by running after the limousine during the shooting. Just as important, Mr. Hill disobeyed Mr. Boring's orders by mounting the rear of the limousine four times briefly prior to the shooting on 11/22/63. Interestingly, Agent Boring just happened to oversee planning the Texas trip for the Secret Service! For his part, #3-man Roy Kellerman indicated to the Warren Commission that on 11/17/63 he was given the assignment to be the nominal agent in charge of the Dallas trip.

Finally, William R. Greer, the driver of the limousine – Ken O'Donnell stated: "Greer had been remorseful all day, feeling that he could have saved President Kennedy's life by swerving the car or speeding suddenly after the first shots." In addition, Greer told Jackie the following on 11/22/63 at Parkland Hospital, shortly after the murder: "Oh, Mrs. Kennedy, oh my God, oh my God. I didn't mean to do it, I didn't hear, I should have swerved the car, I couldn't help it. Oh, Mrs. Kennedy, as soon as I saw it I swerved. If only I'd seen it in time! Oh!" Finally, Dave Powers confirmed Greer's guilt to CBS newsman Charles Kuralt on 11/22/88, also adding that if Greer would have sped up before the fatal headshot, JFK might still be alive today.

Over 70 witnesses and the Zapruder film document Secret Service agent William R. Greer's deceleration of the presidential limousine, as well as his two separate looks back at JFK during the assassination (Greer denied all of this to the Warren Commission). By decelerating from an already slow 11.2 mph, Greer greatly endangered the President's life, and as even author Gerald Posner admitted, Greer contributed greatly to the success of the assassination. When we consider that Greer disobeyed a direct order from his superior, Roy Kellerman, to get out of line *before* the fatal shot struck the President's head, it is hard to give Agent Greer the benefit of the doubt. As ASAIC Roy H. Kellerman said: "Greer then looked in the back of the car. Maybe he didn't believe me." Clearly, Greer was responsible, at fault, and felt remorse. In short, Greer had survivor's guilt.

A sampling of the over 70 witnesses to Greer's gross negligence:

Houston Chronicle Reporter Bo Byers (rode in White House Press Bus) – Twice stated that the Presidential Limousine "almost came to a stop, a dead stop"; in fact, he has had nightmares about this.

Dallas Police Department (DPD) officer Earle Brown– "…The first I noticed the [JFK's] car was when it stopped … after it made the turn and when the shots were fired, it stopped."

DPD motorcycle officer Bobby Hargis (one of the four Presidential motorcyclists)– "…At that time [immediately before the head shot] the Presidential car slowed down. I heard somebody say, 'Get going.' I felt blood hit me in the face and the Presidential car stopped almost immediately after that."

Secret Service Agent John Ready (follow-up car)– "…I heard what sounded like firecrackers going off from my post on the right front running board. The President's car slowed…"

Texas Governor John Connally (rode in JFK's limo and was himself a victim of the shooting)– "…After the third shot, I heard Roy Kellerman tell the driver, 'Bill, get out of line.' And then I saw him move, and I assumed he was moving a button or something on the panel of the automobile, and he said, 'Get us to a hospital quick' … at about this time, we began to pull out of the cavalcade, out of line."

Dallas Morning News reporter Robert Baskin (rode in the National Press Pool Car)– stated: "…the motorcade ground to a halt."

Dallas Morning News reporter Mary Woodward–"…Instead of speeding up the car, the car came to a halt." She saw the President's car come to a halt after the first shot. Then, after hearing two more shots, close together, the car sped up. She spoke forcefully about the car almost coming to a stop and the lack of proper reaction by the Secret Service in 1993.

Alan Smith– "…the car was ten feet from me when a bullet hit the President in the forehead…the car went about five feet and stopped."

Ochus V. Campbell– after hearing shots, "he then observed the car bearing President Kennedy to slow down, a near stop, and a motorcycle policeman rushed up. Immediately following this, he observed the car rush away from the scene."

Peggy Joyce Hawkins– she was on the front steps of the TSBD and "…estimated that the President's car was less than 50 feet away from her when he was shot, that the car slowed down almost coming to a full stop."

First Lady Jacqueline Kennedy (rode in the Presidential limousine)– "We could see a tunnel in front of us. Everything was really slow then … [immediately after shooting] And just being down in the car with his head in my lap. And it just seemed an eternity.… And finally I remember a voice behind me, or something, and then I remember the people in the front seat, or somebody, finally knew something was wrong, and a voice yelling, which must have been Mr. Hill, "Get to the hospital," or maybe it was Mr. Kellerman, in the front seat.… We were really slowing turning the corner [Houston & Elm] … I remember a sensation of enormous speed, which must have been when we took off … those poor men in the front…" Mary Gallagher reported in her book: "She mentioned one Secret Service man who had not acted during the crucial moment, and said bitterly to me, 'He might just as well have been Miss Shaw!'" Jackie also told Gallagher: "You should get yourself a good driver so that nothing ever happens to you." Manchester wrote: "[Mrs. Kennedy] had heard Kellerman on the radio and had wondered why it had taken the car so long to leave." Former agent Marty Venker and C. David Heymann, among others, confirm in their books that Jackie felt Greer was responsible."

The sequence is crucial:

1. First shot (or shots) rings out - the car slows with brake lights on.

2. Greer turns around once.

3. Kellerman orders Greer to "get out of line; we've been hit!"

4. Greer disobeys his superior's order and turns around to stare at JFK for the second time, until after the fatal headshot finds its mark!

As stated before, Greer was responsible, at fault, and felt remorse. In short, Greer had survivor's guilt.

But then, stories and feelings changed.

Agent Greer to the FBI 11/22/63: "Greer stated that he first heard what he thought was possibly a motorcycle backfire and glanced around and noticed that the President had evidently been hit [notice that, early on, Greer admits seeing JFK, which the Zapruder proves he did two times before the fatal head shot occurred]. He thereafter got on the radio and communicated with the other vehicles, stating that they desired to get the President to the hospital immediately [in reality, Greer did not talk on the radio, and Greer went on to deny ever saying this during his Warren Commission testimony] … Greer stated that they (the Secret Service) have always been instructed to keep the motorcade moving at a considerable speed inasmuch as a moving car offers a much more difficult target than a vehicle traveling at a very slow speed. He pointed out that on numerous occasions he has attempted to keep the car moving at a rather fast rate, but in view of the President's popularity and desire to maintain close liaison with the people, he has, on occasion, been instructed by the President to "slow down." Greer stated that he has been asking himself if there was anything he could have done to avoid this incident but stated that things happened so fast that he could not account for full developments in this matter (!) [The "JFK-as-scapegoat" theme … and so much for Greer's remorse from earlier the same day]."

Agent Greer to the FBI 11/27/63: "…he heard a noise which sounded like a motorcycle backfire. On hearing this noise he glanced to his right toward Kellerman and out of the corner of his eye noticed that the Governor appeared to be falling toward his wife [notice that Greer now mentions nothing about seeing JFK hit---he does the same thing in his undated report in the Warren Commission volumes] He thereafter recalls hearing some type of outcry after which Kellerman said, "Let's get out of here." He further related that at the time of hearing the sound he was starting down an incline which passes beneath a railroad crossing and after passing under this viaduct, he closed in on the lead car and yelled to the occupants and a nearby police motorcyclist, "Hospital, Hospital! [Nothing about using the radio this time out]" Thereafter follows a complete physical description of Greer, as if the FBI agents considered him a suspect, including age, height, and color of eyes!

So, if ASAIC Boring didn't convey those "wishes" (no agents on the rear of limo, handicapping you to have to sprint forward from another moving vehicle), if ATSAIC Roberts wouldn't have recalled Rybka & Ready and behaved so lackadaisically, and if Greer would have obeyed Kellerman and stepped on the gas, history *would* have been different. *they* bear the burden. You behaved very admirably, especially under the circumstances.

I would appreciate any/ all comments you would like to make regarding this lengthy commentary.

Sincerely,
Vince Palamara
Carnegie, PA 15106"

On 6/13/05, after not receiving a reply, the author phoned Mr. Hill, who was quite apparently angry – he first pretended not to know about the lengthy letter he had to sign for (of which the author received his signed receipt): "About what?" Hill exclaimed in response to the author's inquiry. Then, forcefully, Hill added: "I'm just not interested in talking to you."

A postscript: author William Law contacted Hill about the contact I had with the former agent. After initially denying that we spoke (and the fact that I sent him a letter), Hill responded: "Maybe he's right, because I apparently turned him down or something, I don't know." [215]

---

215   *In The Eye of History* by William Matson Law (2015 edition), pages 38-39.

CHAPTER NINE

Secret Service Agent Floyd Boring's Interesting ARRB Interview

FLOYD BORING

W ith a few notable, albeit largely overlooked exceptions[216], Floyd Boring was a relatively new name to the research community when this author wrote a detailed article about this former #2 Assistant-Special-Agent-In-Charge (ASAIC) of the White

---

216   18 H 803-809; *The Death of a President* by William Manchester (Perennial, 1988 edition), p. 37.

House Detail (WHD) entitled *Boring Is Interesting* in the May 1995 *Fourth Decade* (based off the author's 9/22/93 & 3/4/94 interviews)."[217]

In October 1995, this author gave a presentation at the 2nd annual Coalition on Political Assassinations conference and wrote a follow-up article entitled *More Boring Details* which appeared in the Nov. 1995 *Fourth Decade*. However, it was from the author's COPA appearance that the name of Floyd Boring perked the attention of Tom Samoluk of the Assassination Records Review Board (ARRB). Samoluk contacted the author, I donated all of my audio tapes and correspondence from all of my Secret Service/ related interviews, and the rest is history.[218] Nevertheless, there is a twist: unbeknownst to me until the publication of a recent book[219], I had no idea that the ARRB actually followed through with one of my suggestions (although they had followed up on two others[220]) and interviewed Mr. Boring...but they did. On September 18, 1996, a mere 2 days after I received the Deed of Gift from the National Archives regarding my donations, Dr. Joan Zimmerman and Doug Horne of the ARRB interviewed Mr. Boring at his home in Maryland. The interview was even audiotaped with Mr. Boring's consent. The ARRB interview of Floyd Boring is in the ARRB's medical documents and depositions box released in July of 1998. It is MD 259. It's a summary of the interview not a transcript.

The interview begins with Boring exclaiming "I didn't have anything to do with it, and I don't know anything." Let's rewind that again: "I didn't have anything to do with it"---what, the assassination or the Texas trip? "I don't know anything"---he sure knew enough about the Texas trip to tell Chief James Rowley via a written report 6 months after the assassination[221] AND in his 1976 JFK Library Oral History, as well as his two talks with me! Boring also claimed that "he had never spoken with anyone at all in the Secret Service about any aspect of the Kennedy assassination," another statement that is very hard to swallow, especially seeing that Boring founded the Retired Secret Service Agent's Association in 1969.[222]

---

217   See the author's numerous books such as *Survivor's Guilt: The Secret Service & the Failure to Protect President Kennedy.*
218   See pages xvii and 138 of ARRB's Final Report.
219   1998 edition of *High Treason* by Harrison Edward Livingstone & Robert Groden, pp. 432-433. The ARRB's interview of Floyd Boring is in the ARRB medical documents and depositions released in July of 1998. It is MD 259.
220   DNC advance man Marty Underwood, interviewed by the author on 10/9/92, and author William Manchester: see the ARRB's Final Report, pp. 112, 117, and 135.
221   18 H 806.
222   See also pp. 66-67 of Boring's Truman Library Oral History. Author Gerald Posner contacted Boring during the writing of *Case Closed*, although this was not revealed in any way in the book (Boring told me that he merely relayed him on to Hamilton Brown, the Executive secretary of the Former Agents' Association---this is noted on p. 503. For more on this matter, see the author's

In any event, Horne writes "Contrary to his disclaimer, the interview proved to be worthwhile and interesting in a number of respects." Boring confirmed that he had never been interviewed by the Warren Commission, the HSCA, or any other government body in regard to the JFK assassination.[223] Boring claimed that he was enjoying a day off at his home on 11/22/63 when he heard the news of the assassination on the radio.[224] This ARRB interview provides startling new information, and that is that Floyd Boring confirms that he was in charge of planning the Texas trip. It also sheds light on the totality of Boring's relationship with Texas trip planning, especially questionable security matters.

First, author Jim Bishop revealed this fact in the 1960's in his book: [225]

"...(LBJ) called Secret Service Chief James Rowley 'Rufe did a brave thing today,' he said. 'He jumped on me and kept me down. I want you to do whatever you can, the best that can be done, for that boy.'" He hung up (this was 11/22/63). It had not occurred to him that Rowley, too, was lonely. If there was any blame, any official laxness, it didn't matter that the planning of the Texas trip had been in the capable hands of Floyd Boring."

And, to the JFK Library in the 1970's:

"Part of my job at the White House during the entire President Kennedy administration was to be in charge of the advance work."

To the Truman Library in the 1980's:

"I was on all the advance work out of there. I was assigned all the advance work, sort of an administrator... I was second in charge [behind Special Agent in Charge Jerry Behn]."

Finally, fellow former agent Sam Kinney (the driver of the follow-up car on 11/22/63):

In regard to SAIC Gerald A. "Jerry" Behn's absence from the Texas trip, leaving ASAIC (#2) Floyd M. Boring to be the agent in charge of the Texas trip, Kinney told this author: "I'll tell you how that happened. We got, as agents, federal employees, 30 days a year annual leave, but they couldn't let us off...there was only "x" number of agents back then in the whole

article in the April 1998 issue of *JFK/ Deep Politics Quarterly*.

223   Although he did speak to Chief U.E. Baughman for *Secret Service Chief* (1962/1963, pp. 68-69), and David McCullough for *Truman* (1992, pp. 364, 385, 434-435, 802, 808-810, and 908) regarding President Truman. Other than to the JFK Library (2/25/76 [released 1/98], the Truman Library (9/21/88), the Discovery Channel program *Inside the Secret Service* (1995), PBS's *Truman*, and this author, no one else has ever interviewed Boring before (and only the JFK Library, me, and the ARRB went into any detail regarding the JFK administration and the assassination). Despite Manchester's quote attributed to Boring on p. 37 of his book *The Death of a President*, Boring confirmed to me twice that he never spoke to Manchester.

224   Boring said basically the same thing in both his presidential Oral Histories cited above.

225   *The Day Kennedy Was Shot*, p. 558 [1992 edition].

country. Jerry Behn probably worked three years without annual leave, so he decided to take some time off ... Roy Kellerman was third in charge- he's qualified. Floyd Boring stayed home – he could still handle whatever came about from his house; there [was] very little correspondence be- tween the agents in Dallas because Win Lawson had the advance."

Back to the ARRB interview: "Boring independently recalled that he was the person who assigned Winston Lawson as the Secret Service ad- vance agent for the Dallas leg of the Texas trip,[226] but could not recall why or how "Win" Lawson was given that assignment." So much for Boring's 'dis- claimer' "I didn't have anything to do with it, and I don't know anything."

Boring initially claimed that his activities on 11/22/63 "were limited to going directly from his home to Andrews AFB to meet the (new) Pres- ident[227] – and that he escorted President Johnson on his helicopter from Andrews to the White House, after which he went directly home"; the latter part of this statement, that Boring went directly home, is not backed up by the documentary record, nor by Boring's own admitted actions. Horne wrote: "When asked who directed him to go to Andrews AFB, Mr. Boring said that nobody asked him to go there – that he just did it on his own...

In about the middle of the interview, Mr. Boring remembered that he and Mr. [Paul J.] Paterni had inspected the President's limousine and the Secret Service follow-up car but was unsure whether they had inspected them the night President Johnson returned to Washington (11/22/63), or the next morning (11/23/63)." Boring and Paterni inspected the limo from 10:10 P.M. the night of 11/22/63 until 12:01 A.M., one minute into 11/23/63 (the FBI inspected the limo afterwards, starting at 1:00 A.M.).[228]

Furthermore, "When asked who directed he and Paterni to search the automobiles, he said that no one had; he said he thought it might be a good idea and had suggested it himself to Paterni, and that they undertook this search as independent action on their own initiative." Interestingly, they also beat Chief Rowley and ASAIC Kellerman to the punch, as the record indicates that they had also thought of the idea while at AAFB.[229] (Just to be clear, Rowley and Kellerman did not inspect the limousine at all.) Continuing: "After recalling that they had searched the cars, Mr. Bor- ing said that he had discovered a piece of skull bone with brain attached[230]

---

226   See also 4 H 336, 337, & 342.
227   See Manchester, p. 389.
228   CD 80; RIF# 180-10001-10041.
229   *The Day Kennedy Was Shot* by Jim Bishop (Perennial 1992 edition), pp. 511-512; Man- chester, 1988 edition, p. 390.
230   Sam Kinney told me that he found a piece of skull in the rear of the presidential limou-

in the rear of the follow-up car (the black Cadillac convertible called the "Queen Mary"), in the footwell just in front of the back seat bench. He said during follow-up questioning that the dimensions of this skull bone-brain fragment were approximately 1" x 2." He said that he never picked it up or touched it himself, but that he simply pointed it out to Mr. Paterni (Mr. Paterni was Deputy Chief of the Secret Service)[231] He said he did not write a report about this, and he did not know whether Mr. Paterni had written a report or not."[232] What makes Boring's recollections of the limo inspection particularly troublesome is the fact that he "made very clear during the [ARRB] interview that this fragment was in the rear of the follow-up car, not in the rear seat of the presidential limousine.

This would be the only known instance of anyone claiming to have found JFK bone fragments in the Secret Service follow-up car. Initially, ARRB staff members Zimmerman and Horne had misunderstood Mr. Boring to mean that the bone-brain fragment was in the rear seat of the President's limousine, and Mr. Boring took specific pains to correct their misunderstanding during follow-on discussion of this matter. However, Boring called Horne the next day to place a correction (and, thus, a retraction) on the record: he now felt that the skull bone-and-brain fragment he saw "must have been in the back seat of the President's limousine, and not the follow-up car. He said that his stroke may perhaps have had something to do with his error." (Boring had a stroke in the early 90's, 1991-1992ish).

During his inspection of the limousine with Paterni, Boring found bullet fragments as well. These bullet fragments were turned over to Orrin Bartlett, the FBI's liaison officer with the Secret Service.[233] Bartlett turned them over to Robert Frazier in person in the FBI lab. These bullet fragments became CE 567 and CE 569.[234] Boring's stroke may also explain why Boring now has no recollection of finding any bullet fragments at all in the limousine (only the skullfragment), and also may explain why he could not remember, one way or the other, the condition of the limousine's windshield and chrome strip.[235]

---

sine while still on board the C-130 on the flight back to AAFB.

231   Paterni was also a former member of the O.S.S., the predecessor of the CIA, and was involved in other matters related to 11/22/63: see the author's article "The Secret Service: In Their Own Words," Spring 1998 *Kennedy Assassination Chronicles journal*.

232   Washington Field Office SAIC Harry Geghlein did write a report about the limo inspection, mentioning Boring, Paterni, and Kinney, among others.

233   3 H p. 435.

234   See CD 80; RIF# 180-10001-10041; 2H p. 90 (Kellerman); 5 H p. 67(Frazier); 7 HSCA p. 389.

235   2 H 90 (Kellerman); 5 H 67(Frazier); 7 HSCA 389; the two bullet fragments retrieved from the front seat of the limousine and turned over to FBI SA Frazier by Paterni and Boring were designated CE567 & CE 569.

The ARRB interview states, "When shown the HSCA summary of its interview with Miami SAIC John Marshall, specifically Marshall's twice expressed opinion that there may have been a Secret Service conspiracy,[236] Mr. Boring expressed surprise at those sentiments and said he had never heard that opinion expressed by SAIC Marshall, a personal friend of his from their previous association as Pennsylvania State Troopers."

"When shown the HSCA interview summary with Miami field officer SA Ernest Aragon, specifically Aragon's allegations of Secret Service security lapses[237], he said he would not agree with that statement and expressed the opinion that SA Aragon may not have known what he was talking about."

"Mr. Boring was asked to read and comment on several pages of the HSCA 6/1/77 interview transcript[238] with former graduate student James Gouchenaur, in which Gochenaur recounted a very long conversation he reportedly had with SA Elmer Moore in 1970. Mr. Boring examined the portions of the transcript in which Gouchenaur quoted Moore as saying that Kennedy was a traitor for giving things away to the Russians; that it was a shame people had to die, but maybe it was a good thing; that the Secret Service personnel had to go along with the way the assassination was being investigated ("I did everything I was told, we all did everything we were told, or we'd get our heads cut off"); and that he felt remorse for the way he (Moore) had badgered Dr. Malcom Perry into changing his testimony to the effect that there was not, after all, an entrance wound in the front of the president's neck. Mr. Boring said that it would be just like SA Moore to give such a lengthy interview, but that he doubted very much whether agent Moore had really said those things."

In addition, "Mr. Boring was shown the HSCA interview of SA [George] Hickey, and was asked to read the portion wherein Mr. Hickey stated that Mr. Boring came down to the garage and told him statements were being collected in the White House, and directed (or suggested) that he go and write down his statement.[239] His response to this was that he did not remember even seeing SA Hickey in the White House garage, nor did he remember seeing SA Kinney, or any other Secret Service agents, or FBI agents, during the automobile searches [plural]. He did have some vague recollection of White House police being there."

---

236   RIF#180-10074-10393: 2/22/78 HSCA interview of Marshall.
237   RIF#10078-10450: 3/25/78 HSCA interview of Aragon.
238   RIF#180-10109-10310.
239   18 H 761-765 (Hickey); see also 18 H 722-802 and 25 H 786-788: these are all the Secret Service reports submitted to the Warren Commission.

Security Stripping Measure #1 – Agents Off the Limo: a JFK Order or An Anecdote?

Evidence against Mr. Boring "not have anything to do with it," meaning his involvement in Texas trip planning include his participation, directly and indirectly through subordinates personally selected by him of what can only be called security stripping measures. The first of which involves removing agents from the rear of the limousine.

"Mr. Boring was asked to read pages 136-137 of Clint Hill's Warren Commission testimony [Vol. 2], in which Clint Hill recounted that Floyd Boring had told him just days prior to the assassination that during the President's Tampa trip on Monday, 11/18/63, JFK had requested that agents not ride on the rear steps of the limousine, and that Boring had also so informed other agents of the White House detail, and that as a result, agents in Dallas (except Clint Hill, on brief occasions) did not ride on the rear steps of the limousine."

"Mr. Boring affirmed that he did make these statements to Clint Hill, but stated that he was not relaying a policy change, but rather simply telling an anecdote about the President's kindness and consideration in Tampa in not wanting agents to have to ride on the rear of the Lincoln limousine when it was not necessary to do so because of a lack of crowds along the street."

I find this admission startling, especially because the one agent who decided to ride on the rear of the limousine in Dallas anyway – and on at least 4 different occasions – was none other than CLINT HILL himself! This also does not address what the agents were to do when the crowds were heavier, or even what exactly constituted a "crowd," as agents did ride on the rear steps of the limousine in Tampa on November 18, 1963 anyway (agents Donald J. Lawton, Andrew E. Berger, & Charles T. Zboril, to be exact)![240]

Furthermore, Clint Hill's written report (as well as his testimony) sure conveys a more strict approach than one stemming from an alleged, kind anecdote; in fact, Hill twice stated he *did not recall* who the agent was who told him, and the other agents, not to ride on the rear of the limousine:

"I, Special Agent Clinton J. Hill, never personally was requested by President John F. Kennedy not to ride on the rear of the Presidential automobile. I did received information passed verbally from the administrative offices of the White House Detail of the Secret Service to agents

240   Excellent security for President Kennedy 11/18/63 Tampa and Miami, Florida (https://www.youtube.com/watch?v=VShezymzQVc)

assigned to that detail that President Kennedy had made such requests. I do not know from whom I received this information. It was general knowledge on the White House Detail, however, that President Kennedy has asked Special Agent in Charge Gerald A. Behn, not to have Special Agents ride on the rear of the Presidential automobile [Behn denied to me that President Kennedy made such a request. Films and photos- from 1963 appear to confirm Behn's story that JFK never made such a request]. No written instructions regarding this were ever distributed."

Hill continues, "I was informed that on November 18, 1963, in Tampa, Florida, President Kennedy had requested through Assistant Special Agent in Charge Floyd M. Boring that Special Agents remove themselves from the rear of the Presidential automobile. I was not on this specific trip with the White House Detail and received this information after the President's return to Washington, D.C. This would have been between November 19, 1963, and November 21, 1963 [Note the time frame!]. I do not know specifically who advised me of this request by the President.."

So, what do we have exactly? Something allegedly happens on the Tampa trip or is attributed to the Tampa trip after the fact by Boring. Yet, no one on the trip left the bumper or recalls being told to leave and stay off the bumper per a presidential request. The Secret Service agents to whom this order would apply to deny this happened. This story does exist though, and spreads through word of mouth, by Boring to agents who were not involved in the Tampa trip such as Clint Hill to whom it is stated as a new policy to be implemented on the next trip, which would be Texas.

Look at what Hill writes: "...I did received information passed verbally from the administrative offices of the White House Detail of the Secret Service to agents assigned to that detail that President Kennedy had made such requests."

Well, who's in this administrative office of the Secret Service's White House Detail? Boring. The "general knowledge" Hill speaks of would more appropriately be coming from Boring, not Behn. Behn denied it outright. Boring was on the Tampa trip from which this information is allegedly coming from. Boring's non-denial denial, that it was only an anecdote denoting the kindness of JFK, is refuted by Boring himself when Manchester pens the tale. Floyd Boring categorically denied what William Manchester reports in his book: "Kennedy grew weary of seeing bodyguards roosting behind him every time he turned around, and in Tampa on November 18 [1963], just four days before his death, he dryly asked Agent Floyd Boring to 'keep those Ivy League charlatans off the back of the car.' Boring wasn't offended. There had been no animosity in the remark."[241]

Boring told me "I never told him that." As far as the merit of the quote is concerned, Boring told me: "No, no, no-that's not true." When asked, point blank, if JFK had ever ordered the agents off the rear of the limousine, including in Tampa on 11/18/63, Boring told me "Well, that's not true. That's not true. He was a very nice man; he never interfered with us at all."

In regard to Tampa, Floyd said "He actually- No, I told them...He didn't tell them anything.... He just – I looked at the back of the car and I seen these fellahs (Zboril and Lawton) were hanging on the limousine- I told them to return to the (follow-up) car. He (JFK) was a very easy-going guy; he didn't interfere with our actions at all."

Boring confirmed what he had previously told me on 9/22/93 and 3/4/94 when he wrote in a letter received 11/22/1997 that "President Kennedy was a very congenial man knowing most agents by their first name. He was very cooperative with the Secret Service, and well liked and admired by all of us."

So, Boring would have you believe it was just routine, as agents would sometimes hop back and forth from the rear of the limousine to the Secret Service follow up car. However, again Boring does not really deny the story as much as he puts a spin on it. All Boring said was he did not speak with Manchester. The tenor and tone of the story are essentially the same. We cannot check if Boring did speak with Manchester as Manchester's materials are withheld from the public.

So, while it is indeed being spread, as policy, Boring can say afterwards it was only a harmless retelling of an anecdote. And he can deny it by saying he never spoke with Manchester. However, Boring is the only one who admits to any truth to the story, and the only one not to totally deny it. Remember, Boring is admitting it came from him, and not JFK. Everyone else totally denies it, it never came from JFK, not even as an anecdotal story. Boring's story, whether actual or not, whether anecdotal or not somehow grows after the Tampa trip into policy. This verbal story is used as policy, though never written down, for the preparation for the Texas trip, something which had never occurred before.

Oddly, if this is a new policy, it goes into practice only in Dallas. Clint Hill does recall hearing it, as policy, though he can't recall from whom he heard it according to his written report. However, he named none other than Floyd Boring as *the* source during his Warren Commission testimo-

---

ny mentioned above" or words to that effect. [It's important to note that Hill was twice coy about naming his source in his written statement yet named the source – Boring – under oath to Arlen Specter of the Warren Commission]. Hill does disobey it four times but that does not necessarily mean the policy did not exist. He may have felt he should be obeying it as he does not stay on the rear bumper for any appreciable length of time. And the other agents do stay on the follow up car.

Interestingly, in viewing slow motion video footage of the Love Field departure,[242] one can see agent Henry J. Rybka[243] attempt to get on the back of the limousine only to be recalled by none other than Emory P. Roberts, who rises in his seat in the follow-up car and hand- gestures Rybka to cease and desist. Giving Roberts the benefit of the doubt, it appears that Borings' orders to not have any agents ride on the back of the limousine were well taken.

After the assassination there are reports that JFK had previously made such requests prior to the Tampa trip. Yet, photos from these trips prove these statements to be false, as well as the lack of any record or document to that effect.

THE TRUTH – JFK NEVER ORDERED SECRET SERVICE
AGENTS OFF THE LIMO

Gerald A. Behn, SAIC of the White House Detail: "I don't remember Kennedy ever saying that he didn't want anybody on the back of his car. I think if you watch the newsreel pictures and whatnot [sic], you'll find agents on there from time to time." As just one of many examples, Behn cited the June 1963 trip to Berlin (There are many others.)[244]

Arthur L. Godfrey, ATSAIC of the White House Detail: "That's a bunch of baloney; that's not true. He never ordered us to do anything. He was a very nice man ... cooperative." Asked if whether Aide Ken O'Donnell did any similar ordering, Godfrey said emphatically "he did not order anyone around." As just one example, Godfrey was on the Italy trip and agents frequently rode on the rear of the limousine- one of the agents was none other than Winston G. Lawson.[245] In a letter dated 11/24/97, Godfrey stated the following: "All I can speak for is myself. When I was working with President Kennedy he never asked me to

---

242   JFK Secret Service agent Don Lawton: rode on rear of limo in Chicago & Tampa + Tampa trip security. (https://www.youtube.com/watch?v=SQUwWGvCMW4)
243   25H787.
244   Interview with author 9/27/92.
245   Interviews with author 5/30/96;6/7/96;11/24/97-letter.

have my shift leave the limo when we were working it," thus confirming what he had also told me telephonically on two prior occasions. Presidential aide David F. Powers: " Unless they [the Secret Service] were 'running' along beside the limo, the Secret Service rode in a car behind the President, so, no, they never had to be told to 'get off' the limo."[246]

Samuel A. Kinney, White House Detail: "That is absolutely, positively false...no, no, no, he had nothing to do with that (ordering agents off the rear of the limo).… No, never-the agents say, 'O.K., men, fall back on your posts' … President Kennedy was one of the easiest presidents to ever protect; Harry S. Truman was a jewel just like John F. Kennedy was … 99% of the agents would agree … (JFK) was one of the best presidents ever to control-he trusted every one of us." In regard to the infamous quote from William Manchester, Kinney said, "That is false. I talked to William Manchester; he called me on the book [sic] … for the record of history that is false – Kennedy never ordered us to do anything. I am aware of what is being said but that is false." Finally, just to nail down this issue, I asked Kinney if an exception was made on 11/22/63: "Not this particular time, no. Not in this case." Kinney also told me that JFK had nothing to do with the limiting of motorcycles during motorcades, and that Ken O'Donnell did not interfere with the agents, "Nobody ordered anyone around."[247]

Robert E. Lilley, White House Detail: "Oh, I'm sure he didn't. He was very cooperative with us once he became President. He was extremely cooperative. Basically, 'whatever you guys want is the way it will be.'" Lilley also refuted the Manchester account, adding that on a trip with JFK in Caracas, Venezuela, he and "Roy Kellerman rode on the back of the limousine all the way to the Presidential palace" at speeds reaching "50 miles per hour" (with the bubble-top on [which Lilley believed "might deflect a bullet."][248]

Donald J. Lawton, White House Detail: When I told Lawton what fellow agent Kinney told me, that JFK never ordered the agents off the rear of the limousine, he said "It's the way Sam said, yes." (Meaning he agrees with Kinney, it happened the way Kinney said.)

Asked to explain how he dismounted the rear of the limousine in Tampa, he said, " I didn't hear the President say it, no. The word was relayed to us- you know, 'come back to the follow-up car.'" According to Lawton, JFK was "very personable … very warm." Asked about the tragedy in Dallas,

246   Letter to author 9/10/93.
247   Interviews with author 10/19/92, 3/5/94 and 4/15/94.
248   Interviews with author 9/27/92; 9/21/93; 6/7/96.

Lawton said, "everyone felt bad. It was our job to protect the President. You still have regrets, remorse. Who knows, if they had left guys on the back of the car ... you can hindsight yourself to death." And, from his letter to the author dated 11/22/97: "Since I am currently employed by the Secret Service, I do not believe it appropriate that I comment on former or current protectees of the Service. If you spoke with Bob Lilley as you stated then you can take whatever information he passed on to you as gospel.[249]

Robert I. Bouck, SAIC of PRS: Bouck confirmed that having agents on the back of the limousine depended on factors independent of any alleged presidential "requests."[250]

Rufus W. Youngblood, ASAIC of LBJ Detail: Youngblood confirmed that "there was not a standing order" from JFK to restrict agents from the back of the limousine - the agents had "assigned posts and positions" on the back of the President's car. On 2/8/94, Youngblood added: "President Kennedy wasn't a hard ass ... he never said anything like that. As a historian, he (Manchester) flunked the course – don't read Manchester!"[251]

Abraham W. Bolden, Sr., White House Detail / Chicago office: In reference to Kennedy's alleged "requests," Mr. Bolden told the author that he "didn't hear anything about that ... I never believed that Kennedy said that."[252]

John Norris, Uniformed Division of the Secret Service: Norris also joined his colleagues in refuting the notion that JFK ordered the agents off the rear of the limo.[253]

Maurice G. Martineau, SAIC of Chicago office: Martineau joined his colleagues in refuting the Manchester story that JFK ordered the agents off the rear of the car. Martineau said this to me in two telephonic interviews.[254]

Cecil Stoughton, WH photographer: "I did see a lot of the activity surrounding the various trips of the President, and in many cases, I did see the agents in question riding on the rear of the President's car. In fact, I have ridden there a number of times myself during trips...I would jump on the step on the rear of the [Lincoln] Continental until the next stop. I have made photos while hanging on with one hand ... in Tampa [11/18/63], for example. As for the [alleged] edict of not riding there by order of the President – I can't give you any proof of first-hand knowledge."

---

249   Interview with author 11/15/95; 11/22/97-letter.
250   Interview with author 9/27/92.
251   Interviews with author 10/22/92 and 2/8/94.
252   Interviews with author 9/16/93 and 4/10/94; 9/10/93, 10/30/93, 12/13/93, 12/31/93, 8/94, and 1/97: letters and correspondence
253   Interview with author 3/4/94.
254   Interviews with author 9/21/93 and 6/7/96; 11/23/97 letter to the author.

Stoughton went on to write: "I am bothered by your interest in these matters"(!). In a later letter, Stoughton merely corroborated his prior written statements: "I would just jump on and off [the limo] quickly- no routine, and Jackie had no further remarks to me." It should be explained that according to Stoughton's book, Jackie had told him to stay close to the limo in July 1963, and he did up to and including the Tampa trip of 11/18/63 AND the Houston, TX trip of 11/21/63 (there are photos that Stoughton made from the follow-up car that day, as well). Then, for some unknown reason, Stoughton was relegated to a position further away from JFK.[255]

Martin E. Underwood, DNC advance man: The advance man confirmed to this author that JFK did not restrict agents from riding on the Presidential limousine (He could not believe that Mr. Behn wrote his report with JFK's alleged "desires," citing Clint Hill's actions on 11/22/63 as just one of "many times" that agents were posted on the back of the JFK limousine).[256]

Press Secretary Pierre Salinger: JFK had a good relationship with the Secret Service and, more importantly, did NOT argue with their security measures.[257]

Jerry D. Kivett, VP LBJ Detail: "[JFK] was beloved by those agents on the detail and I never heard anyone say that he was difficult to protect."[258]

June Kellerman, the widow of Roy H. Kellerman, ASAIC White House Detail: "Roy did not say that JFK was difficult to protect."[259]

Jean Brownell Behn, widow of the late Gerald A. Behn, SAIC White House Detail (see above): Jerry did not like William Manchester's book *The Death of a President* and confirmed that she also did not believe that JFK had ever conveyed to Jerry the idea of having the agents not ride on the rear of the limousine. In a follow-up letter she stated that "The only thing I can tell you is that Jerry always said 'Don't believe anything you hear and only half of what you read.'"[260]

Chief James J. Rowley: "No President will tell the Secret Service what they can or cannot do."[261]

255   12/2/95 and 11/20/97 letters to author; rode close to Kennedy's car from July 1963 until November 22, 1963, authorized by a specific request from Mrs. Kennedy [*The Memories, 1961-1963*, by Cecil Stoughton w/ Ted Clifton and Hugh Sidey (1973), p. 160; see also Stoughton's motorcade films of the trip to Italy (July 1963), as well as his still photos taken from the follow-up car in Tampa, FL (11/18/63) and in Houston, TX (11/21/63) via the JFK Library.
256   Interview with author 10/9/92.
257   Author's correspondence with Roger Peterson, 2/99 (based off Peterson's very recent conversations with Salinger)
258   Letter to author dated 12/8/97.
259   Letter to author dated 12/2/97.
260   Interview with author 11/18/95; letter to author dated 11/28/97.
261   5 H 470.

Charles T. Zboril, White House Detail, Lawton's partner on the rear of the limo in Tampa on 11/18/63 was the only agent I spoke to who did not give me a straight answer, one way or the other, : "Well, Don Lawton and I are just sub-notes [sic] because somebody else testified in behalf of us about what happened in Tampa"- this was Clint Hill, testifying to Arlen Specter about why agents were not on the rear of the car during the assassination. When I asked him if it was true that JFK had really ordered the agents off the limousine four days before Dallas, which I already knew not to be true, Zboril got emotional: "Where did you read that? I … If-if you read it in the Warren Report, that's what happened...do you want me commenting official-ly? I'm speaking to someone I don't know... I gave you more than I would give someone else." Zboril then gave me his address and requested that I send him anything on this matter and he promised to respond to me...he never did.[262]

Jim Bishop sums up the situation best: "no one wanted to weigh the possibilities that, if a Secret Service man had been on the left [or right] rear bumper going down Elm Street, it would have been difficult to hit President Kennedy."[263]

FBI Director J. Edgar Hoover to President Lyndon B. Johnson, 1:40 P.M., 11/29/63: "You see, there was no Secret Service man standing on the back of the car. Usually the presidential car in the past has had steps on the back, next to the bumpers, and there's usually been one [agent] on either side standing on these steps … [ellipsis in text]. Whether the President asked that that not be done, we don't know."[264]

In a letter dated 4/3/64, Warren Commission general counsel J. Lee Rankin had written to Secret Service Chief James J. Rowley "requesting further information concerning expressions by President Kennedy re-garding the placement of Secret Service agents on or near the car during the motorcade," obviously meaning *the* motorcade of 11/22/63.44 Since JFK was conveniently dead and there was nothing in the record to indi-cate that Kennedy had said anything that morning, Rowley mailed back five reports on 4/22/64 to try to "satisfy" the Warren Commission, who obviously were not satisfied by the testimonies of Greer, Kellerman, Hill, or Youngblood on March 9, 1964.[265]

These five reports- by agents Boring[dated 4/8/64], Roberts [dat-ed 4/10/64], Ready [dated 4/11/64], Behn [dated 4/16/64] and Hill [undated]- make much of JFK's alleged comments to agent Boring on

262   Interview with author 11/15/95.
263   Bishop, 1992 edition, p. 558.
264   *Taking Charge: The Johnson White House Tapes, 1963-1964* by Michael Beschloss, editor (Simon & Schuster), pp. 56-57.
265   18 H 803-809. 2 H 61-155.

11/18/63 about getting the agents who were riding on the rear of the limo the hell off of there, as well as "general common knowledge" that this had happened before, even before the Tampa motorcade. However, as I uncovered during the interviews for my manuscript, and which has been demonstrated so far, this was totally fabricated. Each one of these reports is a lie or used for a lie.

Boring already dodgy regarding Tampa, flat out lies about JFK's trip to Italy. The ARRB's Doug Horne writes: "Mr. Boring remembered preparing his written statement and verified that the copy shown to him was indeed his statement." Although primarily about the 11/18/63 Tampa trip, Boring also mentions another time---the July 1963 Italy trip---where JFK had also made an alleged request to not have the agents ride on the rear of the limousine."

However, as with the Tampa trip, agents DID ride on the rear of the limousine, as recently discovered film from the JFK Library, obtained through my efforts.[266] Also, compare Boring's statement here with Arthur L. Godfrey, ATSAIC of WHD statements on the Italy trip above. Roberts' report is merely a confirmation of hearing Boring over the radio in the Tampa motorcade telling the agents to get off the rear of the limousine-it says nothing of JFK's alleged "desires."

Now deceased, Roberts was the commander of the 7 other agents who rode in the follow-up car with him in Dallas. Roberts had, according to the driver of the follow-up car, Samuel A. Kinney, ordered the agents not to move after the first shot sounded![267] Roberts had recognized the first shot as a rifle blast[268], yet recalled agent John D. "Jack" Ready who had begun to move in JFK's direction. Ready was the agent who was assigned to JFK's side of the limousine (as Clint Hill was assigned to Jackie's side[269]).

Roberts came to Ready's rescue in another report: "SA Ready would have done the same thing (as Agent Hill did) if motorcycle was not at President's corner of car."[270] Strange, but this posed no problem at all for Agent Don Lawton on November 18, 1963, in Tampa (but unfortunately, like Rybka, Lawton was left at Love Field and was not in the motorcade detail). This begs the question, were Rybka and Lawton the two agents who were supposed to have ridden the rear of the limousine?

---

266   JFK's Trip to Italy, 7/2/63, courtesy of Jim Cedrone/ JFK Library. This footage was shown at COPA 1996.

267   Author's interviews with Sam Kinney, 3/5/94 and 4/15/94.

268   18 H734-735.

269   18H749-750.

270   18 H 738.

Ready mentions the 11/18/63 Florida trip in his report but he wasn't even there! "Although I was not in Tampa, Florida, Monday, November 18, 1963, it was known to me that President Kennedy requested, through Assistant Special Agent in Charge Floyd M. Boring, that two agents be removed from the rear steps of the presidential vehicle during a motorcade in that city." There is reason to believe Behn did not even write his report as it has a stamped (stamp pad) signature (like other reports contained in the WC volumes and elsewhere; not handwritten). When one considers the fact that a subordinate agent from the Miami office, SA Robert Jamison, signed a vital Secret Service document as if he were the SAIC (in this case, John Marshall), the possibility that someone else merely stamped this type-written report with Behn's stamp pad signature is certainly not above the realm of possibility. (Behn's office was shared with ASAIC's Kellerman and Boring). And Hill's report is undated. Behn's, Boring's, and Hill's reports are not even on any Secret Service or Treasury Dept. stationery, just blank sheets of paper.

All are supposedly evidence of JFK expressing his desire to keep Secret Service agents off the limousine in Tampa and before Tampa.

And, again, there is nothing about what JFK said or "requested on November 22, 1963, the critical day in question!

Security Stripping Measure #2 – Noisy Motorcycles Reduced and Placed Rearward for Conversational Purposes?

The ARRB interview of Boring goes on to say, "When asked whether the Secret Service had any standard procedures regarding size and placement of motorcycle escort for the President's limousine in motorcades, Boring said to the ARRB that there was no standard protocol for this, since local resources were different from site to site. He then stated that the Secret Service would place motorcycles wherever the local authorities would want them, and that the Secret Service would not try to tell local law enforcement authorities where to place motorcycles around the limousine – he said that if the Secret Service had tried to do such a thing, that the local authorities would not have listened anyway. He said that regarding matters like this, local authorities wouldn't take orders from the Secret Service, but instead had to be coaxed. He also stated that placing motorcycles alongside the limousine would not have been a good idea, since they were so noisy that the President would not have been able to have a conversation with the car's occupants."

Now, for the real story:

On November 20th, with no secret service men present, it was agreed that eighteen motorcycles would be used, some positioned alongside the limousine (similar to the plan used in the prior Texas cities of San Antonio, Houston, and Fort Worth). There was another meeting on November 21, 1963, in which those plans were changed. Captain Perdue Lawrence of the Dallas Police testified to the Warren Commission that 2 days before the assassination he met with Chief Lunday and Chief Batchelor and discussed the motorcycle plans for the motorcade. "I was told that there would be these lead motorcycle officers, and that we would also have these other officers alongside the President's car and the Vice President's car, and some of the others that would be in the motorcade, and approximately how many officers would be needed for the escort, and at that time I had prepared a list of 18 solo motorcycle officers, this included three solo sergeants."

"I was also instructed that about this motorcade--that when it reached Stemmons Expressway, Chief Batchelor told me that he wanted a solo motorcycle officer in each traffic lane, each of the five traffic lanes waiting for the motorcade, so that no vehicles, on Stemmons Expressway would pass the motorcade at all and he wanted these solo motorcycle officers to pull away from the escort and get up there on Stemmons Freeway and block the traffic, and some of these officers, he stated, would pull past the Presidential car." Then on November 21, 1963, a change occurs.[271] "This was the first time that I had attended any security meeting at all in regard to this motorcade."

"At approximately 5 P.M. I was told to report to the conference room on the third floor, and when I arrived at the conference room the deputy chiefs were in there, there were members of the Secret Service--Mr. Sorrels, Captain Gannaway, Captain Souter of radio patrol, and Capt. Glen King, deputy chiefs, assistant chiefs, and Chief Curry, and one gentleman, who I assume was in charge of the security for the Secret Service. This was the first time I had attended any conferences in regard to the security of this escort, and I listened in on most of the discussion and I heard one of the Secret Service men say that President Kennedy did not desire any motorcycle officer directly on each side of him, between him and the crowd, but he would want the officers to the rear. This conversation I overheard as Chief Batchelor was using a blackboard showing how he planned to handle this--how plans had been made to cover the escort."[272]

---

271   18 H 789 Grant does not mention the reduction of motorcycles in discussing the November 21, 1963, meeting: *JFK Assassination File* by DPD Chief Jesse Curry (1969), pp.15-16. Curry does and records Grant's presence.
272   7 H 580-581.

Remember, according to Boring, "the Secret Service would not try to tell local law enforcement authorities where to place motorcycles around the limousine."

Secret Service Agent David Grant, who would have known of Kennedy's alleged "desires" via Boring (Grant was an advance man for the Florida and Dallas trips), attended this meeting, along with fellow advance man Win Lawson (who received his assignment from Boring).[273] DPD Captain Perdue Lawrence testified that the Secret Service told them to stay to the rear on the evening of 11/21/63.[274]

DPD Asst. Chief Charles Batchelor wrote in his report that "[Dallas officer Captain Perdue] Lawrence then said there would be four (4) motorcycles on either side of the motorcade immediately to the rear of the President's vehicle [as borne out by his 11/21/63 report]. Mr. Lawson of the Secret Service stated that this was too many, that he thought two (2) motorcycles on either side would be sufficient, about even with the rear fender of the President's car."[275]

DPD Captain Perdue Lawrence's report regarding motorcycle distribution dated November 21, 1963, the day before the assassination [handwritten comments from 7/24/64] stated "In addition to DPD motorcycles officers B.W. Hargis and B.J. Martin, H.B. McLain[276] and J.W. Courson were slated to ride on the left side of JFK's limousine. Also, in addition to DPD motorcycle officers D.L. Jackson and J. Chaney, C.A. Haygood and M.L. Baker were slated to ride on the right side of JFK's limousine!"[277]

If that weren't enough, both DPD motorcycle officer's M.L. Baker and B.J. Martin testified to the Warren Commission (and stated in private interviews) that there was a last-minute change made at Love Field: they were told to stay to the rear of the limousine. Marion Baker told the Commission that he was told on November 22, 1963, at about 8:00 A.M., "My partner and I, we received instructions to ride right beside the President's car." However, when he got to Love Field "When we got to the airport, our sergeant instructed me that there wouldn't be anybody riding beside the President's car."[278] Baker was advised of these 5 or 10 minutes before the motorcade left the airport.

Martin told the Commission, "They [plural = Secret Service] instructed us that they didn't want anyone riding past the President's car

---

273   7 H 580-581.
274   21 H 571.
275   Lawrence Exhibit #2 20H p. 489 (same as the HSCA's JFK Exhibit F-679).
276   See also *No More Silence* by Larry Sneed (1998), p. 162 (based on interview with McLain).
277   3 H 244; 10/98 letter to the author; *No More Silence* by Larry Sneed (1998), p. 123 (based off interview with Baker); 11 HSCA 528.
278   3H244.

and that we were to ride to the rear, to the rear of his car, about the rear bumper."[279] Martin told Jean Hill: "They told us out at Love Field right after Kennedy's plane landed.... Well, while Kennedy was busy shaking hands with all the well-wishers at the airport, Johnson's Secret Service people came over to the motorcycle cops and gave us a bunch of instructions...They also ordered us into the darndest escort formation I've ever seen. Ordinarily, you bracket the car with four motorcycles, one on each fender. But this time, they told the four of us [Martin, Hargis, Chaney, & Jackson] assigned to the President's car there'd be no forward escorts. We were to stay well to the back and not let ourselves get ahead of the car's rear wheels under any circumstances. I'd never heard of a formation like that, much less ridden in one, but they said they wanted to let the crowds have an unrestricted view of the president. Well, I guess somebody got an 'unrestricted view' of him, all right."[280]

Oddly, when these gentlemen were interviewed by the HSCA the story changes: it was now JFK who wanted no motorcycles alongside the car, and not the Secret Service.[281] One wonders whether they changed their stories, or if they had their stories changed for them by the HSCA. We now know the HSCA lied about the Bethesda witnesses supposedly all agreeing as to the nature of JFK's head wound. It would not be a stretch of the imagination if it turns out the HSCA lied by changing what Baker and Martin had to say about no motorcycle placement alongside the presidential limousine.

DPD Chief Curry testified to the Warren Commission about the matter.[282] Included in the actual transcript is a bizarre error involving a clumsy edit:

> **Mr. Curry:** In the planning of this motorcade, we had had more motorcycles lined up to be with the President's car, but the Secret Service didn't want that many.
>
> **Mr. Rankin:** Did they tell you why?
>
> **Mr. Curry:** We actually had two on each side, but we wanted four on each side and they asked us to drop out some of them and back down the motorcade, along the motorcade, which we did.

279   6 H 293; *Murder from Within* by Fred Newcomb & Perry Adams (1974), p.33 (based on interview with Martin); 11 HSCA 528.

280   From Martin's paramour, Jean Hill: *JFK: The Last Dissenting Witness* (1992), pp. 112-114 Hill, quoting Martin.

281   Baker - 11 HSCA 528, 536-537, regarding Baker's 1/17/78 interview with the staff of the HSCA (JFK document No. 014899) Martin - 11 HSCA 528, 536, regarding Martin's 1/17/78 interview with the HSCA staff, done on the same day as Baker's, above (JFK document no. 014372).

282   4 H 171.

Mr. Rankin:. How many motorcycles did you have?

Mr. Curry: I think we had four on each side of him.

Mr. Rankin: How many did you want to have?

Mr. Curry: *We actually had two on each side, but we wanted four on each side and they asked us to drop out some of them and back down the motorcade, along the motorcade, which we did.*

Mr. Rankin: So that you in fact only had two on each side of his car?

Mr. Curry: Two on each side and they asked them to remain at the rear fender so if the crowd moved in on him, they could move in to protect him from the crowd.

Mr. Rankin: Who asked him to stay at the rear fender?

Mr. Curry: I believe Mr. Lawson.

Mr. Rankin: The Secret Service man?

Mr. Curry: Yes, sir.

And what did Secret Service agent Winston G. Lawson have to say about this, in regard to November 22, 1963?

DULLES: "...do you recall that any orders were given by or on behalf of the President with regard to the location of those motorcycles that were particularly attached to his car?'

LAWSON: "Not specifically at this instance orders from him."

[Lawson would go on to say "it was my understanding that he did not like a lot of motorcycles surrounding the car," something not borne out by very recent prior motorcades from 11/18-11/22/63].[283]

The HSCA summed up the situation best:

"The Secret Service's alteration of the original Dallas Police Department motorcycle deployment plan prevented the use of maximum possible security precautions.... Surprisingly, the security measure used in the prior motorcades during the same Texas visit (11/21/63) shows that the deployment of motorcycles in Dallas by the Secret Service may have been uniquely insecure.... The Secret Service knew more than a day before November 22 that the President did not want motorcycles riding alongside or parallel to the Presidential vehicle..."[284]

And, as regards the Dallas Police, in keeping with all prior motorcades in 1963, DPD Captain Glen King stated that the Secret Service was pri-

---

283   4 H 338.
284   11 HSCA 527 & 529.

marily responsible for the President's security, while the role of the DPD was a supportive one.[285]

SECURITY STRIPPING #3 – PRESS & PHOTOGRAPHERS OUT OF THE PICTURE (LITERALLY):

*D*allas *Morning News* reporter Tom Dillard: "We lost our position at the airport. I understood we were to have been quite a bit closer. We were assigned as the prime photographic car which, as you probably know, normally a truck precedes the president on these things [motorcades] and certain representatives of the photographic press ride with the truck. In this case, as you know, we didn't have any and this car that I was in was to take photographs which was of spot-news nature."[286]

Dillard forcefully said the same thing on C-Span on 11/20/93 telling the TV audience that the flatbed truck was "canceled at the last minute" and they were put in Chevrolet convertibles "which totally put us out of the picture." [all previous trips, inc. Florida, has press/photographers very close in front and behind JFK's limousine, including White House photographer Cecil Stoughton, who rode in the SS follow-up car from July 1963 until 11/21/63.][287]

Henry Burroughs, AP photographer (rode in Camera Car #2): "I was a member of the White House pool aboard Air Force One when we arrived with JFK in Dallas on that fateful day. We, the pool, were dismayed to find our pool car shoved back to about #11 position in the motorcade. We protested, but it was too late."[288]

Cecil Stoughton, WH photographer (rode in Camera Car #2): "I did see lot of the activity surrounding the various trips of the President, and in many cases, I did see the agents in question riding on the rear of the President's car. In fact, I have ridden there a number of times myself during trips … I would jump on the step on the rear of the [Lincoln] Continental until the next stop. I have made photos while hanging on with one hand … in Tampa [11/18/63], for example … I would just jump on and off [the limo] quickly- no routine…"[289]

---

285   20 H 453, 463-465; see also Curry, p. 9.
286   6 H 163.
287   *The Memories, 1961-1963* by Cecil Stoughton w/ Ted Clifton and Hugh Sidey (1973), p. 160; see also Stoughton's motorcade films of the trip to Italy (7/63), as well as his still photos from the follow-up car in Tampa, FL (11/18/63) and in Houston, TX (11/21/63) via the JFK Library (shown by the author at COPA 1996).
288   Letter to the author dated 10/14/98.
289   Letters to author dated 11/30/95 & 11/20/97.

SECURITY STRIPPING #4 – WILL FRITZ'S MEN OUT OF THE MOTORCADE:

Seth Kantor's notes: "Will Fritz's men called off night before by SS. Had planned to ride closed car w/machine guns in car behind Pres." [which could mean someplace behind JFK's car, as was the case in Chicago, IL, on 3/23/63 and in New York on 11/15/63].[290]

SECURITY STRIPPING #5 – OTHER VEHICLE SHUFFLING:

Milton Wright, Texas Highway Patrolman (driver of Mayor Cabell's car):

> "As I recall, prior to the President arriving at the airport we were already staged on the tarmac. I do not recall what position I was in at that time, but it was not #1[the number taped to his car's windshield]. At the last minute there was a lot of shuffling, and I ended up in the 5th vehicle. My vehicle was the last to leave downtown after the shooting because the police set up a road block behind my car."[291]

Secret Service Agent Roger Warner stated in his report that, while at Love Field during the forming of the motorcade, "I undertook duties to aid SA Lawson ... in lining up cars for the motorcade, passing out numbers for the automobiles, and other general duties..."[292] During an interview conducted on 9/27/92, Lawson confirmed his handling of the automobile numbers and identification pins in Dallas on 11/22/63. When we consider that several of the vehicles - including the Presidential limousine – were out of their original, numerical order, the trail of suspicion leads to these two men.[293] Lawson oversaw the "car numbers for the windows" at Love Field.[294]

There was even more security stripping attributed to the Secret Service. The Secret Service "prevented the Dallas Police Department from inserting into the motorcade, behind the Vice-Presidential car, a Dallas Police Department squad car containing homicide detectives. Agent Lawson didn't know who canceled the Dallas Police Department car.

---

290   20 H 391; see also 4 H 171-172 (Curry); 11 HSCA 530; RIF#154-10003-10012: Secret Service survey report, Chicago, IL, 3/23/63.
291   9/3/98 e-mail to the author.
292   Roger C. Warner's report 25 H 786-7 CE 2554.
293   11 HSCA 530.
294   17 H 618, 625; 4 H 322.

SECURITY STRIPPING #6 – PERSONNEL SHUFFLING – AN ADDITION, AND SUBTRACTING PEOPLE FROM WHERE THEY NORMALLY WOULD BE:

General Godfrey McHugh (rode in VIP car): McHugh was asked to sit in a car farther back in the motorcade, rather than "normally, what I would do between the driver and Secret Service agent in charge of trip"- he admitted this was "unusual."[295] As the HSCA reported: "Ordinarily McHugh rode in the Presidential limousine in the front seat. This was the first time he was instructed not to ride in the car so that all attention would be focused on the President to accentuate full exposure."[296]

Lt. Col. George Whitmeyer (rode in pilot car): "Mr. Lawson acknowledged that Lt. Col. George Whitmeyer, who was part of the Dallas District U.S. Army Command, who Lawson said "taught Army Intelligence" and who rode in the pilot car, "wasn't scheduled" to be in the motorcade.[297] Mr. Lawson denied that the presence of Col. Whitmeyer had anything to do with Lawson's prior service in the CIC, Army Counterintelligence Corps."[298] Whitmeyer's son told this author: "My father passed away in 1978 and therefore the answers to your questions are somewhat based on personal recollection of his information given to me. Regarding your first question, my father was invited by Col. George Lumpkin (ret.) (deceased) to ride in the point [sic] car of the motorcade. He was not a scheduled participant. I think that Col. Lumpkin was with the Dallas Police Department at the time."[299]

SECURITY STRIPPING #7 – MOTORCADE ROUTE: LARGELY KEPT SECRET, EVEN FROM THE DALLAS POLICE. CHANGES MADE TO IT.

DPD Chief Jesse Curry: testified that he was not even consulted about the motorcade route![300] Curry learned of the route 11/21/63 via agents' Win Lawson and Forrest Sorrels.[301]

---

295   CFTR radio (Canada) interview 1976.
296   5/11/78 interview with the HSCA's Mark Flanagan (RIF#180-10078-10465 [see also 7 HSCA 14]).
297   As 17 H 615, Lawson's scheduled motorcade list, bears out.
298   1/31/78 HSCA interview of Secret Service agent Winston Lawson (RIF#18010074-10396).
299   Letter to author from George Whitmeyer, Jr. dated 9/28/98.
300   4 H 169.
301   CD 5, p. 4.

DPD Asst. Chief Charles Batchelor: "From an administrative stand-point, (DPD's Charles) Batchelor believed that the failure of the Secret Service to inform the police adequately in advance of the exact route to be taken by the president prevented them from adequately organizing their men and taking the necessary security precautions."[302]

DPD Sergeant Samuel Q. Bellah, one of the three advance motorcycle officers in the motorcade: "On the night before his assignment, Bellah reviewed the planned route with his captain. The route was not the original one that was to go straight through Dealey Plaza, but a revised route. The original plan would have skirted the Texas Book Depository building by a block, but the altered plan turned to pass directly in front of the building."[303]

Dallas motorcycle officer Bobby Joe Dale: "Two or three days prior to the President's visit we'd ridden with the Secret Service checking to see where the turns and problem areas might be. We had three possible routes, but we didn't know which one we were going to take, and we were not briefed on it. But by riding during the week, I kept hearing the phrase "escape routes," which dawned on me later that should something happen to any part of the motorcade we had an escape route to either Baylor or Parkland Hospitals.... Once we were assembled and the President was ready to go, we started the motorcade by going out a gate at the far end. At that time, we didn't know which route we were taking; we had three: right, straight, or left. As we were leaving, the word came over the radio that we would use the particular route that went left."[304]

Governor John Connally stated that he was never informed about the exact route to be used on the day of the assassination.[305]

DNC advance man Marty Underwood told Harrison Livingstone: "There were so many things that fell through in Dallas. Any advance man who had any sense at all would never have taken him down that route." When Livingstone commented that the route was changed, Underwood added: "Yeah, I know. You don't take a guy down a route like that."[306]

SAIC Jerry Behn (regarding his unpublished, executive session testimony before the HSCA): Behn told the author that he was asked two things: first, the details about the Florida trip of November 18, 1963; sec-

---

302   Warren Commission document---Griffin to Rankin re: Dallas PD (This is also HSCA RIF# 180-10109-10411.

303   *Fairfield (TX) Recorder*, 11/17/88: based on interview with Bellah [provided to the author by Bellah].

304   *No More Silence* by Larry Sneed (1998), pp. 132-133

305   *NY Herald Tribune*, 11/29/63.

306   *High Treason 2*, by Harry Livingstone, page 442.

ond, why the motorcade route was changed for the Dallas trip! When the author inquired about the second point since it is another crucial matter of security, Behn responded: "I know it was changed but why – I've forgotten completely – I don't know."[307]

SECURITY STRIPPING #8 – OVERPASS NOT CLEARED/ PROTECTED PROPERLY:

Winston G. Lawson: "I recall thinking we were coming to an overpass now, so I glanced up to see if it was clear, the way most of them had been, the way all of them had been up until that time on the way downtown, and it was not.... And I was looking for the officer who should have been there, had been requested to be there ... and I made a kind of motion through the windshield trying to get his attention to move the people from over our path the way it should have been ... we were just approaching this overpass when I heard a shot."[308]

SECURITY STRIPPING #9 – BUILDINGS ALONG THE MOTORCADE ROUTE NOT CHECKED AT ALL.

Lawson told both the Warren Commission and the House Assassinations Committee that he could not recall giving instructions to watch building windows, "although it was his usual practice to do so." Dallas Police Captain Lawrence confirms that no instructions were given.[309]

SECURITY STRIPPING #10 – THE MOST EGREGIOUS LIE: NO ACTIVE DEATH THREATS AGAINST JFK TO BE FOUND IN THE PRS FILES OF THE SECRET SERVICE.

Boring oversaw the advance for Chicago, Florida and Texas trip. The Chicago trip planned for early November 1963 was canceled. There were two separate threats against JFK's life involving arrests of several suspects. The Florida trip revealed a threat against JFK's life that was recorded by a police informant. Grant is there for all three trips. Lawson's check with the Service's PRS for threats against JFK lands on Boring's desk. Boring is directly involved in two of the three known checks with the PRS section. The first check was made on November 8, 1963. Boring replied, "there wouldn't be any information available of any consequence." The second

---

307   Author's interviews with Behn, 9/27/92.
308   4 H 351; see also 4 H 327 and 21 H 564.
309   HSCA Vol. 2 p. 526.

check is done by Kellerman two days later, November 10th. The agent later admitted that it was "unusual" not to have found anything in the PRS files.[310] A third check was done by Rufus Youngblood on the morning of November 22, 1963, again nothing. Yet, Lawson knows nothing of any threat to JFK [see addendum below].

Conclusion

The common links to security stripping? Boring, Lawson, and Grant. ASAIC Floyd Boring can be tied directly to at least 10 instances of stripping security away from JFK. The advance team of Secret Service agents' Winston G. Lawson and David B. Grant, who worked hand-in-glove with ASAIC Floyd Boring, were the in-the-field architects for the planning and implementation of security concerns (read stripping) in Dallas. In fact, although Grant physically joined Lawson on 11/18/63, fresh from his participation with Boring on the Florida trip (inc. the controversial Tampa stop)[311], he was actually working with Lawson and Boring earlier: Lawson's Final Survey Report of 11/19/63, includes this statement: "This survey was conducted by SA Winston Lawson and SAIC Forrest Sorrels, and assisted by SA David Grant, from November 13 through November 22, 1963..."[312] And, as we know, Lawson and Grant had a hand in the motorcycle depletion and realignment, the overpass security, or lack of it, the press' and photographers (dis)placement, and the planning of the motorcade route.[313]

Does Mr. Boring think there was a conspiracy in the death of JFK? Of course not.

"Mr. Boring made clear during the [ARRB] interview that he felt Lee Harvey Oswald had shot President Kennedy acting alone, and that there was no shot from the grassy knoll."

"...I concur 100 % with the Warren Report."[314]

"...I would go with the Warren Commission's report."[315]

At least on *that* point, Mr. Boring is remarkably consistent.

Addendum: Regarding Prior Threats To JFK's Life:

HSCA document180- 10074-10394, an interview with agent Robert J. Jamison states that "the threat of November 18, 1963 was posed

---

310   2 H 107 – 108.
311   18 H 789; *Inside the Secret Service* video 1995 (Lawson).
312   17 H 601.
313   *Mortal Error* by Bonar Menninger, 1992, page 233.
314   Boring's JFK Library Oral History, 2/25/76, RELEASED JAN. 1998.
315   *Mortal Error* by Bonar Menninger, 1992, page 233.

by a mobile, unidentified rifleman with a high- powered rifle fitted with a scope."

In addition, HSCA document 180-10083-10419, an interview with Lubert F. deFreese, states that "a threat did surface in connection with the Miami trip ... there was an active threat against the President of which the Secret Service was aware in November 1963 in the period immediately prior to JFK's trip to Miami made by a "group of people."

In addition to this threat information, and separate from the Joseph Milteer threat of 11/9/63, a CO2 PRS file, released to the HSCA on 5/3/78 and available to all of us only now is the specific name of another individual who made a threat against JFK on 11/18/63: John Warrington (Sam Kinney also told the author of an unspecified "organized crime" threat pertaining to this same trip).

And, as we know, Agent Lawson confirmed that a big, fat ZERO came out of the Dallas check of potential threats to President Kennedy. This is simply impossible, as the rabid right-wing environment, the "Wanted for Treason" mug shots, and the October 24, 1963, attack on U.N. Ambassador Adlai Stevenson make abundantly clear by themselves. When we also couple the 11/2/63 Chicago threats and the 1/9-11/18/63 Miami threats known to the Secret Service before Dallas, we must ask ourselves: was PRS SA Glen Bennett riding in the follow-up car on 11/22/63 actively searching for these known threats?

CHAPTER TEN

MORE THOUGHTS ON
THE KENNEDY DETAIL

I n his book *The Kennedy Detail*, co-authored by Lisa McCubbin (now Clint Hill's wife), Blaine writes in the third person, giving the impression that someone else wrote it. Try writing about yourself in that manner. I can't do it myself. It feels like scratching on a blackboard. Why he chose to go this route is beyond me, unless it was done with the goal of clouding who was the author of a particular alleged fact and giving the impression that he was speaking for all the other agents. Blaine's book has no footnotes, endnotes, links, references, document ed quotes or any confirmations that what he writes is true. It's obvious that Blaine is not presenting his book as a scholarly work, but as a biography of sorts. This is a great shame. Blaine obviously had a great number of inside contacts; people close to the action who would have felt more comfortable talking with Blaine than with a stranger. To not have all those discussions and interviews documented or recorded for the public is a great loss. Then again, it serves the purpose of clouding exactly who can be attributable for all alleged facts and suppositions. Instead of providing insight into the assassination, the book drones on about (1) agent's complaining about not getting to eat meals, being away from their families, being overworked, not getting sleep, etc. (2) how fantastic every agent on the detail was, (3) how they couldn't have done anything more than they did to protect the president (4) how thorough the Warren Commission report was, (5) how emotionally affected each agent was after the assassination and (6) how mean people were suggesting that there was a conspiracy. The book was much more concerned with shaping a fictitious image of the Secret Service (or, CYA) and supporting the government fabrication about the tragedy in Dallas than shedding any light on the truth.

Many of Blaine's comments are in direct contradiction to facts that even government agencies have indicated were true while other comments just gloss over anything that might interfere with his "reality."[316] Just a handful of questions the book raises: Many of the agents in Dallas were out partying into the early morning hours of November 22. Even if, as he states, they were off duty and not inebriated, the question left unanswered is why they weren't back at the hotel sleeping since throughout the book they complain about not getting enough rest. He talks about how stressful they expected the day to be and how important "mental alertness" was for them being able to do their job. And yet, somehow, he doesn't see the inherent contradiction.

Why was Johnson's detail already covering LBJ, who wasn't even a target, while Kennedy's detail still hadn't even reacted because "they weren't sure if what they heard was gunfire?" In what fantasy world does anyone believe that Ruby killed Oswald because of how much he cared about the Kennedy family? Why does agent Paul Landis, who at the time, says he thought at least one of the shots came from the grassy knoll and saw someone running in that direction after the fact, realize "when he thought back with a rational mind" years later that he was wrong? What pressure

---

316   Former Secret Service agent Gerald Blaine claimed in 2010 that actress Marilyn Monroe was in President Kennedy's company only twice, and briefly. In his memoir, he wrote that "These were the only … times that I or any of the agents I have discussed this with remember Marilyn Monroe being in proximity to the president." That same year, Ronald Kessler's book, *In the President's Secret Service: Behind the Scenes with Agents in the Line of Fire and the Presidents They Protect*, hit the bookstores. "According to Secret Service agents, Kennedy had sex with Marilyn Monroe at New York hotels and in a loft above the Justice Department office of then Attorney General Robert F. Kennedy, the president's brother," wrote Kessler.

was applied to give him a clearer memory? Why does Blaine see no validity in any assassination conspiracy theory yet when he couldn't sell the Secret Service IBM equipment, he placed blame on a conspiracy to pay him back for leaving the Service? Blaine says Chief Rowley told agents to lie whenever asked if the president ordered them to stay off the back of his car to "protect the president. "What other lies might have been told in order to "protect" each other?[317] That being said, certain major points are easily refuted: The book claims that the agents "Break Their Silence" in that they have not spoken since 1963, as if the Warren Commission, Manchester's best-seller, the HSCA, various interviews, and several other books, including my own,[318] never happened in the intervening years.

Mr. Blaine states that President Eisenhower almost always rode in a closed car. *WRONG*: the exact opposite is true. In fact, Ike often rode in an open limo, and ironically, Blaine's friend, Clint Hill, corroborated this point in his 2016 book *Five Presidents*.

Mr. Blaine states that JFK hardly ever rode in the limousine with the bubble top on the car. *WRONG*: again, just by doing a Google image search, I over 25 different times – in good weather – that President Kennedy rode under the top (New York, Boston, Caracas, Paris, Ireland, England, etc.). Mr. Blaine, during an earlier interview with myself, thought SAIC Gerald Behn was on the Tampa trip *WRONG*: It was ASAIC Floyd Boring. Mr. Behn was on vacation.[319] This seemingly innocent error is highly disturbing because Blaine speaks so authoritatively about what transpired on the Tampa trip, even using unsourced direct quotes from memory. How can Blaine write so authoritatively that he heard Boring over the radio relaying JFK's alleged instruction to remove Zboril and Lawton from the rear of the limousine in his book when, several years before, he told me it was another completely different agent on the trip? Likewise, his good friend, former agent and Kennedy Detail contributor

---

317   A researcher in Florida wrote me: "Vince, I watched JFK in Tampa 50th Anniversary on PBS in Tampa last night. Guess who 2 of the main narrators were: Agents Blaine and Zboril spreading their usual bullshit about how JFK ordered them off the back of the car in Tampa because he wanted to be seen and how shocked they were. And yet every film, both private and professional in this documentary showed the agents riding on the back of the limo or running alongside. I guess we should believe them and not our lying eyes! It went into detail about how there was an officer on every building and officers and agents in the streets to control the crowds. One film that really stuck out was a clip that showed 4 agents on the sides of the Queen Mary, 2 on the back of the limo and 2 running on the sides. Then you get Blaine smirking about what fun that trip was not knowing what lay ahead later that week."

318   My first book was available in some shape or form as a self-published entity since 1993.

319   "Blaine even erroneously thought [SAIC Gerald] Behn was on the Florida trip, a testament to the frequency of his [Behn's] trips with the president." *Survivor's Guilt*, page 121 [author's interview with Blaine 2/7/04].

Chuck Zboril, also on the Tampa trip (riding on the rear of JFK's limo, no less), erroneously thought Roy Kellerman oversaw the Tampa trip and riding in the front seat of the presidential limo! Again, this is disturbing for the very same reasons, as Zboril vigorously defends Blaine's views in media appearances.[320] How can Zboril support Blaine's later-day Boring story when he thought it was yet another agent on the trip?[321] How can both Blaine and Zboril, with a straight face, endorse the story they attribute to Boring in Blaine's book when both thought it was another person substituting on the trip? I think this is perhaps the biggest clue – the smoking gun – as to the lack of credibility in Blaine's book.

Interestingly, yet another agent I spoke to, Lynn Meredith, admittedly not on the Tampa trip and relying on the stories told by "good friends who were there," also believed Roy Kellerman, not Boring, was on the Tampa trip.[322] Finally, Zboril takes me to task (in his review of my first book on Amazon, of all places) for naming Agent David Grant (Clint Hill's brother-in-law) as an advance agent for the Tampa trip, yet the Warren Report itself confirms Grant's role.[323]

Ironically, Zboril told me: "If you read it in there [the Warren Report], it happened." If that weren't enough, lead advance agent Win Lawson, who worked with Grant, told me that Grant "had been on advance in

320   "Zboril was sure that Kellerman, who wasn't even on the Florida trip, was present in Tampa: "I thought it was Roy Kellerman, not Boring, in the car on the Tampa trip…that's my recollection." *Survivor's Guilt*, page 294 [author's interview with Chuck Zboril 11/15/95]. Interestingly, a 6/1/77 photo of Zboril with President Jimmy Carter and Vice President Walter Mondale comes with the caption stating that "Zboril was a young agent scheduled to be on the back of President John F. Kennedy's limousine on the day he was assassinated in Dallas, Texas" [Alamy.com; Ken Hawkins Pictures].
321   Postscript: it is a total non-issue about Boring telling the agents to not ride on the rear of the limousine right before the Texas trip. I BELIEVE this indeed happened (page 43 of my first book) and I also have no doubt that, if I was given the chance to speak to many of Blaine's colleagues circa late 1963-1965 (or perhaps even later), those gentlemen would have "rained on my parade" in droves and told me the fib that JFK ordered the agents off his limo (bottom of page 52 of my first book). The point is the credibility of this action by Boring, NOT that Boring performed this action of telling the agents not to ride there (albeit disobeyed by Agent Clint Hill – 4 times – on Main Street in Dallas!). By credibility, I mean that I do NOT believe JFK had anything to do with this – this was a decision made by Floyd Boring for reasons that appear sinister yet, at the same time, seem hard to fathom (according to what Tampa motorcycle officer Russell Groover told me, the point is a moot one: agents did not ride on the rear of the limo during the FINAL LEG of the long journey because the limo was going at a fast rate of speed in a residential area. In any event, both Groover and Congressman Sam Gibbons, both told me that they heard no order from JFK. Even believing Boring's 1996 "story" to the ARRB, what JFK allegedly conveyed to him was hardly an order of any kind… and it was one that Hill ignored in any case). It was only with the advent of time, the release of films, photos, records, the ARRB, the internet, etc., as well as contacting White House aides/ non-Secret Service agents like Dave Powers with no horse in the race (no reason to lie and cover-up) that the truth came out. Take your pick: were the agents lying in 1963-1965 or were they lying to me?
322   *Survivor's Guilt*, page 32.
323   Warren Report, page 445.

Florida."[324] Mr. Blaine blames Kennedy for the top not being on the car in Dallas – *WRONG*: agent Sam Kinney was adamant to me that he (Kinney) was solely responsible for the top's removal. Mr. Blaine, in an online video, said that fellow agent Art Godfrey "gave his blessings" to his book *WRONG*: by his own admission, Mr. Blaine did not even begin his book until over three years after Mr. Godfrey passed away![325] Mr. Blaine states in an online video that he "has never spoken to an author of a book"[326] *WRONG*: He spoke to both William Manchester and myself. Manchester's book references a 5/12/65 interview. What's more, Mr. Blaine is thanked by Mr. Manchester in his other JFK book *One Brief Shining Moment*. Thus, Mr. Blaine is 2 for 2: he is in both Manchester JFK books. In addition, Mr. Blaine spoke to me in both 2004 and 2005, as well as corresponding via e-mail during this time. And, incidentally, Blaine told me he spoke to Manchester.

Mr. Blaine states, in yet another online video, that he specifically never spoke to Mr. Manchester.[327] *WRONG*: (see above). Mr. Blaine writes on page 201 of his book that the presidential limo "just didn't gather speed as quickly as he [Agent Greer] would like." *WRONG*: Agent Kellerman told the Warren Commission under oath "we literally jumped out of the God-damned Road"[328] and many films depict the limousine traveling at a very high rate of speed (Agent Lilley told me that the limo reached speeds of over 50 mph – with both him and Agent Kellerman on the rear of the car – during one motorcade).

Mr. Blaine, on pages 221-222 of his book, referring to the president's physician, Admiral George Burkley, writes: "Normally the admiral rode in a staff car in the motorcade, or in the rear seat of the follow-up car, but he and the president's secretary, Evelyn Lincoln, had misjudged the timing of the motorcade's departure from Love Field and wound up scurrying to the VIP bus. He was furious for not having been in his normal seat but had nobody to blame but himself." *WRONG*: Burkley protested that the Secret Service placed him further away from JFK than he normally rode (on 11/18/63 he rode in the lead car) – see Burkley's JFK Library oral history, among other sources.

---

324   *Survivor's Guilt*, page 268.
325   JFK Secret Service Agent Gerald Blaine talks to a dead man?!?!?- Kennedy Detail, Clint Hill. (https://www.youtube.com/watch?v=U_YqC5NJASA)
326   JFK Secret Service Agent Clint Hill vs Vince Palamara Part 1. (https://www.youtube.com/watch?v=IbD1shPmla8)
327   Gerald Blaine DENIES that either himself or Floyd Boring were interviewed by William Manchester! (https://www.youtube.com/watch?v=LxZVgPlt05o)
328   2 H 74.

Mr. Blaine writes, on page 74 of his book: "...the only way to have a chance at protecting the president against a shooter from a tall building would be to have agents posted on the back of the car." *WRONG/NOT COMPLETE*: as he himself wrote in his final survey report for the Tampa trip, the other way to guard against a shooter is to have the building roof-tops guarded (as they were in Tampa and many other cities).

The Kennedy Detail repeats the legend that Clint Hill came within a split second of saving JFK and taking the fatal bullet. But he's not even in the Moorman photo (taken at the moment of the fatal head shot) and in the Muchmore film he's only climbing down from the follow up car after the head shot. Also, in the Altgens photo (which was taken after the second shot), Hill is still on the running board and staring at JFK but not running towards him.

For her part, Lisa McCubbin, co-author (for Blaine and Hill) of *The Kennedy Detail, Mrs. Kennedy & Me, Five Days in November, Five Presidents,* and *My Travels with Mrs. Kennedy,*[329] posted the following on 11/24/10 on the official Facebook edition of *The Kennedy Detail*: "Contrary to Vince Palamara's claims, the book was absolutely NOT written to coun-teract his letter to Clint Hill. Mr. Hill never read Palamara's letter–it went straight into the trash. Gerald Blaine wrote this book on his volition, and Mr. Hill contributed after much deliberation." For his part, Hill told Brian Lamb on C-SPAN four days later: "I recall receiving a letter which I sent back to him. I didn't bother with it ... he called me, and I said "Hello" but that was about it. But he alleges that because he sent me a letter 22 pages in length apparently, and that I discussed that with Jerry. I forgot that I ever got a 22-page letter from this particular individual until I heard him say it on TV and I never discussed it with Jerry or anybody else because it wasn't important to me." Yet, in the biggest contradiction of all, Blaine quoted from my letter to Hill when I spoke to him on 6/10/05 and men-tioned his deep friendship with Hill, as well, extending back to the late 1950's! For the record, I received Hill's signed receipt for the letter, and it was never returned to me, either. What's more, Hill conceded to author William Law: "Maybe he's (me, Vince) right, because I apparently turned him down or something, I don't know."[330]

During yet another 6th Floor Museum appearance (with Hill and Blaine, hosted by Gary Mack), co-author Lisa McCubbin mentions that,

---

329   Interestingly, a John McCubbin was Captain of the White House police force in 1922 and hailed from the same area Lisa did – the MD/VA part of the country: https://ghostsofdc. org/2012/10/26/white-house-policeman-mccubbin/
330   The 2015 edition of *In the Eye of History* by William Law, page 39.

during the writing of the book, she would find things that contradicted what Blaine was telling her. Ultimately, she copped out, stating "he was there" …no, he wasn't there on 11/22/63 in Dallas and what about all his colleagues who refute him? Geez. McCubbin strikes me as a good investigative reporter. One wonders if her closeness to Blaine (she grew up with him, dated his son, and now married to his best friend Hill) along with the allure of big money, swayed her to "look away," so to speak, at all the conflicting and contradictory evidence. On page 124 from his book *Five Days in November*, Hill writes: "It strikes me that perhaps we should keep an agent with President Kennedy's body – out of respect for both President and Mrs. Kennedy, and in light of the questions that were raised at Parkland Hospital about taking the body back to Washington for the autopsy. This way, if there is ever any doubt about whether Dr. Burkley stayed with the body until the autopsy, or suspicions about tampering, there will be a Secret Service agent who also remained with the casket and can vouch for the integrity of the body. Agent Dick Johnsen is selected for the post because he is an agent who was with President Kennedy from the beginning and is familiar to Mrs. Kennedy, O'Donnell, and Powers." Beyond the absurdity of picking an agent as somehow relieving any person's suspicion that something could possibly be amiss ("oh, an agent was there? Alright, no suspicion there"), the agent chosen was none other than the official keeper of CE399, aka the magic bullet. What's more, Lifton's best-selling book did not appear until the early 1980's and the issue of body tampering/ alteration was not on anyone's minds until the early-mid 1970's at the earliest … why would Hill write these comments? And, from the excerpt above as written, are we to somehow infer that it was HILL (not Kellerman, for example) who made the decision to have an agent stay with the body and decide that the specific person should be the magic bullet holder? Hmmm…

On pages 138-139 from his book *Five Days in November*, Hill writes: "The doctor points to a wound in the throat and explains that this is where the emergency tracheotomy was done at Parkland Hospital, which covered up the area where a bullet had exited. He rolls the president slightly onto his left side and points to a small wound just below the neckline, slightly to the right of the spinal column in the upper back. This, he says, is where the bullet entered, and then came out the front of the neck. The bullet that caused these wounds hit nothing but soft tissue. Those wounds, I knew without a doubt, came from the first shot. It corroborates what I saw – the president suddenly grabbing his throat immediately after the first explosive noise. The doctor points to a wound on the right rear of the head. This, he says, was the fatal wound. He lifts up a piece of the scalp, with skin and hair still attached, which reveals a hole in the skull, and an area in which a good portion of the brain matter is gone." To his "credit," as he also recently demonstrated on television, Hill repeats what he has said since 11/22/63 (and in all his other Lisa Mc Cubbin co-authored books) that the right rear of JFK's head was missing (page 107), but what up with the above? Amazingly, Hill is now on record in his 2016 book *Five Presidents* denouncing the Warren Commission's single bullet theory, the entire keystone to their Oswald-acted-alone scenario, as is his colleague Paul Landis, according to an interview Landis did with the *Cleveland Plain Dealer* on 11/22/2016.

5/27/12 C-SPAN: Clint Hill addresses me, Vince Palamara –

HILL: Well, my wife and I are not together and haven't been for some time.

LAMB: She's still alive?

HILL: Yes.

LAMB: Did you – did you keep notes?

HILL: I did, but I destroyed them a few years ago which really made it more difficult.

LAMB: Why did you destroy them?

HILL: I promised that I would never write a book. I vowed that I would never do so, never contribute to a book, never talk to anybody about it and so just to kind of make sure I would never get myself involved, I burned everything. There are a few mementos I kept, but for the most part, I burned all my notes. And now, when the opportunity presents itself and I decided to do it, I had to go back and talk to other agents who I worked with, who did have – still have some notes. And to check everything through newspaper archives for dates and times and places to make sure I was accurate and so it was very tedious to go through this and write the book.

LAMB: Do you remember the year you burned your notes?

HILL: It is 2012 [now] – it was [long pause] maybe 2005, something like that [Note: 2005 was the year I contacted Hill for the first time with my 22-page letter referenced above, so I find the specific timing of his note burning suspicious, to put it mildly].

LAMB: As an aside by the way, the fellow we talked about in the last interview, Vince Palamara.

HILL: Yes.

LAMB: You've seen his letter about your book?

HILL: I have not read it, no.

LAMB: I'm sure you probably know that he said that *Mrs. Kennedy and Me* is highly recommended to everyone for its honesty and rich body of truth." He actually fully endorsed your book[331] even though he's been critical of (pause)... are you worried that he's not being ...? (Cutting Lamb off)

HILL: Maybe he has some secret agenda, I don't know. But I accept his praise, thank you."

11/10/10 C-SPAN: Gerald Blaine and Clint Hill, both address me, Vince Palamara –

LAMB: Now, we got some video from YouTube – one of the things you say in your book that made you want to write this book was all the conspiracy theories and you talked about the movie from Oliver Stone. This is a man named Vince Palamara. Do you know him?

BLAINE: I am familiar with him; I don't know him.

LAMB: He says that – and I guess we'll talk about this, that he sent you a 22-page letter?

HILL: I recall receiving a letter which I sent back to him. I didn't bother with it.

LAMB: You didn't talk to him ever?

HILL: He called me, and I said" Hello" but that was about it.

LAMB: And over the years, have you both been called about this assassination on many occasions.

HILL: I had been called numerous times.

LAMB: What has been your attitude, how have you approached the people...

HILL: For the most part, I just said I have no comment, I just have nothing to say.

LAMB: And why is that?

---

331   Well, not entirely, although I like most of it.

HILL: Well, most of it is from people who are writing conspiracy theory books that don't make any sense to me so if they are not going to deal in facts, then I don't want anything to do with it.

LAMB: And how about you?

BLAINE: I have never talked to any author of a book and that – I just felt we had it on our commission books: "worthy of trust of confidence" – and I felt those were issues that you should never talk to anybody on the outside about. And it was – I had to weigh and evaluate when I wrote this book because I felt I wasn't talking about the Secret Service, I wasn't talking about the Kennedy Family, but I was talking about the agents that I work with and the incidents that occurred and those were my friends. So that's when I decided to write.

LAMB: Did you have to get permission to do this from the secret service?

HILL: No.

LAMB: So, this wasn't cleared by the Secret Services?

HILL: No.

BLAINE: No, but we had lunch today with the director of the Secret Service who thanked us very much for our contribution.

LAMB: Here is this video, it's not very long and this man's name is Vince Palamara, he is a citizen who has taken it on his own to become an expert. He is from Pennsylvania, and I don't know him, I haven't talked to him, and I have just seen it on the web, and he is – I believe he is a graduate of Duquesne University so let us watch this and I'll get your reaction.

BLAINE: OK.

[START OF VIDEO].

VINCE PALAMARA: Hi, this is Vince Palamara, the self-described Secret Service expert that Jerry Blaine accuses me of without naming me, OK? Back with my obsession about *The Kennedy Detail*. I have to read this, this is rich. Page 287 [of Blaine's book] is where Blaine is claiming what Rowley said. [Quoting from the book] "Rowley turned to Jerry Blaine. "And Jerry, since you were in the lead car, did you ever hear this over your radio as well?" " Yes, sir. I did. I heard exactly what Floyd just told you." The thing about this-this is the whole 'Ivy League charlatans' crap. Jerry Blaine told me that the 'Ivy League charlatans' thing "came from the guys. I can't remember – I can't remember who said it." (Said sarcastically) Boy, his memory got real good five years later because now, he is claiming he heard it over the radio from Floyd Boring. It's unbelievable, and it's just amazing to me – you know, there never would have been a book if I didn't send a 22-page letter to Clint Hill that pissed him off so much that his very good friend, Jerry Blaine, came out with his book as a counter. OK? These are some good things in it. I recommend everyone to buy it, no censorship, it's my First Amendment rights, OK? There are some nice pictures and there are even some good assassination related things in here, but it's very odd. Other people have picked up on this, that's why there are some really bad reviews on Amazon right now, mine is the best-mine at three stars too. It's very obvious that it's a thinly veiled attempt to rewrite history and blame President Kennedy – without trying to blame him – for his own assassination.

[END OF VIDEO].

LAMB: First of all, his is not the best of the reviews, there are seven with five stars just for the record that I saw today when I looked on Amazon. What's your reaction, could you hear?

BLAINE: Well, he wrote an assessment of the book about the – first time about five weeks before it was released. The second time on Amazon.com, he and four of his friends or four of his aliases put a statement on assessing the book a one, a two, and a three (stars). My assessment of Mr. Palamara is that he called probably all the agents, and what agent who answers a phone is going to answer a question "was President Kennedy easy to protect?" Well, probably he was too easy to protect because he was assassinated. But the fact is that the agents aren't going to tell him anything and he alludes to the fact that when I wrote the book, most of these people were dead. Well, I worked with these people, I knew them like brothers, and I knew exactly what was going on and always respected Jim Rowley because he stood up to the issue and said" Look, we can't say the President invited himself to be killed so let's squash this." So that was the word throughout the Secret Service and he – Mr. Palamara is – there are a number of things that had happened (sic) that he has no credibility. He is a self-described expert in his area which I don't know what it is, he was born after the assassination, and he keeps creating solutions to the assassination until they are proven wrong. So he is… (Cutting Blaine off)

LAMB: A lot about–

HILL: But he alleges that because he sent me a letter 22 pages in length apparently, and that I discussed that with Jerry. I forgot that I ever got a 22-page letter from this particular individual until I heard him say it on TV and I never discussed it with Jerry or anybody else because it wasn't important to me. And so far as him being an expert, I don't know where the expert part came from. I spent a long time in the Secret Service in protection and I'm not an expert, but apparently, he became an expert somewhere up in Pennsylvania, I don't know where."

But Blaine wasn't finished with me just yet: "The Zapruder film, when the Zapruder film was run at normal speed, another theme that Palamara throws out is that Bill Greer stopped the car, when it's run at its normal speed, you will notice the car absolutely does not stop at all. This happened in less than six seconds after the President was hit in the throat and moving along."

Oh, so you agree with my "solutions" that JFK was shot in the neck from the FRONT, do you, Mr. Blaine? And there were close to 60 witnesses to the limousine slowing or stopping, including 7 Secret Ser vice agents and Jacqueline Kennedy – not my "theme" or theory, just the facts. Returning directly to *The Kennedy Detail* documentary, Agent Ron Pontius specifically refers to one of my articles (also a part of a chapter in my book) without naming me. As the narrator, Martin Sheen, notes: "The most painful theories point fingers at the agents themselves." Who needs theories when we have facts: former agent Chuck Zboril served in the Marines with Lee Harvey Oswald! QUA Company, 1st Battalion, 2nd Infantry Training Regiment, Marine Corps Base, Camp Pendleton, California between 20th January 1957 and 26th February 1957: Oswald and Zboril. I only discovered this in October 2016 – no one ever reported this before I did.

GERALD BLAINE'S HANDWRITTEN "NOTES"

The Gerald Blaine documents, submitted to the National Archives in 2013 when Blaine got word of my first book *Survivor's Guilt* that was due to come out that same year,[332] consist of 28 pages – mostly duty assignments and travel vouchers, but there are two survey reports – one for Tampa and the one for a post assassination State Department reception between foreign dignitaries and LBJ. There is also a brief statement, a denial of having consumed any alcoholic beverages at the Press Club or the Cellar in Ft. Worth. There are also three pages of handwritten notes, two

332   Papers of Gerald S. Blaine | National Archives (https://www.archives.gov/research/jfk/finding-aids/blaine-papers.html)

pages written over a schedule dated from Nov. 8 to November 30 that I transcribe below. Gerald Blaine's handwritten notes (undated):

"Frank Yeager and myself have the advance in Tampa, Fla. Everything goes well and I feel real good. Never a thought of the tragedy that is due to occur on the 22nd. Kennedy makes the first of fateful steps that seem to lead toward the tragedy. He states that he wants no agents riding on the rear of his car as we did in Europe. If one was there the assassination might not have occurred. An agent's life is a frustrating one. You can set all of the security in the world, but it's only as good as the President lets it be. The day will come when the only way the public will be able to see the president is by television. The country seems to be loaded with eccentrics and potentials. I don't think I have ever been filled so low emotionally by anything like the president's assassination. There wasn't a thing anyone could have done to stop it and the Secret Service did everything it could do [can I puke now? VMP]. My shift worked midnight in Ft. Worth on the 22nd.

We took them to the airport – they flew to Dallas, went to Austin to sleep for the next nights duty. I had been asleep about ten minutes in the Commodore Perry Hotel. Art Godfrey came in the room and almost broke the door down. 'The boss was hit in Dallas.' I was groggy but the sickening truth seemed to sink through and I couldn't do anything but swing my legs over the bed and when the shock hit me I couldn't find the strength to stand and I was hit with a sudden wave of chills. Then I tried to fight off the despair and asked Art if he was sure. He said he knew that Kennedy was shot, but didn't know if it was fatal. We turned on the radio and finally got through on the security phone to hear the horrible truth. We just withdrew in our own thoughts.

We flew back in a SAC Bomber, myself, Art Godfrey, Bob Faison, Jerry O'Rourke, Paul Burns and John Bailey (National Democratic Chairman). We arrived back after Kennedy's body and set up security at the Johnson residence. (What a disgusting settlement – Kennedy replaced by Johnson – like a pro-ball player going from the Yankees to the bottom of the league.) They say that not many single things have an influence on history, but I am sure this one will. Even though we could have done nothing to prevent it, nor was there anything anyone could have done except use a bulletproof automobile, we are all suffering from guilt and failure in our one task. *The ordeal we were to all go through for the next few months was a sad one,* but we all came out with a feeling of hope far greater than we had ever had before. We shall all be stronger for the experience in the years to come. President Kennedy left us a little of his courage and we lost not only a fine president but a friend we will never forget and always admire." (Emphasis added)

"The ordeal we were to all go through for the next few months was a sad one"? I thought these notes were contemporary to the assassination. And why weren't they used for his book or documentary?

Blaine's book came out in 2010. I submit that these so-called contemporaneous "notes" originated not in 1963 but in 2013.

CHAPTER ELEVEN

PRESIDENT KENNEDY SHOULD HAVE SURVIVED DALLAS – A SYNOPSIS

I magine this stunning scenario- President Kennedy survives Dallas on November 22, 1963. There is no Vietnam War as we know it today; no ground troops– merely a few thousand advisors as the low-key conflict grinds to a halt and fades away like a poor man's Korean Conflict, at best. In turn, imagine no civil unrest, no drug culture, no prolonged Cold War, no J. Edgar Hoover reigning for another decade, no 1968 Democratic National Convention violence – without the Vietnam War, there is no real reason to protest the government now, is there? With JFK alive to fulfill a second term, there is no LBJ presidency, no Nixon revival (and, thus, no Watergate, the other historical event, like the JFK assassination and the Vietnam War, that tore the country apart and created decades of mistrust in government); no Ford Presidency (no Nixon – no Ford), thus, no reason for a "protest" Carter vote; presidents Reagan thru Trump may or may not have ever happened. I am not saying it would have been utopia

… it wouldn't have been. I am not saying President Kennedy was a God, a saint, or an unflawed man … he clearly was not. What I am saying is this: if the Secret Service would have done their usual, thorough, 1963-era standard job, President Kennedy survives Dallas and probably doesn't even become wounded in an attempted attack! So, the next time someone says "Oh, c'mon now – it's over 60 years later; a new century; post 9/11 – what does it all matter now?" Tell them no Vietnam War, no Watergate, the large mistrust in government probably never would have reached the levels it has today (or, at least, as soon), the Cold War would have ended long ago, and, perhaps – perhaps: the need to keep the military-industrial "war machine" going wouldn't have led to our heavy hand in the Middle East and all the inherent problems that have arisen from it – 9/11, the war on terror, the draining of our economy, etc. The real "domino theory" came to fruition – with the death of JFK, several presidencies were spawned that never would have happened (again, at least LBJ thru Carter, at a minimum) and the respect and trust in government would have been felt for a far longer time.

The scars from the JFK assassination truly are with us today. Keep in mind – President Kennedy was our last assassinated president and only 10 presidents ago: in the big scheme of things, with new best-selling books and audio/visual reminders plentiful on the internet and shared by millions, not ancient history. As for myself, my interest in President Kennedy, the Secret Service and the JFK assassination began at the age of 12 in 1978, coinciding with both the HSCA re-investigation of the assassination and reruns of the classic fictional television series about the Secret Service of the 19th century, *The Wild, Wild West*. Coupled with two parents who were rabid Kennedy fans, and you have a very interested son in myself. My original research truly took off shortly after 1988, the 25th anniversary of the assassination. I started to key on the Secret Service, especially in comparison to the assassination attempt on President Reagan on March 30th, 1981. I said to myself: "Hmmm – theories about the Mafia, the CIA and other possible culprits are all fascinating, but what did the Secret Service agents do to try to prevent the assassination? Why was the assassination a success?" In 1991, at the age of 25, I made my first major presentation at Jerry Rose's *Third Decade* conference in Fredonia, New York and, if I do say so myself, amazed an audience of 60 older authors and researchers, many of whom admitted they really didn't pay the Secret Service any mind – as Robert Groden told a friend of mine, "I guess that is why the Secret Service is secret." I was the first to popularize the fact that the driver of JFK's limousine, Bill Greer, turned around not once but twice during the shooting, slowing the limousine down to a near stop; disobeyed common sense, training and a direct order from his superior, fellow agent Roy Kellerman, to get out of the line of fire; and was chiefly responsible for the success of the assassination no matter who was the shooter and no matter who was behind the murder. The reaction from the audience, which included authors Harrison Livingstone, George Michael Evica, and Bob Cutler, among others, made me realize that I was on to something. With their encouragement and inspiration, I went further than mere photo and film analysis and secondary sources.

In short, my goal was to do something unique: attempt to interview and/or correspond with every former agent and surviving family member I could find. From 1991 until the present time, this is what I have done. I am now the author of four books on both the Secret Service and the assassination; I have a major part in both part seven of *The Men Who Killed Kennedy* from 2003 (a major ratings success and popular DVD) and the recently released DVD/Blu Ray called *A Coup in Camelot*. I have appeared in over 200 other author's books ... and so on and so forth. I have interviewed and/corresponded with over 80 former agents, White House aides and sundry other important people, far more than the Warren Commission, the HSCA or the ARRB. In fact, I am in the ARRB's final report, and the Board was inspired by me to go interview a couple important former agents, but I digress. But enough about my background – this is all a labor of love and a commitment to truth and history; I have a life and a job; not in this for the money, folks – far from it. So, what is the bottom line from all my research and hard work? Here it is:

President Kennedy should have survived Dallas, and the Secret Service agents truly are the men who killed Kennedy! No, there was no agency plot, per se, and many of these men – the vast majority – were merely following orders or, at most, were negligent. I have three – just three – major suspects who I feel crossed the line into (at the least) gross negligence and (at most) actual participants in aiding the success of the assassination (I will get to them in a moment). Sure, there are a very small handful of other agents I am suspicious of regarding the assassination and/or the cover-up, but, again, we are talking a very small number. Other parties were the shooters, masterminds and power brokers ... what the agency provided was action through inaction – no pulling of triggers or firing of bullets but allowing those triggers and bullets to act in an unimpeded fashion. All it takes is a few precious seconds, folks, and we had both a dead president as well as a dead president who cannot defend himself against claims that he brought it on himself (the old blaming-the-victim mythology- I will also get to that in a moment). So, from about 1991 to 2005, I worked hard on my research part time as I pursued a working career and other interests. However, 2005 was a watershed moment. Via a tip from former agent Lynn Meredith, I was able to obtain the unlisted address and number for former agent Clint Hill, a very reclusive man who, up to that time, testified to the Warren Commission but not the HSCA or the ARRB, spoke to author William Manchester but no other author and, other than an iconic *60 Minutes* interview and a couple Secret Service television programs, pretty much became the Howard Hughes of the Secret Service – again, reclusive and never granting private researchers and authors any interviews. After all, as I said, he had an unlisted address and phone number and, if you notice, he only spoke to official bodies and spouted pretty much official history – just "name, rank and serial number" and a few other notions ... that was it.

Then in 2005 came my 22-page, registered, signed-receipt-required letter to Hill, summarizing my work up to that time, basically saying that the agents were handicapped that fateful day in Dallas because a couple senior agents laid down the law – thru actions and words – that hampered the agent's abilities to do their jobs while, at the same time, falsely blaming JFK for these so-called handicaps. In addition to all the other former agents I spoke to, I also contacted former agent Gerald Blaine. This will become important momentarily. In a nutshell, one of my major discoveries was the fact that, despite official mythology, President Kennedy did not order the agents off his limousine, nor did he order the agents to do anything else! This I learned via many interviews and correspondence with dozens of actual former agents and White House aides who would most certainly know first-hand. The list includes the head of the White House Detail, Gerald Behn; his top assistant, Floyd Boring; one of the three Shift Leaders, Art Godfrey; the driver of the follow-up car in Dallas, Tampa, and many other trips, Sam Kinney; JFK's good friend and aide, Dave Powers; and many more. This was all a huge surprise to me – although I focused on Secret Service negligence, I reluctantly bought the "JFK-as-scapegoat" myth from roughly 1988 until 9/27/92, when I spoke to the number one agent, Gerald Behn, who demolished this notion in no uncertain terms.

Back to the matter at hand: I included a self-addressed, stamped envelope with my bold letter to Clint Hill, encouraging him to contact me with comment. It was a pipe dream, I knew, but, hey – nothing ventured, nothing gained. Having heard nothing from him, I decided to call him … and, boy, was he livid! The conversation was short, sweet and awkward – Hill denied receiving my letter, although I was staring at his signed receipt, then, after an equally awkward pause wherein I asked him if he was still on the other line, he ended the conversation with "Yes, I am still here. I just have no interest in talking to you." Ouch. Through happenstance, I spoke to Gerald Blaine the next day and he shocked me by bringing up my private letter to Hill and quoting from a segment from it! It turns out the two long-retired men were dear friends for decades (since the 1950's) and, in fact, Blaine had just attended Clint Hill's son's wedding (along with fellow former agent Bill Livingood, the former Sergeant at Arms for the House of Representatives who you are actually all familiar with – if you watched any of the State of the Union addresses for Presidents Clinton, Bush or Obama from about 1995 to 2012, he was the man who shouted "Mr. Speaker- the President of the United States!" Small world, indeed, … and, yes – I had also spoken to and corresponded with Livingood previously, but, again, I digress). Up to this time, my first book was a self-published affair and, although I was stunned by these developments regarding Hill and Blaine, I thought that was basically it. I would have my blogs and appearances in other people's books to spread the word, but I thought, at the time, it was the end of the road. Boy was I wrong. In late 2009, I received word that Gerald Blaine of all people – yes, him: Clint Hill's good friend whom I spoke to and who quoted from my letter to Hill! – was coming out with a book about the Kennedy Detail (which turned out to be the title of the book: *The Kennedy Detail*). It went from initially being just a small publishing house affair into a huge Simon and Schuster release with all the inherent huge publicity machine, no mean feat for a first time, very obscure agent turned author. I then received a letter from Gerald Blaine's attorney, asking me to take down my one blog post wherein I mentioned his upcoming book – they thought I was trying to say I was the co-author of the book, an asinine notion that was the farthest thing from the truth. They threatened me with obtaining a court order to remove my little blog, so I decided to let them have their way – for the moment. But why little ole (ok, big ole) me … and why Blaine, a very obscure agent who was on the Texas trip but not the Dallas stop that next-to-no-one had ever heard of? Why, indeed.

No sooner could I digest all these bizarre out-of-the-blue happenings then I found out Clint Hill – yes, him: the reclusive agent with the unlisted address and number I had boldly sent that alarming letter to – was writing the foreword to Blaine's book, as well as contributing to its contents, appearing on the inherent media blitz (MSNBC, Fox – you name it), and also appearing in the Kennedy Detail television documentary. These two men (one famous, one very obscure) were long retired and had no compunction to write a book, let alone appear in public again. In fact, Sam Kinney proudly told me "All of us old timers would never sell out or write a book for any amount of money – I am taking Clint Hill, me and all my buddies. This is the old school of 'no kiss and tell.'" In the interest of time, read my first book – no delusions of grandeur here: it was my 22-page letter to Hill that awakened a sleeping giant, so to speak.

In 2010, when Blaine's book came out, I discovered much of it was a direct response to my work, including Blaine sarcastically calling me a Secret Service expert on pages 359-360. Also in 2010, both Blaine and Hill would appear on C-SPAN with network CEO Brian Lamb and mockingly discuss my work, even showing a You Tube video of me speaking – little ole me of all people! Why? Why, indeed. If it isn't obvious by now, you haven't been paying attention. Events would springboard from here: Co-author Lisa McCubbin would go on to help in the writing of the *Kennedy Detail*, but also all of Clint Hill's books; all four of them. No TMZ tabloid tidbit here – a factual truth they both admit to. 84-year-old Hill left his wife of 50-plus years for 52-year-old McCubbin, also married with kids at the time (McCubbin had gone to the prom with Blaine's son years ago, but I digress. All this information is easily verifiable via You Tube and, of all things, the *Irish Times*. McCubbin lived in Qatar in the Middle East during the early millennium, was sought out by the Saudi government to help them in dealing with the Western press – no joke! – and scored an exclusive interview with George Bush, all before the age of 37; despite her relatively young age, no spring chicken here, if you catch my drift. Interestingly, John McCubbin was head of the White House Police in the 1920's and was from Lisa's same home state of Virginia).

The following events occurred not long after Blaine's book came out – Hill would appear on C-SPAN with network CEO Brian Lamb in 2012 discussing Hill's first book in his own right and – you guessed it – I was mentioned out of the blue once again (yep, little old me, the as-yet-unpublished researcher at that time [Hill also mentioned on the same program that he burned all his personal notes in 2005 – what? As a reaction to my letter sent the same year?]); I was then harassed at my prior place of employment from a good friend of Blaine's; and, most important of all,

Blaine and Hill would do their best to propagate the myth that President Kennedy had it coming and ordered them off the limousine, despite what Blaine told me in 2004 and 2005 that greatly contradicts this false notion.

You can thank me or curse me – take your pick. I am responsible for both Hill and Blaine coming out of the woodwork, writing their huge *New York Times* best-selling books for the biggest publishing house in the world that has garnered them all quite a bit of money, appearing on television numerous times since (include the Emmy-nominated documentary they made) and, sadly, reinvigorating the false debate about blaming JFK for his own death. It probably would have ended there around 2012 or 2013, but I had a big surprise for them – I obtained a publisher for my first book, *TrineDay*, and it was released in time for the 50th anniversary. That is when the harassment at work began, my blogs and Amazon reviews started getting hacked, and another obscure agent and dear friend of Hill and Blaine, Chuck Zboril, would go on to write a one-star review of my book (while McCubbin also gave my book a one-star on *Good Reads*, with Blaine marking it as a "to-read" item), no doubt all with the goal of suppressing what I had to say ... because it is very damaging – for them. It shows they are liars profiting on the death of the man they failed to protect.

In addition, nine agents drank the night before the assassination ... guess who one of them was? Clint Hill, the same man who had the audacity to criticize the nine agents who drank in Cartegena, Columbia in 2012 when another President was scheduled to appear and who now goes around telling people who want his autographed books that he did not drink the night before, despite his official report in the Warren Commission volumes, and his prior statements, stating the exact opposite. But President Obama lived and wasn't blown away like he was under your watch now, was he, Clint Hill? Hill is a false hero – what I call the Jessica Lynch of the Secret Service: he got to the limousine when the shooting was all over and done with; he did not protect JFK and, furthermore, Jackie got in and out of the limo of her own volition; they never even touched. Hill performed the equivalent of a foul tip out in baseball or even striking out swinging; he tried to do something, albeit too late. Hill would go on to receive a medal for this attempt from LBJ for this so-called heroism (never mind the drinking incident which Secret Service regulations show were grounds for removal from the service! Yes – him, Paul Landis, Jack Ready and Glen Bennett – all in the follow-up car – and five other agents drank hours before Kennedy got his head blown off. Alcohol consumption and sleep deprivation wreak havoc on even the best trained reflexes. They all went to bed between 2 and 5:30 A.M. and had to report for active duty at 8 am! For his part, Gerald Blaine was there, too, but claimed to have only drank fruit juice, if he can even be believed.)

See, for me, this is most certainly *not* a 50-plus year-old murder mystery. In addition to how history was changed and how it all affects us today, you have two old men traveling the world, smiling widely, making very big money (a Hill book movie is allegedly in the works), and peddling lies against the man they failed to protect; Hill even rode in an open limousine down Elm Street in one program without breaking a sweat; so much for being traumatized by the event. In effect, JFK was assassinated three times: his actual murder, the character assassination regarding his private life (to which several agents held him in contempt) and this blame-the-victim mythology.

Now, after providing you with the background, here is the foreground- the details; the nuts and bolts):

1) A major discovery of mine in two parts: President Kennedy did not order the agents off his limousine in Tampa four days before his death, there is zero evidence this was even invoked for Dallas in any case, and agents on or near the rear of the limousine would have saved the presidents life. The lack of agents on or near the limo was a secret service decision. Many times, agents walked, ran or jogged near the rear of his limo and/ or rode on the rear of his limo. The second major discovery, one touched on in my first book and expanded in my next book: the Secret Service is the boss of the president, not the other way around. Even if a president wanted to order the agents around, they would ignore him. Take, for example, an *Associated Press* story from November 15, 1963: "The (Secret) Service can overrule even the President where his personal security is involved." Shockingly, perhaps with an eye toward real history after he is long gone, Hill admitted in 2010 in his Sixth-Floor oral history, with Blaine right by his side: "[The president] can tell you what he wants done and he can tell you certain things but that doesn't mean you have to do it. What we used to do was always agree with the President and then we'd do what we felt was best anyway."

2) President Kennedy had nothing to do with the limiting or placement of motorcycles by his limousine as has been alleged by some. Three to six motorcycles normally rode on each side of his limousine, as had been the case on the prior stops on the Texas trip, the Florida trip and

countless other trips. This was a Secret Service decision to limit their use in Dallas, something the HSCA rightfully said was "uniquely insecure."

3) President Kennedy had nothing to do with another major discovery of mine- the lack of security covering multi-story buildings along the parade route. It was common practice from the FDR era thru and including the JFK era (and beyond) to have agents and/or police and/or a branch of the military to guard and monitor buildings, sometimes even using a helicopter to help monitor both the route and the buildings themselves. This does not mean just watching the windows as the cars passed but by stationing men on the rooftops themselves, as was the case in San Antonio, Florida, Nashville, Germany, Ireland, and many other trips. I corresponded twice with former Secret Service Chief Inspector Michael Torina. The position of Secret Service Chief Inspector was very influential – it was Torina himself who completed the Secret Service's Manual. Torina contributed significantly to a book by author Wayne Hyde written in 1962 in which it is plainly stated: "If the President is to appear in a parade, agents and policemen are assigned posts atop buildings and on the street along the parade route." This lack of coverage in Dallas was a Secret Service decision. We would learn even more from Secret Service records of the era except for one thing – the ARRB noted in their final report from 1998: "Congress passed the JFK Act of 1992. One month later, the Secret Service began its compliance efforts. However, in January 1995, the Secret Service destroyed presidential protection survey reports for some of President Kennedy's trips in the fall of 1963."

4) Agent Sam Kinney was adamant to me, on three different occasions, that he was solely responsible for the bubbletop's removal on 11/22/63 – JFK had nothing to do with it. It was briefly on the car on 11/22/63 and was then removed. Although not bulletproof or bullet resistant in the traditional sense, many people thought it was, thus making it a psychological deterrent: would someone fire onto the car with it on? In addition, many agents thought it would deflect a bullet and/or shield the president via the sun's glare off the top. Many times, the top was on the car in either full or partial formations (meaning, just the front and rear pieces were used so the president could stand intermittently and offer some semblance of protection at the same time, like the famous Eisenhower bubble). In addition, the top was used in bright, no-rain conditions: I found it was used on approximately 25 good-weather trips, roughly a third of all JFK motorcades.

5) Normally, a flatbed truck (sometimes two) carrying still and motion photographers from the press was used in motorcades and rode in front of the presidential limousine, as it was used on the prior trip in Florida and many other occasions. It was cancelled at the last minute by the Secret Service at Love Field.

6) SAIC Behn or his immediate assistant, #2-man Floyd Boring, accompanied the president on trips outside of Washington. Behn took his first vacation of the JFK era coinciding with both the Florida and Texas trips, while number two assistant Boring manned the Florida trip, yet was absent from the Texas trip, allowing a third-stringer, Roy Kellerman, to make only his second major trip without either Behn or Boring (there is a possibility Texas was the very first, as it is unclear if Behn was also on a part of the Nashville trip, possibly Kellerman's first trip alone with JFK). However, there were stark contrasts between Nashville in May 1963 and Dallas in November: building rooftops were guarded, and a helicopter guarded the motorcade, as well as other strict security measures were invoked.

7) The Secret Service knew of prior threats to the president's life in the month of November in Chicago (that trip was cancelled at the last minute) and Florida, yet the Dallas trip went forward as scheduled, despite all the warnings from Senator J. William Fulbright and others.

8) With regard to these threats, another major discovery of mine was the existence of two major agency covert threat monitors on the Texas trip that they did not admit to: PRS agent Glen Bennett, riding in the follow-up car, and fellow PRS agent Howard K. Norton, on the Austin trip. Bennett was temporarily added to the White House Detail on 11/10/63, the day after the infamous Joseph Milteer tape was made, an investigation the Secret Service was very much aware of. Bennett lied under oath to the HSCA, saying he was not on the Florida trip, while not volunteering that he was also on the 11/14-11/15 New York trip. Secret Service records released only in the late 1990's, as well as agency identification of Bennett's appearance in photographs, conclusively proves that Bennett was indeed on the New York, Florida and Texas trips – every stop– often riding in the follow-up car. Howard Norton was also on the Florida trip and his background was only made known to me via an interview with fellow PRS agent Dale Wunderlich. When I tried to obtain more information on Bennett and Norton, former agent Jerry O'Rourke told me: "I don't want to do it. I don't want to do it. I'm afraid for my agency." Bennett passed away in 1994 and Nor-

ton's current whereabout are unknown. I contacted the Secret Service, and, after a check of records, they could not even tell me how long he served in the agency! This is in addition to the presence (or lack thereof) of military intelligence operatives in Dealey Plaza, including James Powell, who took a photo of the Texas School Book Depository after the shooting.

9) SAIC Behn confirmed to me that the route was changed for the Dallas trip! He gave me no details other than to say, "I know it was changed but why – I have forgotten completely – I don't know." Needless to say, the Secret Service was responsible for the terrible route JFK took that fateful day in Dallas and there were alternate routes, as agents Sam Kinney, Win Lawson, and others confirmed, including the one going from Main to Industrial Boulevard, a route that would have bypassed Elm Street altogether and had the limo moving further away from the knoll and the Depository (and moving at a faster rate of speed, as well). Straight down Main Street is the route FDR took in 1936; it was also the ceremonial route, as Governor Connally admitted under oath.

10) As most people are aware, Sheriff Bill Decker ordered his men not participate in the security of the motorcade, as verified by Deputy Sheriff Roger Craig. Decker said this after agreeing to offer security to Secret Service agent Forrest Sorrels the previous day. Not enough police were guarding the route; the sheriff's department weren't doing their jobs; and no branch of the military augmented security, as was standard procedure (you see, agents weren't always on the back of the car, and they were often short-staffed back then – this is why they relied on the local police and the military to help them out).

11) Godfrey McHugh, military aide to President Kennedy, said he was told, for the very first time, to not ride in the presidential limousine. Who told him not to ride there? The Secret Service. He said that he normally rode between the driver and senior agent in the front seat observing and taking notes.

12) In conjunction with the above, Dallas Police Chief Jesse Curry and Dallas Chief of Homicide Will Fritz each wanted a car full of policemen in the motorcade and these requests were nixed by – you guessed it – the Secret Service, yet, not only did they originally agree to their presence in the motorcade, there was a precedent for their usage, as previous motorcades usually had a police and/or a detectives car in the motorcade, in addition to the Secret Service follow-up car.

13) The overpass in Dealey Plaza was not cleared of spectators as it should have been.

14) As mentioned previously, nine agents drank the night before and morning of the assassination, including four agents in the follow-up car.

15) JFK, the president, and LBJ, the vice president, were in the very same motorcade in open cars moving at a slow pace – this never happened before and hasn't happened since.

16) The presence of fake or unauthorized Secret Service agents in Dealey Plaza when, officially speaking, no agents were there.

17) Another major discovery of mine: one of two main drivers of JFK's limousine, Secret Service agent Tom Shipman, passed away suddenly of an alleged heart attack at, of all places, Camp David on 10/14/63. He was buried quickly, and no toxicology tests were given. I have much more on Shipman in this book, as I tracked down several surviving family members. One wonders what would have happened if Shipman – and not Greer – drove the presidential limousine.

18) Suspect number one: ASAIC Floyd Boring, the number two agent of the White House Detail, was (as I discovered and as documents and interviews confirm) the actual planner of the Texas trip from the Secret Service's point of view. He gave out the assignments of advance agents and so forth and was responsible for what did – and did not – happen, security-wise, in Dallas. He was the originator of the myth that JFK did not want agents on the rear of his limousine and that President Kennedy allegedly told him this in Tampa. Clint Hill testified that, during the period from 11/19 to 11/21/63 (note the time frame!), Boring told him and other agents of this alleged request. Yet, Boring was adamant to me – on three different occasions, not to mention his 1976 JFK library oral history – that JFK was very cooperative and did not order the agents off the limo (debunking the Manchester book on this score in the process), while also telling the ARRB that there was "no policy change" and he was merely conveying an anecdote of "kindness and consideration" from the president that the agents need not stand on the rear of the car if the crowds were sparse. Yet, not only did Congressman Sam Gibbons, who rode in the car inches away from JFK, state to me that there was no order from JFK in Tampa, Tampa motorcycle police officer Russell Groover agreed with Gibbons and further told me that agents were on the rear of the car

for the whole trip (as many films and photos confirm) except for the very end of the trip when the public motorcade was essentially over and the cars were on their way to the airport, travelling at a high rate of speed! In other words, JFK had zero to do with the agents not being there at this final part of the motorcade – they weren't there because of the speed of the cars on the highway heading home, so to speak. What's more, he confirmed (as the Secret Service's final survey report also confirms) that multi-story buildings were guarded during this very long motorcade, the longest domestic motorcade JFK ever undertook (far longer than Dallas) and that police and military units lined the streets and faced the crowds, in addition to the high volume of flanking motorcycles, his own cycle included. I had the ARRB contact Floyd Boring. Boring told the ARRB the same bizarre thing he first told me: "I didn't have anything to do with it and I don't know anything." Boring rose to the coveted position of Inspector and retired in 1967. I was the first private researcher to talk to him about JFK.

19) Suspect number two: Driver William Greer, having no competition from the dead Thomas Shipman, turned around during the start of the shooting, either braking and/or taking his foot off the gas pedal, and looked directly at JFK; this is his first turn to the rear. Kellerman then ordered him to get out of line ... Greer disobeyed a direct order (and his own training and common sense) and turned around for the second time to stare directly at JFK until the fatal head shot occurs. Only after this did he face forward and hit the gas pedal. Greer denied under oath that he ever turned around to see JFK, let alone twice. As Kellerman told Manchester: "Greer then looked in the back of the car: maybe he didn't believe me." Yet, Greer, after initially giving the impression of guilt and remorse for his horrific actions and inactions, told the FBI the night of the murder that the president sometimes told him to slow down, agent number two who propagated the "blame the victim" mythology (Boring, as we saw before, was first, pre-dating the actual assassination!). Greer retired in 1966, serving LBJ, a president he allegedly despised, for several years after the assassination. Greer died in 1985. When I spoke to his son in 1991, I asked him "What did your father think of JFK?" A very innocent question, to put it mildly. He avoided the question ... so I asked him again. He then answered: "Well, we're Methodists and JFK was Catholic"!! It is important to note that Bill Greer was born and raised in County Tyrone, Ireland, a country infamous for its religious wars, coming to this country

around the age of 18 and later serving Henry Cabot Lodge, Jr., JFK's two-time political opponent and, later, ambassador to Vietnam.

20) Suspect number three: Shift leader Emory Roberts. As I discovered and popularized way back in 1991 and have demonstrated at conferences since 1995 (and, later, on *The Men Who Killed Kennedy* and *A Coup in Camelot*), Roberts rises in his seat during the start of the motorcade rolling out at Love Field airport and recalls agent Don Lawton, who stops in his tracks and raises his arms three different times in disgust. Paul Landis makes room for Lawton on the running board of the car, yet Lawton does not budge. Previous to Lawton's recall (literally only moments before), another agent, Henry Rybka (as seen in films and photos and as verified in his report) joined Lawton in walking/jogging beside JFK's side of the limo, only to walk away, no doubt also a victim of shift leader Roberts' order (interestingly, Rybka was "accidentally" placed in the follow-up car in three different reports after the fact, only to be corrected later, as Rybka and Lawton remained at Love Field).

As a side note, as with the death of Shipman, I have more on Lawton in my books, but I can add here that he told me in 1995 that the agents had regrets about 11/22/63 and quote: "Who knows – if they had left guys on the back of the car. You can hindsight yourself to death." Notice he did not blame JFK for the agent's removal and the "they" he referred = the Secret Service. Lawton told a trusted colleague shortly after the assassination that, quote, "I should have been there" (on the back of the limo). Indeed. Lawton rode on the rear of the limo in Chicago in March of 1963 and in Tampa four days before Dallas. Returning to Roberts, he went on to recall agent Ready who made some forward movement toward Kennedy during the assassination and, much more importantly, ordered the agents not to move during the shooting, as confirmed by an agent sitting inches away from him, driver Sam Kinney (see *A Coup in Camelot* for more on this). Incredibly, Roberts achieved infamy after the assassination as the only agent to ever become appointment secretary to a president (in this case, LBJ, fulfilling the role once accomplished by Dave Powers), also rising to the level of Inspector, receiving a medal in the process and, as I demonstrate, being the object of an attempt by LBJ himself to name him to the federal parole board – why? To make sure LBJ and his cronies were safe?

Regarding motive, I believe it was a combination of a couple major factors: some of the agents (notably, follow-up car agents Tim McIntyre and Emory Roberts, among others) were angry and disgusted with Pres

ident Kennedy's private life, while others, such as Forrest Sorrels and Elmer Moore, were angry at President Kennedy for his foreign policy views.
Chief U.E. Baughman, like Allen Dulles, was fired by the Kennedy brothers – in Baughman's case, the reason was because he did not believe the
Mafia existed, a view shared by J. Edgar Hoover of the FBI. Baughman
was made the Chief on November 22 of 1948. Interestingly, the following
agents and White House aides believed (or, in some cases, knew) that
there was a conspiracy: Abraham Bolden, Maurice Martineau, Sam Kinney, Bill Greer (yes-him), Roy Kellerman, Robert Bouck, Gerald O'Rourke, John Norris, Marty Underwood, and John Marshall. A few other
agents – Forrest Sorrels, Lem Johns and Paul Landis- believed at least one
shot came from the front. See, that is all it took – not an agency "conspiracy"; not many men; not dozens of men … three – the driver of the
limousine, the shift lead er who was the commander of the follow-up car
agents, and the planner of the Texas trip. It is action thru inaction– by not
doing certain things (hitting the gas pedal, having agents on or near the
rear of the limousine, and blaming JFK for the lack of security, among
other items), the agency was made to purposely fail and, thus, had to run
with this JFK-is-to-blame myth to cover up and hide their gross, purposeful negligence or face the consequences – Congressional hearings,
press inquiries, loss of pensions, prosecutions, and the end of the agency,
at least their role as protectors of our nation's highest officials. Further,
by covering up the drinking incident (as Rowley testified, he didn't want
to stigmatize the agents, never mind that they broke a sacred rule that
was grounds for dismissal and they lost a president) and giving out two
awards (one arguably undeserving – to Hill, the other dubious – to agent
Youngblood, who allegedly covered LBJ a little sooner than even Youngblood believed was possible), the agents got away with a verbal slap on the
wrist coupled with great praise for their heroism and courage. In an age
before Watergate and true investigative journalism, with a dead president
unable to defend himself and a naïve and trusting public, should we have
expected anything else? And, when a certain amateur researcher, on his
own time and his own dime, started asking the hard questions, should we
be surprised when he was subjected to harassment, ridicule and a campaign by two sad old men to blame the president they failed to protect for
huge profit, all the while feeding a gullible public seeking their books and
the autographs that they willingly and sickeningly affix to autopsy photos
and assassination scenes.

CHAPTER 12

WHAT THE SECRET SERVICE AGENTS (AND OTHERS) TOLD ME

GERALD BEHN

Special Agent in Charge of the JFK detail, Gerald Behn, told me on 9/27/92: "I don't remember Kennedy ever saying that he didn't want anybody on the back of his car."

FLOYD BORING

Assistant Special Agent in Charge of the JFK detail, Floyd Boring, told me the same thing on three different occasions between 1993 and 1997: "[JFK] was a very easy-going guy ... he didn't interfere with our actions at all. He was a very nice man; he never interfered with us at all. President Kennedy was very cooperative with the Secret Service." Boring also told the JFK Library on 2/25/76: "Of all the administrations I worked with [FDR-LBJ], the president and the people surrounding the president were very gracious and were very cooperative. As a matter of fact, you can't do this type of security work without cooperation of the people surrounding the president." (In my interviews with Mr. Boring, he was adamant that he never spoke to William Manchester and denounced the substance of the made-up quote attributed to him [the whole "Ivy League charlatans" nonsense attributed to JFK]. Ironically, none other than Gerald Blaine himself went on record stating that Boring was never interviewed by Manchester! The archivist of the entire collection of Manchester papers wrote to me: "I can confirm that there is no transcript of an interview with Floyd Boring in the papers." I have always suspected – as I spelled out in my first book – that Gerald Blaine was the source for the quote in Manchester's book attributed to Boring. Blaine's good friend Frank Badalson wrote in an online review contesting my book: "Could it mean that Manchester simply confused the men?" Oh, really? This was my suspicion all along – Blaine, who was interviewed for the book instead of Boring, was the source of this made-up quote, just as Blaine submitted handwritten notes to the National Archives that were clearly written long after 11/22/63, as well as writing about a meeting that never occurred: as a fellow former agent, Talmadge Bailey, said, it is "horseshit"!

Clint Hill

During former Kennedy era agent Clint Hill's 11/19/10 Sixth Floor Museum oral history, the former agent revealed the full, unvarnished truth about JFK: he did not order the agents to do anything; they did what they wished to do, security-wise: "He can tell you what he wants done and he can tell you certain things but that doesn't mean you have to do it. What we used to do was always agree with the President and then we'd do what we felt was best anyway."

Winston G. Lawson

Winston G. Lawson, the lead advance agent for the Dallas trip, wrote to me in a letter dated 1/12/04: "I do not know of any standing orders for the agents to stay off the back of the car ... it never came to my attention as such."

Art Godfrey

Shift Leader Art Godfrey, also on the Texas trip, told me on three different occasions between 1996 and 1997: "President Kennedy never ordered us to do anything. He was a very nice man ... cooperative...President Kennedy never asked me to have my shift leave the limo when we were working it."

Sam Kinney

Agent Sam Kinney, the driver of the follow-up car on the Florida and Texas trips (among many others), told me on three different occasions between 1992 and 1994: "[the idea that JFK ordered them off the limo] is absolutely, positively false ... no, no, no: he had nothing to do with that ... No, never – the agents say, 'O.K., men, fall back on your posts' ... President Kennedy was one of the easiest presidents to ever protect; Harry S. Tru man was a jewel just like John F. Kennedy was ... 99% of the agents would agree ... [JFK] was one of the best presidents ever to control – he trusted every one of us ... for the record of history that is false – Kennedy never ordered us to do anything. I am aware of what is being said but that is false." (Sam believed there was a conspiracy and knew the back of JFK's head was missing, corroboration for a shot from the front, as he had the piece in his hand and put in a phone patch aboard the C-130 to Dr. Burkley. What became of this specific fragment is a mystery. Sam's grandchild contacted me, telling me that Sam's wife Hazel believed LBJ was involved in JFK's death!)

BOB LILLEY

Agent Bob Lilley conveyed to me on four different occasions between 1992 and 1996:" JFK was very cooperative with us once he became President. He was extremely cooperative. Basically, 'whatever you guys want is the way it will be.'"

DON LAWTON

Agent Don Lawton told me on 11/15/95 that he agreed with his friends Sam and Bob, above: "It's the way Sam said, yes. You can take whatever information [Bob Lilley] passed on to you as gospel. JFK was very personable ... very warm. Everyone felt bad. It was our job to protect the President. You still have regrets, remorse. Who knows, if they had left guys on the back of the car ... you can hindsight yourself to death." In fact, in new information from an obscure local news article (*Idaho State Journal* 11/24/13) that was totally overlooked by everyone on the 50th anniversary of the assassination comes some explosive new information regarding Lawton and his feelings on the matter at hand: "Former Marine officer Jacquee Alvord is convinced the theory that Lee Harvey Oswald acted alone in the assassination of President Kennedy 50 years ago is false. Her skepticism is born from intimate knowledge about the military and CIA and the fact a good friend of hers was a Secret Service agent in Dallas that fateful day. His name was Donald Lawton and his job with the Secret Service was how they met. 'Don had a personal like for the man,' Alvord said. 'He said Kennedy had a great personality and was easy to talk to.'" A few days before Kennedy's Nov. 22 visit to Dallas, she talked to Lawton about his duties in Florida where the president had just visited. Lawton talked about how he had ridden on the rear platform of the presidential limousine just behind the president. It was a job requiring balance and concentration that Lawton had perfected [note: Lawton also rode on the rear of the limo 3/23/63 in Chicago]. "He told me he was going to Texas next," Alvord said. "He said his job had been to secure the airport in Dallas and that he had not been with the motorcade." [Right after the assassination] I asked him if he was OK and he said, 'No,'" Alvord said. "He said, 'I

187

should have been there.'" It wasn't until February of 1964 that Alvord was able to meet Lawton again in person. She said he was nervous because he was going to be interviewed by lawyers with the Warren Commission. The commission was a group of government officials, led by Chief Justice Earl Warren, charged with investigating the Kennedy assassination. There was some concern that Secret Service agents had been out drinking late the night before the fatal shooting and might not have been completely fit to protect the president. But Alvord said something else was bothering Lawton and he wouldn't talk about it. "I knew he felt guilty," Alvord said. "That's why he kept saying, 'I should have been there.'" It wasn't until later that Alvord realized the significance of Lawton's statements. She watched the documentary film *Four Days in November* and saw Lawton at Love Field in Dallas as the president's motorcade was preparing to depart. He was running alongside the rear of the car with his hand behind the president. It was a position he had mastered before jumping aboard the platform at the rear of the limousine. It was something Lawton had done in Florida and Chicago during presidential parades earlier in 1963. Suddenly, someone pulled Lawton away from the car. The motorcade proceeded without him or any agent manning the rear platform on the president's limousine. To this day, it's a mystery to Alvord and others why there were no Secret Service agents on the back of that limo. "If Don had been standing there, he would have been killed or prevent ed it," Alvord said. "That's why he kept saying, 'I should have been there.'" Lawton passed away in 2013. His nephew, Richard James Lawton, wrote to me and thanked me for the information I had about his uncle.

DAVE POWERS

Presidential aide Dave Powers, President Kennedy's best friend and political helper, who rode in the Secret Service follow-up car in Dallas and was on many other trips, wrote to me on 9/10/93:" [The agents] never had to be told to 'get off' the limousine." For the record, Agent Bob Lilley endorsed Mr. Powers' view: "Dave would give you factual answers." Frank Vamos wrote me on 12/6/10, "I developed a friendship with Dave Powers, and he told me that the President never asked the agents to get off of the limo." Assassination Records Review Board (ARRB) Director Tom Samoluk told me in 1996 that JFK's longtime friend and Presidential Aide Dave Powers, "agreed with your take on the Secret Service," based on a lengthy interview Samoluk had with the gentleman.

Researcher Will Ruha wrote to me on 11/11/13 concerning his in-person interview with Dave Powers: "Zboril, Blaine, et al, are full of it in their sorry refusal to accept responsibility and properly expiate their failure in Dallas. What is so pathetic, indeed so meretricious about their current spate of lies is that they now choose to posthumously assault the very victim their past actions managed to help assassinate. And this I know to be true because shortly after the JFK Library opened, I was invited by JFK's aide, Dave Powers, to meet privately with him in his office, wherein we engaged in an almost hour-long discussion of JFK, his career, presidency, and alas, the assassination. Dave had been with Jack as a trusted aide and companion since Kennedy first ran for political office in 1946, and he was with him during countless motorcades, including right behind his vehicle in Dallas. Perturbed by Manchester's claim that JFK was irked by Secret Service agents being too close, I asked him whether the president ever ordered agents away from his vehicle. Dave told me, "No. Not to my knowledge. He respected them and their performance of duties and left the matter of his security and personal safety entirely to their well-trained expertise. I know of no time that he ever ordered agents away from their assigned positions in his security detail."

I mentioned to him early reports that JFK outpaced or tried to avoid Secret Service agents after his election, to which he replied, "Well, you must understand. He was 43, the youngest elected president in history – following the oldest. So, it was natural that the Secret Service may have found it more difficult to keep up with him than Eisenhower. But I can tell you, that almost three years in office and after numerous threats, the president pretty much stuck to their security directives. He believed in them." I won't go into all that we talked about, but Dave, you, and I all know that JFK would have never ordered Secret Service agents away in the fall of 1963 for the very fact that he was aware of numerous death threats and plots. Increasingly, he had begun to openly speak about the possibility of his assassination – to Jackie, Bobby, Dave, Kenny, Paul Fay Jr., authors like Jim Bishop, and even, with gallows humor, to Secret Service agents assigned to his protection. A few Sundays before his death, he teased one agent about the possibility of an assassin shooting him from the church's choir balcony, asking him if he would leap forward to throw himself over his president. Jack was deploying his self-deprecating humor as a way of "acting out" what seemed to be almost an inevitability. At one point that season, alighting from the yacht, *Honey Fitz*, behind Jackie and Anita Fay, Jack acted out his being shot, grabbing his chest and falling to the pier before the mock horrified eyes of Paul Fay. The entire episode was filmed. Jackie was not amused. It was Kennedy's way of trying to deal with the stress and tension under which he had increasingly been thrust following his back-to-back addresses on detente and civil rights in June. Animosity toward him had spiked and with it, death threats sharply escalated. In November, he repeatedly expressed reluctance to travel both to Florida and Texas in no small part for this very reason – especially to Texas. Senator Smathers (then, the only US. Senator named in the burgeoning Bobby Bak er scandal) heartily encouraged him to travel to both places. Bill Fulbright strongly advised him not to go. So did numerous others.

On the night of his departure, Kennedy family members and friends were celebrating Bobby's 38th birthday, but the Attorney General was anything but festive. He was dour, worried, and highly anxious about his brother's trip to Texas. And during JFK's stops and talks during the journey – particularly, the evening before his assassination, those behind the podium noticed how violently his hands trembled as he addressed the audience. Some attributed this to his medication, others to his essential reticence before a crowd, but in truth it was his foreboding that somewhere there in Texas he was to be targeted.

On the morning of November 22, 1963, perusing the Dallas newspaper, he noticed the black-bordered ad taken out by right-wing extremists and commented on it. Everyone in the room was concerned, very worried. Noticing this, Jack did what he always did in similar circumstances, he showed courage. "If anyone wanted to shoot me," he explained, "It wouldn't be that difficult. All he would need would be a high-powered rifle fired from a tall office building and there would be nothing anyone could do about it." He said this to show that, in almost three years, it hadn't happened yet, and then he reassured them by telling them not to worry, that the Secret Service would do their jobs. But his comment wasn't so much prophetic as it was simply based on what he had discovered to be foiled plots against him elsewhere. They hadn't materialized and so he simply hoped to get through Dallas to LBJ's ranch and then back home to Washington. And to help ensure this, he assuredly did NOT order any agents away from his car. No way. It never happened."

RUFUS YOUNGBLOOD

Rufus Youngblood, Vice President Johnson's lead agent in Dallas who rode in the same limousine as LBJ, told me on more than one occasion between 1992 and 1994: ""President Kennedy wasn't a hard ass … he never said anything like that [re: removing agents from limo]."

PIERRE SALINGER

Press Secretary Pierre Salinger conveyed to a colleague of mine that JFK had a good relationship with the Secret Service and, more importantly, did not argue with their security measures.

CECIL STOUGHTON

Cecil Stoughton, the White House photographer on both the Florida and Dallas trip (among many others), wrote me the following:" I did see a lot of the activity surrounding the various trips of the President, and in many cases, I did see the agents in question riding on the rear of the President's car. In fact, I have ridden there a number of times myself during trips ... I would jump on the step on the rear of the [Lincoln] Continental until the next stop. I have made photos while hanging on with one hand ... in Tampa [11/18/63], for example ... I would just jump on and off [the limo] quickly – no routine.... As for the edict of not riding there by order of the President – I can't give you any proof of first-hand knowledge."

MICHAEL TORINA

Michael W. Torina, Chief Inspector of the Secret Service on 11/22/63 who wrote the Secret Service manual, and to whom I corresponded twice in 1997 and 2003, contributed significantly to a book about the Secret Service written in 1962, in which it is plainly stated, "Agents of the White House Detail ride in the same car with the President. Others will walk or trot alongside, while still others ride in automobiles in front of and behind the Presidential car." Indeed, agent Mike Reilly, the SAIC of the FDR detail, wrote in his book: "There were two inviolate rules. The man running or riding at the President's shoulder never left that position unless relieved. The other, if a situation got out of hand, empty all cars and get as much Secret Service flesh between the crowd and the Boss as possible."

SAM SULLIMAN

Former agent Sam Sulliman, on the Florida and Texas trips (among many others), told me on 2/11/04 that agents were frequently on the back of the limousine. When told of Art Godfrey's comments on the matter, the former agent agreed with his colleague. Regarding the notion that JFK ordered the agents off the car, Sulliman told the author twice, "I don't think so."

Frank Stoner

Agent Frank Stoner, a PRS agent during the Kennedy era, told me on 1/17/04: JFK was "very personable. He was an old Navy man. He understood security. He wouldn't have ordered them off the car."

Gerald O'Rourke

Agent Gerald W. "Jerry" O'Rourke, also on the Texas trip, told me on 1/15/04: ""Did President Kennedy order us off the steps of the limo? To my knowledge President Kennedy never ordered us to leave the limo." The agent added, "President Kennedy was easy to protect as he completely trusted the agents of the Secret Service."

Vincent Mroz

Agent Vincent Mroz, famous for protecting President Truman on 11/1/50 and who also went on to protect Presidents, from Eisenhower to Nixon, told me on 2/7/04 that President Kennedy was "friendly, congenial – he was really easy to get along with … just like Truman." When asked point blank, if JFK had ever ordered the agents off the car, Mroz said forcefully, "No, no – that's not true." When asked a second time, the former agent responded with equal conviction: "He did not order anybody off the car."

Larry Newman

JFK Agent Larry Newman told me on 2/7/04 that there was "no policy" regarding the use of agents on the rear of Kennedy's car, further adding that the question was "hard to answer: it depends on the crowd, the threat assessment, and so forth. There was not a consistent rule of thumb." Newman phoned me unexpectedly on 2/12/04 to say that "there was not a directive, per se" from President Kennedy to remove the agents from their positions on the back of his limousine.

Jim Goodenough

Agent Jim Goodenough, on the Texas trip, told me on 3/16/04 that "President Kennedy was a pleasant and cooperative person to work for."

Lynn Meredith

JFK agent Lynn Meredith wrote to me on 3/9/04: "I do believe if agents had been riding on the rear of the limo in Dallas that President Kennedy would not have been assassinated as they would have been in Oswald's line of fire.… To elaborate a little more on the assassination in Dallas, I have always believed that the following adverse situations all contributed to the unnecessary and unfortunate death of President Kennedy: (1) No Secret Service agents riding on the rear of the limousine. Meredith wrote to me again on 5/22/05: "I do not know first-hand if President Kennedy ordered agents off the back end of his limousine."

DARWIN HORN

Agent Darwin Horn told me on 1/30/04: "You asked about Kennedy. I have worked him primarily in Los Angeles on several occasions ... and never heard him tell the agents to get off the car. Agents on the rear of JFK's car might have made a difference. They may have been hit instead of the President. That would have been all right with all of us. Agents normally would have been on the sides [of the car]."

ROBERT BOUCK

Robert I. Bouck, SAIC of PRS/Intelligence Division, told me on 9/27/92 that having agents on the back of the limousine depended on factors independent of any alleged Presidential "requests": "Many times there were agents on his car." On 4/30/96, the ARRB's Doug Horne questioned Bouck: "Did you ever hear the President personally say that he didn't want agents to stand on the running boards on his car, or did you hear that from other agents?" Bouck: "I never heard the President say that personally." The former agent also told the ARRB that JFK was the "most congenial" of all the presidents he had observed (Bouck served from FDR to LBJ).

MARTY UNDERWOOD

DNC Advance man Martin E. "Marty" Underwood, on the Texas trip, told me on 10/9/92 that JFK never ordered the agents off the rear of the car.

ABRAHAM BOLDEN

JFK Agent Abraham W. Bolden, Sr. told me, in reference to Kennedy's alleged "requests," on numerous occasions from 1993-1996 and beyond to the present day that he "didn't hear anything about that ... I never believed that Kennedy said that [ordering removal of agents]."

MAURICE MARTINEAU

Maurice G. Martineau, SAIC of the Chicago office, joined his colleagues in refuting the Manchester claim that JFK ordered the agents off the rear of the car. Martineau said this to the author in two telephone interviews conducted on 9/21/93 and 6/7/96, respectively.

WALT COUGHLIN

Agent Walt Coughlin, also on the Texas trip, told me on several occasions between 2003 and 2004: "In almost all parade situations that I was involved with we rode or walked the limo. We often rode on the back of the car." Walt Coughlin stated on video in 2014 for the Sixth Floor Museum oral history project that JFK was "very cooperative" with the Secret Service. In addition, Walt said the only time he ever heard that JFK ever ordered the agents off the limo was in Dallas. However, Walt was not in Dallas, so what he "heard" is what we all heard: second-hand stories via some of the agents. Also, Walt was on the Florida trip. It is telling that he didn't hear of any alleged orders there. During his 2/18/11 Sixth Floor Museum oral history, Coughlin said, "He was a wonderful man to work with. I loved the job.... But he would listen if you told him not to do something. He would, as long as you didn't 'cry wolf' all the time. If you said, you know, 'Don't do that', he assumed you had a good reason. He was good about that ... had an agent been allowed to stay on that right bumper, he would have blocked the shot.... And it's a terrible thing to say, but Kennedy really helped improve the Secret Service."

TOBY CHANDLER

JFK Agent Toby Chandler said the following during his 11/20/10 Sixth Floor Museum Oral History: "They [Presidents] have all, in my experience, listened to us. Almost all of them, within reason, have made their point or, in the end, accepted our advice. I don't know of anybody who deliberately or blatantly over-ruled a Secret Service suggestion. Most of them observe our suggestions."

WILLIAM DUNCAN

William Duncan, the advance agent for the Fort Worth trip, said during his 10/15/05 Sixth Floor Museum oral history that JFK was a "real fine gentleman with a magnetic personality" who was "very friendly" and "very concerned about the people around him – a real pleasure to work with" who was also "easy to work very hard for." Most importantly, the former agent stated that President Kennedy "let you do your job." Duncan went on to guard President Nixon. One of Duncan's colleagues, Mike Endicott, wrote in his book that, during the 1968 campaign, he told Nancy

Reagan, wife of presidential candidate Ronald Reagan, that she and her family "must respond at once to what any agent told them."

J. FRANK YEAGER

Agent J. Frank Yeager, who assisted in the advance work for both Tampa and Austin, stated in a letter dated 12/29/03: "I did not think that Pres ident Kennedy was particularly 'difficult' to protect. In fact, I thought that his personality made it easier than some because he was easy to get along with." In response to the author's question, "Did President Kennedy ever order the agents off the rear of his limousine?" Yeager wrote, "I know of no "order" directly from President Kennedy … I also do not know who actu-ally made the final decision, but we did not have agents on the rear of the President's car in Dallas. While Yeager was one of three agents in corre-spondence (O'Rourke and Ron Pontius were the other two) who seemed to indicate that this alleged order may have originated with Chief of Staff Kenny O'Donnell, I was granted permission to view the transcript of O'Donnell's interviews with author William Manchester – nothing what-soever is mentioned concerning any alleged presidential security-related orders of any kind. O'Donnell does not mention anything about telling agents to remove themselves from the limousine during his lengthy War-ren Commission testimony, nor in his or his daughter's books. The same is true for the other two Presidential aides: Larry O'Brien and Dave Powers. In fact, as mentioned above, Powers refutes this whole idea. JFK's staff is not mentioned as a factor during any of the agents' Warren Commission testimony, nor in the five reports submitted in April 1964. Agents Rowley, Behn, Boring, Godfrey and Kinney denounced the "staff/O'Donnell" no-tion (see chapter one of my first book *Survivor's Guilt*). It is interesting to note that, like JFK, O'Donnell was not blamed for any security deficien-cies and the like until after his death in 1977, when he was thus unable to refute any allegations.

RON PONTIUS

As for agent Ron Pontius' personal knowledge, on page 162 of *The Ken-nedy Detail* he stated, "I've never heard the president say anything about agents on the back of the car." Perhaps the coup de grace comes from Helen O'Donnell, daughter of JFK Chief of Staff Ken O'Donnell. In a message to the author, based on both her memory and her father's au-dio tapes, Helen wrote, "Suffice to say that you are correct; JFK did not order anybody off the car, he never interfered with my dad's direction on the Secret Service, and this is much backed up by my dad's tapes. I think and know from the tapes Dallas always haunted him because of the might have-beens – but they involved the motorcade route."

GERALD BLAINE

Agent and *Kennedy Detail* author Gerald Blaine, on the Florida trip (advance agent for Tampa, working with agent Yeager, above) and the Texas trip (among many others), told me on 2/7/04, years before he published his 2010 book, that President Kennedy was "very cooperative. He didn't interfere with our actions. President Kennedy was very likeable – he never had a harsh word for anyone. He never interfered with our actions." When I phoned Blaine on 6/10/05, he said the remark regarding "Ivy League charlatans," made infamous in both Manchester's book and his own book, came "from the guys … I can't remember who [said it] … I can't remember." Thus, Blaine confirms that he did not hear the remark from JFK. Blaine now denies that either himself or Floyd Boring were interviewed by William Manchester! And so, it goes. The bottom line: the whole "Ivy League Charlatans" remark was made up – Boring and others told me JFK did not say that! As author and researcher John Onesti wrote on 11/10/13: "I highly doubt JFK would use the language "Ivy League Charlatans. "Whoever made it up (Blaine?) obviously doesn't know much about east coast schools and that Harvard is in the Ivy League. JFK having graduated from Harvard cum laude would not have used such words having taken school seriously. Now if he said "Get those Skull and Bones lackeys and freemasons off my car" that still would not sound like him, but it would ring truer. For JFK to use those terms would be like me (a University of Illinois graduate) saying "get those Big Ten [expletives] off my car!" It makes no sense. It is just another example of liars like Hill, Blaine & Manchester not being able to play both sides of the chess board.

FLORIDA CONGRESSMAN SAM GIBBONS

I wrote to former Florida Congressman Samuel Melville Gibbons on 1/7/04 and asked him if he had heard President Kennedy order the agents off the rear of the limousine. Gibbons rode in the rear seat with JFK and Senator George Smathers on the Tampa trip of 11/18/63. Here is Gibbons' response in full, dated 1/15/04: "I rode with Kennedy every time he rode. I heard no such order. As I remember it the agents rode on the rear bumper all the way. Kennedy was very happy during his visit to Tampa: Sam Gibbons."

JACQUELINE KENNEDY

Jacqueline Kennedy "played the events over and over in her mind ... She did not want to accept Jack's death as a freak accident, for that meant his life could have been spared – if only the driver in the front seat of the presidential limousine [Agent William R. Greer] had reacted more quickly and stepped on the gas ... if only the Secret Service had stationed agents on the rear bumper."[333]

ROCKY STONE

Rocky Stone, Fort Worth (Texas) police department – in a newly dis covered film from WBAP-TV (KXAS) NBC 11/22/63: Talking about the Kennedy Detail, President John F. Kennedy's Secret Service men: "They had nothing but praise for President Kennedy and his manner in which he felt about the Secret Service men. They said that by far he was more considerate of them and their feelings than any of the previous presidents they had been taking care of. They said that he always went by their decisions to protect him. That he was always considerate of their (sic) fact that he never tried to do anything that they thought was against the rules in which to protect him. They stated that President Kennedy referred to them as 'his boys' and that at times when there were large crowds of people that the president always looked around to see where 'his boys' was (sic) at so, at a moment's notice, they were able to be at his side and get him out of the crowds as he possibly could be in danger. In the moments after, they said the Secret Service was very, very short of money and that even some of the agents had to buy the two-way radios they used out of their own pocket and they did need more money to operate on to hire more men in order to be successful in protecting the president out of state [presumably Washington, D.C.]."

JAMES J. ROWLEY

Chief James J. Rowley testified under oath to the Warren Commission: "No President will tell the Secret Service what they can or cannot do."[334]

U.E. BAUGHMAN

In fact, Rowley's predecessor, former Chief U.E. Baughman, who had served under JFK from Election night 1960 until he was fired ("retired") by the Kennedy brothers in September 1961, had written in his 1962 book *Secret Service Chief*, "Now the Chief of the Secret Service is legally

333   Just Jackie: Her Private Years, pp. 58-59 & 374: based on an interview Klein had with Kitty Carlisle Hart re: Hart's conversation with Jackie.
334   5 H 470.

empowered to countermand a decision made by anybody in this country if it might endanger the life or limb of the Chief Executive. This means I could veto a decision of the President himself if I decided it would be dangerous not to. The President of course knew this fact."

Indeed, an *Associated Press* story from November 15, 1963, stated, "The [Secret] Service can overrule even the President where his personal security is involved."

President Harry Truman agreed, stating, "The Secret Service was the only boss that the President of the United States really had." This was brought up during Chief James Rowley's LBJ Library oral history. In fact, Chief Rowley heard this exact sentiment again repeated by none other than LBJ on 11/23/68. President Bill Clinton also used Truman's words as a reference before a gathering of Secret Service officials (including former directors Eljay Bowron, John Magaw and Stu Knight, as well as SAIC Larry Cockell) and other dignitaries for the dedication of the United States Secret Service Memorial Building on 10/14/99: "Harry Truman once said, the Secret Service was the only boss he had as President, with the exception of Mrs. Truman. And even when I don't like it, I have to admit that's true." In an 11/23/63 *UPI* story, titled "Secret Service Men Wary of Motorcade," based in part on "private conversations" with unnamed agents, Robert J. Serling wrote, "An agent is the only man in the world who can order a President of the United States around if the latter's safety is believed at stake ... in certain situations an agent outranks even a President." In addition, Democratic National Committee advance man Jerry Bruno, who played a role in planning the Texas trip, wrote, "[The Secret Service's] word on security was final. They could by law order a President not to go someplace on security grounds, and he was bound to obey them."

GEORGE J. McNALLY

Former Agent George McNally, also on the Texas trip, among many others, wrote, "Legally the Secret Service could forbid a President to do such and such or go to this or that place."[335]

MIKE REILLY

Former Agent Mike Reilly, the SAIC for FDR, wrote: "Incidentally, every schoolboy knows that the White House Secret Service boss can order the President of the United States not to go here or there if he chooses...

---

335   *A Million Miles of Presidents*, p. 110.

presidents usually accept the laws of the land and follow Secret Service advice with little or no question."[336]

BILL CARTER

Former JFK Secret Service agent Bill Carter wrote, "The Secret Service still had absolute authority … complete authority when it came to a presidential visit."[337]

JOHN F. NORRIS

John F. Norris, Uniformed Division of the Secret Service: On 3/4/94, in an interview with the author, Norris also joined his colleagues in refuting the notion that JFK ordered the agents off the rear of the limo: "I would doubt that very much," Norris said. "The whole JFK-is-to-blame, the very pervasive myth found in a myriad of dubious sources, is officially debunked."

---

336   *Reilly of the White House* by Mike Reilly (1947), pages 13-14.
337   *Get Carter* by Bill Carter, pp. 34-35.

APPENDIX

SECRET SERVICE AGENT NEMO CIOCHINA AND THE CHICAGO TRIP

Nemo Ciochina in his military days.

Readers of my sixth book *The Plot to Kill President Kennedy in Chicago* were introduced to Secret Service agent Nemo Ciochina, a name that was relatively new to everyone. Well, thanks to newly discovered documents concerning the cancelled Chicago trip of 11/2/63, Ciochina's name appears once again. Included are the most relevant and interesting pages from the lengthy document:

REFER TO FILE NO. 1-16-602.111

TREASURY DEPARTMENT
UNITED STATES SECRET SERVICE
FIELD FORCE

White House Detail

Washington, D. C.

November 1, 1963

PROTECTIVE SURVEY REPORT

Re: The President's visit to
Chicago, Illinois, to attend
the football game between
Army and the Air Force Academy,
November 2, 1963.

Mr. James J. Rowley
Chief, U. S. Secret Service
Washington, D. C.

Sir:

INTRODUCTION

This report relates to a protective survey conducted at Chicago-O'Hare
International Airport, military side, the Conrad Hilton Hotel, Soldier Field,
Chicago, Illinois, and connecting routes of travel, by Special Agents
David B. Grant and Robert Kollar (1-16) and Acting SAIC Maurice G.
Martineau and Special Agent James S. Griffiths (2-1), from October 25 to
November 2, 1963.

The President, on this occasion, will arrive at Chicago-O'Hare International Airport, military side, and proceed via motorcade to the Conrad
Hilton Hotel, where he will lunch privately in the Imperial Suite.

The President, after the completion of his luncheon, will then proceed
via motorcade to Soldier Field to witness the football game between Army
and Air Force. The game is expected to be a sellout, with approximately
75,000 fans attending.

The appropriate dress on this occasion will be business suit.

ITINERARY

Saturday, November 2, 1963

11:00 a.m.   The President and party will arrive by Air Force 1, USAF
               Plane #26000, at Chicago-O'Hare International Airport,
               military side, Chicago, Illinois. The President will be

202

Mr. James J. Rowley   - 5 -   1-16-602.111
                                    November 1, 1963

In addition to the standard security measures employed by this Service
at affairs of this type, additional precautions will be effected at the
time the President changes sides; i.e., a cordon of uniformed Chicago
Police officers will be across the field, backs to the Cadets.

Routes

A motorcycle escort will be employed on this occasion. All intersections
of travel, underpasses, and overpasses will be controlled by uniformed
officers of the Chicago Police Department.

Uniformed officers will also be positioned along the parade route at
predetermined intervals.

POST ASSIGNMENTS

Chicago-O'Hare International Airport

1. Point where President's plane spotted   SA Grant
                                                ASAIC Martineau

2. Ramp gate   SA Ciochina
                                                2 uniformed officers

3. Press area   SA Stocks
                                                SA Tucker

4. Barricade - Public area   40 uniformed officers

5. General ramp area   15 uniformed officers
                                                10 detectives

6. Building roofs overlooking ramp area   3 uniformed officers
                                                3 detectives

Conrad Hilton Hotel

1. Point where President's limousine spotted   SA Griffiths
                                                6 detectives
                                              40 uniformed officers

2. Lobby   25 uniformed officers
                                              8 detectives

Mr. James J. Rowley   - 8 -   1-16-602.111
November 1, 1963

SA Tucker will ride in the Chicago Police Department pilot car.
ASAIC Martineau and SA Grant will ride in the Chicago Police Department
lead car. SA O'Leary will ride in the Chicago Police Department tail car.

The general supervision of all activities and post assignments will be under
the direction of ASAIC Boring and SA's Grant and Kollar, Office 1-16, and
ASAIC Martineau and SA Griffiths, Office 2-1.

To properly establish their identities, all special agents will wear their
RED permanent lapel buttons. White House Staff and WHCA personnel will
wear theirs.

Chicago Police Department detectives will wear orange lapel buttons.
Employees at O'Hare Field will wear yellow lapel buttons. Employees at the
Conrad Hilton Hotel will wear white lapel buttons. Employees at Soldier
Field will wear green lapel buttons. Chicago Fire Department employees will
wear gold lapel buttons.

PROTECTIVE RESEARCH

SAIC Bouck, Protective Research Section, has been apprised of this movement.
If it develops that there are any active protective research subjects at
large in this area, all pertinent information concerning them will be given
to the personnel participating in the security measures.

Information has been received that the Student Non-Violent Coordinating
Committee is planning to picket at the Conrad Hilton Hotel and at Soldier
Field. The Chicago Police Department will deal with these pickets as the
occasion warrants.

INSTRUCTIONS TO AGENTS

SA Grant, ASAIC Martineau, and SA's Tucker, Stocks, and Ciochina will report
to Chicago-O'Hare International Airport at 9:30 a.m. to set up security
arrangements prior to the President's arrival.

SA's Griffiths, Strong, and Gorman will report to the Conrad Hilton Hotel
at 9:30 a.m. to set up security arrangements prior to the President's
arrival.

SA's Kollar, Cross, Bolden, McLeod, Motto, and Plichta will report to
Soldier Field at 9:30 a.m. to set up security arrangements prior to the
President's arrival.

Mr. James J. Rowley   - 9 -   1-16-602.111
                                                               November 1, 1963

ATSAIC Roberts and SA's deFreese, Yeager, Lawton, Zboril, and McIntyre
will report to SA Grant upon arrival of the press plane for transportation
via police car to Soldier Field. They will report to SA Kollar at the
Field for post assignments.

ATSAIC Godfrey and SA's Giannoules, Paolella, Burns, and Faison will report
to SA Grant at Chicago-O'Hare Airport, the Conrad Hilton Hotel, and Soldier
Field for post assignments.

SA Kinney will report to Chicago-O'Hare International Airport, Military
Side, with SS 100-X and SS 679-X at 9:30 a.m.

SA's Griffiths, Strong, and Gorman will depart the Conrad Hilton Hotel after
the arrival of the President at the Imperial Suite and proceed to Soldier
Field, where they will report to SA Kollar for post assignments.

SA's Stocks, Ciochina, and Burke will remain at O'Hare Field and maintain
security for the President's departure.

SA O'Leary will ride in the Chicago Police Department tail car.

SA Maynard will remain on duty in the Chicago field office during the
President's visit.

AUTOMOBILES

SA Kinney will arrive in Chicago, Illinois on October 31, 1963, with Secret
Service cars 100-X and 679-X. The cars will be stored in the Chicago Police
Department garage with a police officer assigned to them at all times.

The Ford Motor Company has supplied nine cars for the motorcade. The local
telephone company is supplying a wire service car for the motorcade. The
City of Chicago is supplying a bus to transport the members of the press.

The Chicago Fire Department is supplying the drivers for the automobiles
in the motorcade.

A list of car assignments in the motorcade is attached to this report.

PRESS AND PHOTOGRAPHERS

Arrangements have been made whereby four cars will be placed in the motorcade directly behind the follow-up car. They will be for the use of the
wire service reporters, still photographers, newsreel photographers, and

James J. Rowley

- 10 -

1-16-602.111
November 1, 1963

one car for local newsreel and still photographers. All other members of the press will be transported in a bus which will be placed at the rear of the motorcade.

Press facilities have been set up at Chicago-O'Hare International Airport, the Conrad Hilton Hotel, and Soldier Field.

All press activities will be under the direction of Press Secretary Pierre Salinger and his assistant, Andrew Hatcher.

COMMUNICATIONS

Communication arrangements were made by White House Communications Agency (WHCA) and consist of the following.

A Chicago White House switchboard will be in operation in the Conrad Hilton Hotel, telephone No. 427-7135. Direct telephone service will be provided to Washington, local Chicago services, all areas to be visited by the Presidential party, and all security posts. The long distance telephone numbers of the Chicago White House switchboard are Chicago LD numbers 451 and 452.

Radio base stations will cover all aircraft, motorcades, and arrival locations. The motorcade will be equipped with radio in the pilot, lead, Presidential, and follow-up cars.

A center for teletype, classified messages will be operating in Chicago. For receipt or dispatch of classified traffic call the Chicago White House switchboard for courier service.

CONCLUSION

The following number of personnel will participate in the overall security measures:

White House Detail Agents	17
Office 2-1 Agents	13
Detectives - Chicago Police Department	103
Uniformed Officers - Chicago Police Department	1,248
Firemen - Chicago Fire Department	50
Hotel Security Officers	5
Total - - - - - - - - - -	1,436

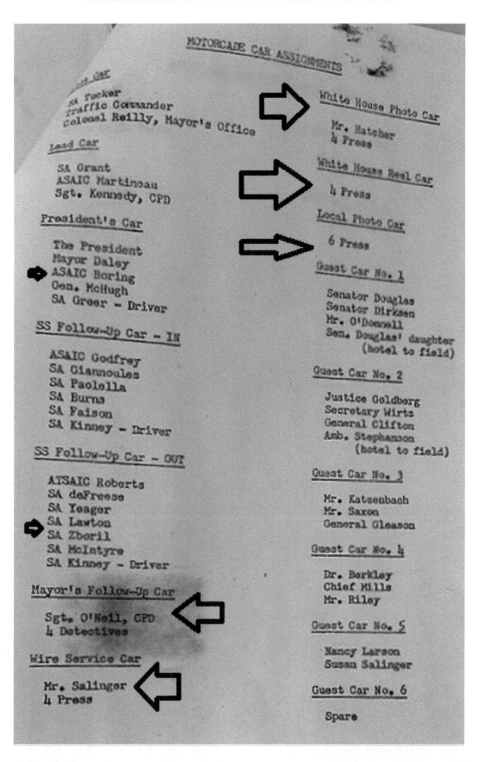

MOTORCADE CAR ASSIGNMENTS

Pilot Car

SA Tucker
Traffic Commander
Colonel Reilly, Mayor's Office

Lead Car

SA Grant
ASAIC Martineau
Sgt. Kennedy, CPD

President's Car

The President
Mayor Daley
ASAIC Boring
Gen. McHugh
SA Greer - Driver

SS Follow-Up Car - IN

ASAIC Godfrey
SA Giannoules
SA Paolella
SA Burns
SA Faison
SA Kinney - Driver

SS Follow-Up Car - OUT

ATSAIC Roberts
SA deFreese
SA Yeager
SA Lawton
SA Zboril
SA McIntyre
SA Kinney - Driver

Mayor's Follow-Up Car

Sgt. O'Neil, CPD
4 Detectives

Wire Service Car

Mr. Salinger
4 Press

White House Photo Car

Mr. Hatcher
4 Press

White House Reel Car

4 Press

Local Photo Car

6 Press

Guest Car No. 1

Senator Douglas
Senator Dirksen
Mr. O'Donnell
Sen. Douglas' daughter
(hotel to field)

Guest Car No. 2

Justice Goldberg
Secretary Wirtz
General Clifton
Amb. Stephanson
(hotel to field)

Guest Car No. 3

Mr. Katzenbach
Mr. Saxon
General Gleason

Guest Car No. 4

Dr. Berkley
Chief Mills
Mr. Riley

Guest Car No. 5

Nancy Larson
Susan Salinger

Guest Car No. 6

Spare

Index

Sherman, Tony 8
Shipman, Thomas 7, 69, 70, 181-183
Sibert, James 32, 33, 101
Silbernagel, Bob 4
Six Seconds in Dallas 67
60 Minutes 6, 83, 104, 173
Smathers, George 110, 190, 196
Sneed, Larry 28, 93-95, 146, 152
Sorrels, Forrest 7, 13, 28, 97, 145, 151,
154, 180, 184
Souter, J.M. 97, 145
Specter, Arlen 15, 16, 33, 34, 43, 107,
108, 110, 116, 122, 138, 142
Starling, Edmund 76
Starling of the White House 76
Starr, Kenneth 110
Steuart, Robert 7
Stevenson, Adlai 28, 69, 98, 155
Stoner, Frank 7, 117, 192
Stone, Rocky 197
Stoughton, Cecil 5, 30, 100, 115, 116,
140, 141, 149, 191
Stout, Stu 7, 17, 18, 68, 76
Sulliman, Samuel E. 8, 14, 90, 117, 118,
191
Sullivan, Mark 5
Survivor's Guilt: The Secret Service &
The Failure To Protect President
Kennedy, 3, 11, 17, 21, 22, 35,
52, 69, 74, 75, 77-79, 82, 83, 85,
88, 130, 158-160, 167, 195

T

Tague, James 35
terHorst, J.F. 29
Thacker, Elliot 7
The Secret Service: The Hidden History
of an Enigmatic Agency 6, 13,
133
Third Decade 171
Thompson, Josiah 67, 86, 87
TMZ 55, 175
Tolson, Clyde 116
Torina, Michael 178, 191
Towner, Tina 58
Truman (book) 76

Truman, Harry 9, 77, 83, 89, 114, 118,
121, 122, 130, 131, 139, 192, 198
Trump, Donald 86, 170
Twenty Years in the Secret Service: My
Life With Five Presidents 76

U

Underwood, Marty 22, 33, 102, 112,
130, 141, 152, 184, 193

V

Vancouver Sun 51
Vanity Fair 55, 59, 62, 66
Venker, Marty 32, 33, 126
Very Stable Genius, A 86

W

Warner, Roger 8, 13, 150
Warren Commission 1, 6, 9, 11, 13, 15,
16, 19, 22, 25, 30, 32-35, 40, 43,
44, 56, 58-60, 71, 83, 91, 93, 98,
99, 104, 105, 107-109, 115, 123,
124, 127, 131, 134, 135, 137, 138,
142, 145-147, 152-154, 157, 158,
160, 163, 172, 173, 176, 188, 195,
197
Warren, Earl 13, 107, 188
Warrington, John 155
Wells, Tom 8, 50, 67, 68
White, Ricky 66
White, Roscoe 66, 67
Whitmeyer, George 151
Wiesman, Ken 8, 68
Wild, Wild West, The 104, 171
Wildy, Ed 7
Willis, Rosemary and Linda 58
Within Arm's Length 39
Wright, Milton 29, 58, 101, 150
Wunderlich, Dale 8, 179

Y

Yeager, Frank 8, 18, 20, 41, 120, 168,
195, 196
Youngblood, Rufus 7, 13, 20, 29, 76, 81,
83, 111, 112, 121, 140, 142, 154,